English Historical Sociolinguistics

Edinburgh Textbooks on the English Language – Advanced

TITLES IN THE SERIES INCLUDE:

Corpus Linguistics and the Description of English
Hans Lindquist

A Historical Phonology of English
Donka Minkova

A Historical Morphology of English
Dieter Kastovsky

Grammaticalization and the History of English
Manfred Krug and Hubert Cuyckens

A Historical Syntax of English
Bettelou Los

English Historical Sociolinguistics
Robert McColl Millar

A Historical Semantics of English
Christian Kay and Kathryn Allan

Visit the Edinburgh Textbooks in the English Language website at www.
euppublishing.com/series/ETOTALAdvanced

English Historical
Sociolinguistics

Robert McColl Millar

EDINBURGH
University Press

Edinburgh University Press Ltd
22 George Square, Edinburgh EH8 9LF

www.euppublishing.com

Typeset in 10.5/12 Janson
by Servis Filmsetting Ltd, Stockport, Cheshire, and
printed and bound in Great Britain by
CPI Group (UK) Ltd, Croydon CR0 4YY

A CIP record for this book is available from the British Library

ISBN 978 0 7486 4181 9 (hardback)
ISBN 978 0 7486 4180 2 (paperback)
ISBN 978 0 7486 6438 2 (webready PDF)
ISBN 978 0 7486 6440 5 (epub)
ISBN 978 0 7486 6439 9 (Amazon ebook)

Contents

Figures

Tables

Acknowledgements

This book has been a long time in the making, in the sense that I have been concerned with its subject matter in my research and teaching for over twenty-five years. Although I cannot mention everyone who has inspired me over the years, I would like to record my debt to the late Michael Samuels (whose *Linguistic Evolution* I read regularly and with the same pleasure as when first exposed to it in 1984), Marina Dossena, Paul Kerswill, John Kirk, Gunnel Melchers, Terttu Nevalainen, Dani Schreier and Jeremy Smith. I am sure that all would take issue with something I have written here, but my gratitude and respect are considerable. I would also like to record my debt to my colleagues at Aberdeen, in particular Mercedes Durham and Janet Cruickshank, for much conversation on these matters. Heinz Giegerich has been the best of series editors, providing feedback and support whenever necessary. Gillian Leslie has been very tolerant of my foibles in producing a manuscript.

I have taught the History of the English Language and Historical Linguistics to a great many students, undergraduate and postgraduate, native speakers and non-native speakers. I have learned a great deal from their questions and responses to the subject matter. Some of their concerns are included in both the subject matter and the points to consider found within this book.

Finally, a few words about my family: my father died in the last months of the composition of this book. I can never repay the debt I owe him and my late mother. Both showed great interest in my work and would regularly engage with it, in particular in relation to the history and present state of the dialects of Scots. My beloved wife Sandra and our dear daughter Mairi saw this book from inception to completion with their usual support and tolerance. Sandra read the book on a number of occasions during its development; Mairi became a speaker and a living embodiment of linguistic variation and change during the same period. This book is dedicated to them both.

Foreword: Towards a sociolinguistic history of the English language

A search for origins is attractive to most of us: we need to know where we come from, in the hope that this will tell us who we are. If this is true for the individual, it is also true for the language we speak, particularly since, if we have lived long enough (and this need not be *very* long) we will be aware of change taking place, just as we see fashions shifting rapidly from those we considered fashionable in our youth. This is one of the reasons why students of a particular language – often their own, but also a language they learned as (young) adults – regularly study the history of that language. Some do so because of requirement; most have at least some interest in the subject which, if the topic is well enough taught, will lead to further interest in the subjects involved and, it is to be hoped, to the study of linguistic change itself, historical linguistics.

But *how* the history of the English language, for instance, is taught, and *what* is included from course to course, differs considerably. While English is blessed in having at least fourteen centuries of written history behind it, the first ten centuries at least of this history is associated with varieties of the language which are now largely opaque to present speakers. A student's first introduction to Old English (spoken up to about 1100–1150) can be unsettling, since, unless you have German, even the grammatical precepts upon which the language is based – grammatical gender and case, marking of definiteness on the adjective, and so on – are quite foreign to a speaker of Modern English (spoken from about 1400–1450 on). Relationship therefore has to be taken on trust, at least to begin with. But while an unsettling sensation may actually be a good thing when a subject is being studied, some students can find this off-putting. Certain features of the early history of the English language which are more readily comprehensible to contemporary students, such as the French influence on English lexis, may well be given priority over morphological and syntactic change, since this takes a considerable degree of prior work before understanding comes and, perhaps justifiably, it is often felt that teaching this 'special knowledge' is not necessary for most students, who merely need to understand that English has changed significantly but *not* how this happened.

It is not surprising, therefore, that many teachers of the history of the English language tend to place most concentration upon the Modern English period, both because there is a great deal more material to consider and this material is relatively approachable for most students – indeed, since many people who are taking a course of this type are students of English literature, they may well feel more at home in what is covered. This concentration on the modern also includes the description of the spread of the language geographically, important since the United States, not England, is now the economic and political centre of the English-speaking world; indeed, many more students will be studying the subject in North America than in the British Isles at any given time.

Most, but not all, history of the English language courses are based upon a textbook. This makes perfect organisational sense, since almost everything that is needed in a course can be found in this one resource, if the course is tailored accordingly. A number of single-volume histories of the English language are available, ranging from the highly scholarly, such as the *Oxford History of English* (Mugglestone 2006) or its Cambridge University Press equivalent (Hogg and Denison 2008), through to works intended for a wider audience and often not written by academic specialists on the subject (although that need not make these works in any way worthless), such as Bragg (2004) or McCrum, MacNeil and Cran (2011). While reference might be made to these works in an introductory University course, most course leaders would probably prefer a scholarly work designed for those with little background in either linguistics or early varieties of English, the most used being probably the long-standing and developing tradition of the *History of the English Language*, first written by Albert C. Baugh and continued in various editions by Thomas Cable over the last thirty years and more. I would be very surprised if a copy of this work in whatever edition is *not* to be found in at least most universities in the English-speaking world and in many beyond. It can also be regularly found in public libraries and schools (indeed I read it first early in my high school career). Does such an impressive distribution mean that it is a useful and comprehensive survey of the subject?

The answer, to a degree, is, of course, yes. At an introductory level, most of what is necessary to know is present; this knowledge can readily be built upon for more advanced courses on the history of the English language. In other ways, however, it can be seen as a rather conservative work which has not kept up with the aspects of the subject which have interested scholars in the last thirty years. Indeed, if you went to one of the biennial International Conferences on English Historical Linguistics (ICEHL), you would be surprised at how little the narrative found in Baugh and Cable's work is being refined or even discussed. As an example: most historical linguists concerned with the English language would not consider the French influence upon the language (dating largely from the Norman Conquest of England in 1066-7) as being as important, in particular in relation to the structure of the language, as the influence of contact with Scandinavian or (in a relatively recent development) Celtic speakers in the Old English period (as we will discuss further in Chapter 5 of this book). Yet Baugh and Cable emphasise the French influence, largely (and understandably, given their brief), because the reality of lexical borrowing is easier to get across to students than structural change. Students in more advanced courses therefore need to go further into the subject, using more developed resources from a wider range of scholarly backgrounds.

A further feature not always covered in mainstream survey textbooks – although likely to be covered to some extent in a survey course – is the social and cultural history underlying change, a feature about which students do not necessarily know much, although they often find what is covered interesting. A number of Histories of the English language (such as Knowles 1997) give this side of the subject free rein. Since the culture towards which speakers felt tied obviously affected how they viewed their language, and the ways in which that culture was formed and influenced by historical forces obviously also caused (or hindered) contact between speakers, as well as increased or lowered literacy, and so obviously must be factored in to our understanding of linguistic change, it needs to be recognised that the analysis of how these forces worked is not carried out in a systematic manner. In other words, it can sometimes feel as if special pleading is taking place.

In the last fifty years, however, a more structured version of this tendency has made itself felt. As has long been recognised, humans are *social* beings ('political animals', as Aristotle termed us), interacting socially and collectively with other individuals and groups to build and maintain social constructs, from means of government to the concept of art. How these constructs came into being, how they were governed and who gained most benefit from them differed, of course, from place to place and from period to period, but social relationships, social distance and social proximity have been and remain a commonplace of human existence. Language use is a marker and feature of how these social relationships work.

As we will see in greater depth in the first chapter of this book, *sociolinguistics* acts as a scientific means of weighing up the effects of these relationships, comparing them to class, gender, ethnicity and further social features. Almost since the inception of this field, scholars interested in linguistic change have attempted to use the findings of sociolinguistics as explanations for what was happening in a given language at a particular time, in the process producing a new field, *historical sociolinguistics* (also known as *sociohistorical linguistics*). Again this will be dealt with in the next chapter. In the following paragraphs, however, I will make reference to two books which have attempted to read the history of the English language – for the purpose of teaching a course on the subject – through a sociolinguistic lens.

Possibly the most available example of this tendency is Fennell (2001), in many ways an admirable treatment of several sociolinguistic features visible in the history of English. It has to be recognised, however, that even at a somewhat greater length than most histories it is still not comprehensive enough to carry through everything it intends to carry out. Moreover, its chronological treatment also does not lend itself to thematic analysis. In terms of this book a sociolinguistic view of the history of the language is best treated with a focus on the last 500 years (for reasons which we will come to recognise on occasion in the following chapters), meaning a rather sketchier treatment of earlier change. The treatment of the geographical diversity of English is particularly well handled (although more recent evidence and theoretical advances may have made this material somewhat outdated).

The other commonly used textbook of this type is Leith (1997), which describes itself as a 'social' rather than 'sociolinguistic' history. In some senses this book lies on the cusp between 'cultural' and 'sociolinguistic' history traditions. Leith's work does not demonstrate the micro-sociolinguistic attention to detail in patterns and evidence Fennell's book attempts, something which makes Leith's book rather 'anecdotal' to some. But the social history of the speakers is genuinely related to the development of their language. I have used it as a secondary text for relatively basic history of the English language courses both within and outside the English-speaking world. My students have responded with considerable interest and even enthusiasm. But as a primary textbook it is rarely 'linguistic' enough to give the students sufficient depth to understand what is happening.

Another 'school' on teaching the subject can be found in works like Watts and Trudgill (2002). This collection is not so much a discussion of the history of English as of the histories which can be constructed and, indeed, the 'Englishes' which can be related to it. Like many sociolinguistically driven works, the last five or six centuries dominate, but, in my experience, most students derive a great deal from it. Of a similar nature, although intended for a rather less advanced audience, is Graddol, Leith and Swann (1996), updated as Graddol (2007). Again, the modern period is given most commentary; on this occasion, as with Leith (1997), the treatment is often 'social' rather than sociolinguistic. All of these works are primarily discussions of specific periods or themes in the history of the English language rather than being essentially chronological.

Finally, two other treatments of the historical development of English should also be mentioned: Samuels (1972) and Smith (J. J. 1996). Samuels' work is a masterly portrayal of the different ways in which English – and, indeed, all languages – has changed, dealing with the subject not according to chronology, but rather themes. Given when it was published, it is not surprising that, while social (and indeed proto-sociolinguistic) evidence is discussed, this is treated as being at best ancillary to system-internal explanation. Smith (J. J. 1996) takes what might be termed an 'ecological' view of the language's development, heavily influenced by sociolinguistic insights, developing the idea of theme rather than chronology as being vital to our understanding of the subject. Unlike the works presented in the previous paragraphs, however, their single authorship encourages a sense of coherence and an overarching narrative. On the other hand, the books would be more useful as additional reading to most history of the English language courses primarily because they are intended as scholarly rather than pedagogical works (although they are both very well written and approachable to enthusiastic and bright students even at a relatively early stage of their academic careers).

A feature which none of these works has to any extent is a *macrosociolinguistic* grounding. An exact discussion of the distinction between this and the *microsociolinguistic* study of individual and group use of linguistic variables must wait until the first two chapters of this book. Essentially, however, macrosociolinguistics represents ways in which our understanding of the structure of, and change in, society can be mapped onto language use (and vice versa). What varieties are used under certain circumstances and what status a particular variety has in a society in relation to other varieties are mapped and analysed by the macrosocoiolinguist, along with what prolonged high or low status might mean to the variety and its speakers. As with microsociolinguistics, the subject's findings can, with some caution, be applied to the past (see, for instance,

Millar 2010c). All microsociolinguistic studies, whether contemporary
or historical, have to include macrosociolinguistic elements in their
analysis; this book is unusual in placing these features on occasion in the
foreground rather than the background.

The present book, *English Historical Sociolinguistics*, attempts to employ
and develop some of the best points of the works discussed. It is thematic rather than chronological and keeps sociolinguistic insights in the
forefront, both microsociolinguistic and macrosociolinguistic. A more
traditional 'social' interpretation is also inherent, however. When it is
necessary, social history is discussed in some detail. It makes no claim
to being comprehensive, since it is intended to be used in an advanced
course where students have already studied the history of English in
a traditionally linear way and more time can be devoted to patterns
of change in the language's development, their analysis and origin. It
can also serve as a secondary work in a chronological survey course,
however. On all occasions I would encourage readers to seek out other
case studies related to the topics discussed. Suggestions for reading are
given at the end of each chapter, along with suggested issues for discussion. Naturally, there is often no single answer for any of these points.
The idea is to encourage students and other readers to think about the
subject within a broader framework.

The book is organised in the following way. Chapter 1 contains a
brief discussion of sociolinguistic theory, methodology and findings.
Both *microsociolinguistic* and *macrosociolinguistic* concepts are considered,
in particular as they relate to language change. Chapter 2 considers
sociolinguistic approaches to language change, involving case studies
both from the relatively recent past and at a rather great remove. In the
rest of the book these theories and analytical techniques will be driven
in tandem with more macrosociolinguistic concerns.

Chapters 3 and 4 are in some ways variations on the same theoretical issues, since both are concerned with the standardisation of English.
Chapter 3 is particularly concerned with the process itself and how this
relates to changes in wealth, status and technology in late medieval
England. Chapter 4 is concerned with the ideology of standardisation
and how this relates to social changes in the English-speaking world in
the modern era.

Chapters 5 and 6 are concerned with the effects linguistic contact has
had on the development of English; the closely related phenomenon
of language shift is also considered. In Chapter 5 the major typological changes English passed through in the late Old English and early
Middle English periods will be considered in relation to the major

contacts speakers of English had had with speakers of other languages. Chapter 6 is concerned with how new varieties of English come into being and how contact between varieties of the language (and also often other languages) must be understood if we are to explain why territorial varieties are often similar to, but different from, each other.

1 Sociolinguistics: an overview

1.1 Historical linguistics and sociolinguistics

Since the inception of a scientifically informed historical linguistics during the course of the nineteenth century, it has been generally recognised that language changes constantly. Inherent in this viewpoint – although its full meaning was long partly obscured by the Neogrammarian belief in the absolute centrality of systemic lack of exception to change – was the awareness that variation is the norm in everyday language use, even if it was only with the advent of variationist sociolinguistics in the late 1950s that the meaningful nature of this variation was first recognised. Variation is intrasystemic, in the sense that it occurs naturally within a system due to changes in that system. Yet it also has social roots. Modern sociolinguistics has demonstrated that ethnicity, social background, gender and context may affect the way people speak their native (and indeed other) language(s). Moreover, the way a society is constructed affects how language is used at a less individual, rather more collective, level. Social forces dictate which language varieties are considered prestigious and to be enforced by educational and governmental actors, for instance. The study of individual and group variation is often described as *microsociolinguistics* (although *variationist sociolinguistics* is also common); the study of language within society will be described as *macrosociolinguistics* in this book, although *sociology of language* could be used as readily.

Sociolinguistic features are not confined to the present, of course. Human beings have been, we think, essentially at the same level of intellectual and emotional development for tens of thousands of years, although obviously social structures have changed greatly even since the rise of urban cultures in the last five thousand. Nevertheless, sociolinguistic explanations for change should be possible, for as long as humans have interacted with each other. Sometimes we are not able to produce such explanations because we do not know enough about

1

social relationships and society at a particular time. This does not mean that forces of this type were not present, however. One of the most famous large-scale changes is what is termed *Grimm's Law* (otherwise the *First Germanic Consonant Shift*), a set of systematic changes in consonant pronunciation which affected the Germanic languages, probably towards the beginning of the Christian era. It is certainly possible that the growing population of Germanic speakers pressed onto the Roman Rhine-Danube frontier (an artificial border which has rarely if ever been enforced in its entirety at any other time before or since) may have encouraged looser social networks (of which more in the following), thus bringing about change. But we have practically no evidence to back this up. In more documented past societies, however, it is quite possible to extrapolate sociolinguistic insights and findings into the past. This extrapolation into the past can be described as *historical sociolinguistics*, as it is here, but an older term, *socio-historical linguistics*, is also valid. The first might be said to concentrate on the sociolinguistic nature of language change, while the latter demonstrates how a combination of sociolinguistic and historical linguistic analyses and explanations for change can be achieved. The boundary between the two is blurred, however.

In relatively well-documented societies, such as those associated with the English language throughout most of its history, we know a considerable amount about the societies in which the language was spoken, so that the task of bringing sociolinguistic analyses to bear upon the past, while not always straightforward, is perfectly possible. It is with this task that this book is concerned.

In this chapter we will consider what microsociolinguistic variation means *synchronically* (from the viewpoint of any one place in time). This will then be interpolated backwards in the following chapter into past stages of the English language to provide *diachronic* depth between two stages of a language's history. Macrosociolinguistic concepts will also be briefly discussed, although more in-depth discussion must wait until later chapters.

1.2 Sociolinguistics

1.2.1 Formal linguistics and language variation

In the period following the Second World War a general move towards abstraction (or idealisation) became the mainstream in linguistics. Primarily associated with the work of Noam Chomsky (1928–), this tendency generally avoided discussion of how individuals spoke, instead focusing on the rules which governed what was assumed to be a homogenous language variety. This concern was essentially based upon earlier insights, such as those voiced by the main claimant to the title of 'founding father' of modern linguistics, Ferdinand de Saussure (1857–1913). Saussure (1916) proposed that our linguistic experience could be split into *parole* and *langue*. *Parole* is everyday language: variable, rarely fully realised and often ill thought out. He contrasted this with *langue*, a system where, as he put it, 'everything holds together'. *Langue* is, by its nature, idealised, in the sense that everyone uses *parole*. Nevertheless, it is *langue*, Saussure claimed, which lies at the heart of our ability to use language in a structured and meaningful way. Possibly in relation to this theoretical construct, Saussure (who started his career as an historical linguist) was troubled by what appeared to him a truth: language change is everywhere and occurring all the time, yet observing it is apparently impossible. This paradox was based upon the idea – common in the formal linguistics which Saussure inadvertently helped inspire – that linguistic variation, present everywhere and always, is inherently meaningless. This view was overturned by variationist sociolinguistics.

1.2.2 The origins of variationist sociolinguistics

There had been a counter-current from an early period in the history of linguistics which embraced variation and held that the *parole* was generally the only real representation of language, especially, perhaps, in the spoken form. Evidence, it could be said, trumped idealisation. Initially associated largely with dialectology, this variation-centred viewpoint only became fully codified in the 1950s and 1960s when linguistic analyses were combined with insights and methodologies derived from the social sciences, in particular sociology. The problem (if that is the correct word to use) with dialectology is that, despite the ways in which it is laid out – most noticeably, perhaps, through the use of atlases ostensibly marking the distribution of pronunciations, word use and structural preference – its findings were generally based on a very small sample, primarily because of the length and complexity of the research instruments employed but also because representativeness was downplayed in favour of 'genuineness', demonstrating dialectology's origins in Romanticism. Older rural male speakers who had not been geographically (or for that matter socially) mobile were often foregrounded in this process, primarily because it was assumed that informants of this sort were likely to have maintained the most conservative (or 'traditional', depending on your viewpoint) speech forms, a boon since dialectology naturally fed into the discourse of linguistic change and development central to historical linguistics (for a discussion of these matters, see the first three chapters of Chambers and Trudgill 1998).

The speech of the inhabitants of urban areas was often ignored, primarily because it was *less* traditional, due to the recent advent of full-blown urbanisation caused by mechanically aided industrialisation in western Europe from the late eighteenth century on, and was spoken by people who were often mobile geographically and socially. The patterns found were not – at least from the older viewpoint – either as categorical or as interesting. By the middle of the twentieth century, however, urban living patterns had become prevalent – or even dominant – in many parts of the industrialised world. Findings skewed towards rural districts were, from this point of view, highly unrepresentative and becoming increasingly so. Sociolinguistics presented the opportunity of lessening the problems in representativeness inherent in dialectology by harnessing it to the methodologies of sociology.

The first sociolinguists (led in the English-speaking world by scholars such as William Labov) were particularly interested in the ways in which the barriers placed between people by society – social background, ethnicity, gender, and so on – were reflected in the variation in use of individual speakers and groups. This belief that variation was *not* meaningless (as the tradition descending from Saussure asserted) was backed up by the use of quantitative methodologies emanating from the social sciences. For the first time, linguists could derive explanations for social language use from statistics and plotting of use across various sample populations.

In this early period, the question of register was also broached. As with many other sociolinguistic 'discoveries', this breakthrough was primarily based upon everyone's experience. All literate people are much more linguistically formal when they are, for instance, reading a passage aloud than they are when having a conversation with someone with whom they are related or on friendly terms. This formality is even greater when the audience for the reading aloud is unknown to the speaker or of a social background considered prestigious by the speaker. This formality – which might even be defined as discomfort – is more acute when we are asked to read aloud a list of words. The general supposition is that tasks of this type encourage speakers to move towards more prestigious, metropolitan and standardised usages. Along with other linguists, Labov took this set of insights and essentially proved them, as we will discuss in the following section.

1.2.3 The three waves of microsociolinguistics

Central to the first wave of sociolinguistics, as part of a schematisation put forward by Eckert (2005; my emphases may be somewhat different) was a traditional, almost essentialist, view of class structure and how this affects language (although other features, such as gender and ethnicity, were also of considerable importance in analysis). Thus Labov in his work on New York City speech (see, for instance, Labov 1972b) demonstrated how members of different social classes behaved linguistically in different ways. A central feature of this work was the demonstration, long suspected by linguists and others, that the lower middle classes may actually become *more* standard in their speech in formal contexts than do members of the upper middle classes, evincing a fundamental insecurity expressed through language. This can actually lead to *hypercorrection*, a prototypical historical example being the pronunciation (current from the nineteenth century on) of *forehead* as (in my pronunciation) /for'hɛd/ rather than the earlier /fər'ıd/, because the former apparently represents the spelling better than the latter (a near-contemporary analysis of which can be found in Steadman 1926).

While this analysis has undoubtedly produced useful results, issues have inevitably come to light. In the first instance, there have been a number of occasions in this early research where class identity has been assumed without there necessarily being irrefutable evidence. For instance, in what is probably Labov's most famous piece of fieldwork (although not central to the development of his views on New York City speech patterns), a rapid survey of /r/ use among assistants in three New York department stores associated with particular demographics (see, for instance, Labov 1966 or 1972b: 43–64), the assistants in the store associated with 'lower class' shoppers are themselves associated with that demographic background. It has to be accepted, however, that while a conclusion of this type may well be true on occasion, it is quite possible to imagine temporary staff, including students, who were born into a different class background but work in the store because work was available, remunerative or convenient there. It is quite possible that someone from a lower middle class background would take on aspects of working class speech when working in a store aimed at a working class clientele, but that cannot be seen as a 'natural' expression of his or her linguistic identity. We will return to this survey and issue in the next chapter.

1.2.3.1 'First wave'
A number of practitioners of the first wave (this included Labov in his fully developed work) recognised these problems and included them

within the expanding paradigm of the discipline. In his research on the speech of Norwich, a city in south-east England, Trudgill (for instance, in Trudgill 1974 and 1975) demonstrated that middle-class men appeared to choose to take on local features in their speech in certain contexts – such as football matches – where masculinity is favoured. On the other hand, these men even claimed to use local forms when they did not actually do so. Trudgill termed this feature *covert prestige*. Interestingly, Trudgill's data appeared to suggest that working class women regularly took on more standardised (and less local) features in their speech, a feature he termed *overt prestige*.

We can see something of this in his treatment of a range of three variables which are marked both for class and regional associations in Norwich: (yu) in *beautiful*, where variants without /j/ are less overtly prestigious than those with; and (er) in *hair* and (o) in *slow*, where differing vowel combinations are highly marked between Received Pronunciation (RP; or its near relatives) and vernacular Norwich speech. The differences between what informants *said* they did linguistically and what they actually *did* is very striking, as the following tables demonstrate (Trudgill 1975: 95–6). *Over-r(eporting)* is where someone claims they use the overtly prestigious form, bur actually used the vernacular one; *Under-r(eporting)* is the opposite, representing where someone claims to use the vernacular pronunciation, but actually uses the overtly prestigious one:

It is immediately striking that men, of whatever social background, tend at least to *claim* that they use covertly prestigious forms, while women tend to do the opposite. The difference between these particular variables might be because (yu), unlike the other variables, is a marker of Norfolk identity, both inside and outside the county. People are likely to be highly conscious of the variable and a degree of local pride might accrue to its use (as well as, naturally, a degree of cultural cringe, the unease felt by some locals with speech features which are not always compatible with middle class norms). The other two variables are less well known outside the immediate area and may well be the features most focussed upon in relation to the identification of prescriptive norms in educational and other formal contexts. Trudgill termed this the *sociolinguistic gender pattern*.

Leaving to one side for the moment the discussion of how gender interacts with language use, we can say that Trudgill (and others in the same period) had begun to bring to light the ways in which identity construction acted (often unconsciously) upon language use. Labov himself had been highly aware of how membership of closely-knit associations could affect language use, as shown, for instance, in the

Table 1.1 Variable production and report based on gender in Norwich

Percentage of informants over- and under-reporting (yu):

	Total	Male	Female
Over-reporting	13	0	29
Under-reporting	7	6	7
Accurate	80	94	64

Percentage of informants over- and under-reporting (er):

	Total	Male	Female
Over-reporting	43	22	68
Under-reporting	33	50	14
Accurate	23	28	18

Percentage of informants over- and under-reporting (o):

	Total	Male	Female
Over-reporting	18	12	25
Under-reporting	36	54	18
Accurate	45	34	57

essentially inward-looking and exclusive friendship connections found in the Harlem street gangs his team analysed in the late 1960s (Labov 1972a). Many of these insights lead into the findings of Trudgill and others (notably Cheshire 1982) in the 1970s, although it quickly became apparent that the level of exclusivity inherent in a street gang was not found to be necessary to create social ties with and of language.

1.2.3.2 'Second wave'
These views were codified and extended in the second wave of socio-linguistics, initiated by the work of James and Lesley Milroy from the late 1970s on (see, for instance, L. Milroy 1987). The language varieties of the Irish city of Belfast on which they worked, at that time going through a thirty year period of social division and unrest which, while deeply regrettable from a personal and societal viewpoint, was particularly productive in relation to sociolinguistic analysis. The Milroys discovered that, although social and ethnic background (and, indeed, gender) was central to a person's linguistic identity, how different people interacted with the social variables dealt to them differed according to a person's sense of belonging to a given social unit. Thus, while it was true in Belfast that people from working class

neighbourhoods were more inclined to realise local features in their speech, some people within these neighbourhoods who, for whatever reason, did not integrate socially with other local people, tended to produce fewer local vernacular features.

The Milroys organised this awareness through harnessing the concept of *social network* from sociology, demonstrating that the higher the number of ties you had with the people with whom you lived – through work, relationship, voluntary ties associated with politics or religion, and so on – the more likely you were to use local features in your speech. These *dense* network ties encouraged the linguistic local-ism of members' language and were associated almost wholly with working class speech. On the other hand, middle class (particularly lower middle class) people would participate in much looser and more geographically diffuse social networks. It was unlikely, for instance, that a lower middle class man would live near either his place of work or colleagues. He might well be a member of a number of voluntary organisations, but these would not be so likely to be locally based.

In general it must therefore be accepted that loose network ties are likely to encourage more standard forms of language, since the people with whom a member of a loose network interacts are far less likely to associate vernacular features with a particular place with which they feel solidarity. Instead a person is judged on her linguistic behaviour according to more prestigious and less local standards. Having said that, however, perhaps the greatest single discovery the Milroys made was that while dense networks encouraged linguistic innovation (as well as retention – the two are not always distinguishable across the wider society), it was loose networks which encouraged the spread of these innovations, possibly because of their number and demographic and geographical extent. The linguistic insecurity of the lower middle classes could therefore be said to be one prop of the edifice of linguistic change and its transfer and duplication.

1.2.3.3 'Third wave'

To some sociolinguists, however, the idea that class, however analysed and constructed, is the primary pole of meaningful social linguistic vari-ation is an over-simplification. People also form social (and linguistic) groups because of what they do and what they perceive their interests to be. In pioneering work based upon fieldwork from the early 1980s in the suburbs of Detroit, Eckert (in particular 2000) demonstrated that background (which could be seen at least somewhat parallel to class), aspirations and plain friendship could lead a person to behave (again probably mainly in an unconscious way) linguistically like their associ-

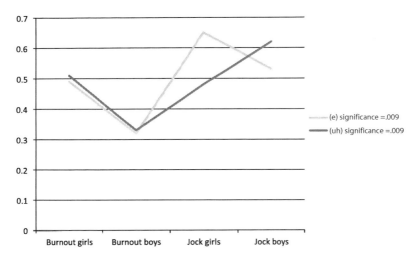

Figure 1.1 Backing of (ʌ) – represented by (uh) – and (e) in Belten High

ates. The fact that Eckert based her findings upon the language use of adolescents gave them extra focus, since there is never as much a sense of close friendship (and also peer pressure, for good and bad) as there is during that period in someone's life. The need to conform – even in favour of nonconformism – is considerable for most adolescents. American high schools, with their dualistic natures (played out in Eckert's work between often middle class and aspirational *Jocks*, earnest collaborators in extra-curricular school life, and locally-oriented, communally committed, generally 'blue collar' *Burnouts*) also lend themselves to stark contrasts, as seen, for instance, in this diagram (adapted from Eckert 2000: 117), where (particularly male) Burnouts generally favour one vowel variant and Jocks favouring another (with girls on this occasion being more inclined to use the 'Jock variable' than their male equivalents; more could naturally be made on these gender distinctions than is possible here).

This type of relationship was also teased out through an anthropological view of how linguistic variation should be analysed, with long-term participant observation becoming the norm. Eckert's great contribution to the debate was the suggestion that choice of variant could be group-centred. The group might be perceived as a *community of practice*; speaking in a particular way is a central marker of group membership. Inherent in this idea, of course, is the recognition that speakers may be members of more than one group and that their linguistic behaviour might differ from group to group, normally unconsciously.

It is, of course, unlikely that linguistic variables can be assumed in a 'pick and mix' manner according to which network and context (*domain* in the language of macrosociolinguistics) a particular speaker wishes to identify himself with at a particular time. But the 'third wave' of sociolinguistics *has* demonstrated that language use is not fully essentialist in its nature. We can to a considerable degree mould ourselves linguistically to a domain in order to fit in that context, although much of this moulding is probably semi-conscious. This extended 'palette' of linguistic ability helps to explain why we are capable of considerable linguistic variation, variation which readily leads to linguistic change.

1.2.4 Change in apparent and real time

Most of us make the assumption that people's language is representative of the speech of their childhood (or, extended, their teenage years). Thus, my father, born in 1926, might have been expected to represent the speech of working class males from the industrial west of Scotland who grew up immediately before and during the Second World War. There are problems with such an assumption, however. Retaining the personal interpretation, my father, after naval service towards the end of the war, attended university (the first in his family) and qualified as a schoolteacher. In this profession he eventually rose to the rank of Primary School Headteacher. He was also actively involved at both a local and Scottish level in the largest of the Scottish teachers' unions. It could be argued – indeed, it is practically provable – that his speech was affected by a professional trajectory rather different from most of his primary schoolmates, who would generally have left school at 14 and eventually sold their labour – skilled or unskilled. This analysis does not take into account a further contributory and complicating factor – that there was Gaelic in my father's family and that he was exposed to that language as a child.

Moreover, the assumption of lack of change over a lifetime does not acknowledge the ways in which linguistic (and indeed other) fashions affect us at different times in our lives. In non-linguistic terms, there is a period, roughly from the ages of fourteen to a little under thirty, when we feel obliged either to follow the current fashions or to make a statement in our dress (as was suggested in our discussion of *communities of practice* above). Of course, some people continue to take an interest in fashion and most of us do not go out of our way to be desperately unfashionable; nonetheless, it is not an issue which troubles most of us. Linguistically, there are periods in our lives where – we might postulate – we are more likely to move towards a rather homogenised view of linguistic appropriateness, one where we are likely to coincide in use with many of our age cohort across a relatively wide space, rendered practically global in the last twenty years (indeed Eckert's analysis of behaviour – and language use – in an American high school discussed above essentially proves these points). At other times, most notably both in childhood and later in life, we are more inclined to be 'conservative' in language, employing norms which have been learned closer to home (or through overt prestige), rather than through the fashions of that particular era. Of course, this retrenchment is unlikely to be complete: some of the elements of language which you picked up in your teenage years are likely to be retained later in life; during your teenage years, moreover, many of the presiding elements in your linguistic makeup – where you were born, your social background, your gender, and so on – are unlikely to be completely obscured, except through a radical – and often traumatic – restructuring of character and status.

Thus *change in apparent time* in many ways prompts as many questions as it answers, since we cannot normally know the personal (linguistic) history of all informants in a study. Nevertheless, if analysed intelligently, we can begin to build up an idea of how change is passing through a community (for an in-depth discussion of how information of this type can be used, see J. Milroy 1992: 136–54, where he also deals with what is to follow). *Change in real time* gives a more accurate sense of how these changes affect individuals and groups, but is also inherently challenging.

In many regions today a contemporary linguistic analysis may be partly replicating some of the material found in earlier studies; at the very least, recordings (or, earlier, transcriptions and descriptions) exist which can be compared with modern data. Thus recordings made with 40-year-olds in 1950 can be compared with data from 40-year-olds recorded in 2000. If the informants come from essentially the same backgrounds, we can probably assume that the linguistic differences evinced demonstrate actual change over the period (although what this change truly represents is another matter). Of course there are always a number of issues skewing this assumption – working class women in their forties in 1950 would probably not have been as used to being recorded (never mind the size of the recording devices) as would have been the case with a similar sample from 2000, for instance, making the former group's language more stilted or formal than that of later groups. But generally we are comparing like with like.

Even more interesting is where we can compare the same groups – perhaps even at times the same speakers – across time. Thus a group of 20 year olds in 1950 could be compared with a group of 70 year olds in 2000. If the backgrounds of the two groups are similar – or, as is often the case, the actual groups are very similar – we can assume that what we analyse represents the change in language inculcated in an individual across a significant part of a lifetime (in a sense, therefore, coming close to answering some of the problems associated with *change in apparent time* discussed above).

1.2.5 Change from above and below

Connected to these concepts is a further binary opposition: *change from above* and *change from below*. These concepts can be – and often are – interpreted in two ways, both of some importance to the kinds of sociolinguistics discussed in this book. From one viewpoint, the two terms refer to our conscious awareness of a change or feature. If a change comes from above, we are consciously aware of it, while when it comes from below, it is something which we take on board without being fully aware of it (since, Keller 1994 suggests, most change spreads through the working of the 'invisible hand', at work in all communities, but not normally discernible to members). An example of the former is the spread of gender neutral and non-sexist vocabulary in English from the 1970s on (for a recent discussion, see Pauwels 2011). No matter a person's ideological position, assuming these changes was not effortless and, for a long time, demanded a concentration to remember what terms to use (and *not* to use) not normally necessary for vocabulary items.

Change from below is a very different matter. In the course of the 1970s and 1980s, the /u/ used by people in Aberdeen, previously pronounced in the back of the mouth, came to be pronounced in the middle or even the front, thus bringing local pronunciation in line with pronunciation in the more populous central regions of Scotland. This was quite a major change, involving alterations in the pronunciation of a considerable number of words. And yet hardly any native Aberdonian is aware that it happened; generally it was long-term residents who grew up somewhere else who noticed it, because, I imagine, the connections they had built up between the patterns of their native dialect and Aberdonian had been complicated by the change (Millar 2007a: 48).

An alternative view of these terms can be put forward, based upon an essentially hierarchical model of society, present in most cultures. Linguistic change from below is the result of (overtly) less prestigious linguistic varieties influencing more prestigious ones. Thus, until the 1960s, speakers of the RP accent socially dominant in (south-east) England used a not completely low front vowel /æ/ in words like *cat*; at the same time, speakers from the English Midlands and elsewhere had a completely low pronunciation (/a/: often termed 'flat' in the popular literature on the subject). From the beginning of the 1960s on, younger RP speakers began to use this less prestigious pronunciation (Upton, Davis and Houck 2008). It might be suggested that this was possibly because the period was one in which 'classlessness' (in other words, the reinforcement of lower middle class political as well as linguistic hegemony) was becoming central to the ideology of a new Britain. This suggests, in fact, that other kinds of prestige, not associated with large-scale sources of power within a society, are available as speakers, consciously and unconsciously, construct their identity (of which more will be said in the following section).

Change from above, from this point of view, represents essentially the opposite tendency. Linguistic features which were previously only found in more overtly prestigious varieties influence the pronunciations of less prestigious. Thus the use of /ʌ/ in words like *cut* and *sulk* in southern English varieties, including RP, has gradually affected, largely through mass education, the pronunciation of speakers from the English midlands and north, where /ʊ/ was historically the norm. Many speakers from the latter regions have maintained the traditional pronunciations, although almost all can produce some centralised vowel compromise (see, for instance, Wells 1982: II, 351–3). The lower middle classes of the English midlands and north in particular have assimilated the southern vowel, however, often through elocution classes, at least in the past. The fact that hypercoristic pronunciations such as /kʌp əv 'ʃʌgə/ (for 'cup of sugar') exist demonstrates how salient this feature is to the identity construction of speakers from these backgrounds. They could also, of course, be interpreted as change spreading through loose social networks. The two interpretations are not mutually exclusive, naturally.

It should be noted, however, that the prestige involved may not be of the most obvious type. Fifty years ago, vernacular speech in Norfolk (in the south-east of England) was /h/-full (although Norwich, the county seat, is /h/-less), in the sense that words like *help* begin with this consonant. Most working class varieties from the south-east of England are /h/-less, however. This includes the working class speech of London (often termed 'Cockney'). Although Cockney pronunciations have always been frowned upon by educationalists and other gatekeepers of traditional prestige, there is no doubt that its associations are attractive to both working class people from elsewhere in the region and some middle class speakers (whose variety is often termed 'Mockney'). This kind of influence can be seen in Norfolk, where /h/-less pronunciations appear to be becoming the norm in working-class speech (Trudgill

1983: 77; see also Trudgill 1986). The level to which this change (and its identity associations) has been consciously adopted by speakers is probably of a different order to that discussed in the preceding paragraph: there can be little doubt that conscious efforts are being made.

1.2.6 Macrosociolinguistics

As well as the microsociolinguistic features discussed above, macrosociolinguistic interpretations can be found throughout this book. Most of these will be discussed in depth in the following chapters; but it does make sense to give some idea of how the field constructs itself here.

Macrosociolinguistics (sometimes termed the 'sociology of language') might be interpreted as representing a view of language use associated with the idea of relationships between different language varieties and different groups of speakers. At times these relationships can be highly stable and normally peaceable. At other times, however, struggle is omnipresent. In any such relationship, however, it can be assumed that some language varieties have greater 'cultural capital' invested in them, as Bourdieu (for instance, 1986) would describe it, than others. This 'capital' is also regularly associated with economic and political force.

In this brief introduction we will consider only one major macrosociolinguistic tendency: *diglossia*, a feature which has turned up regularly in English, but which can be seen most readily in the relationship between French and English (and their speakers) in the two centuries following the Norman Conquest of England of 1066–7. Initially popularised in English by Ferguson (1959), diglossia refers to a situation where in a particular society one language variety occupies High (H) position, while another occupies the Low (L). It might be assumed that everyone would choose to use H in order to give themselves more assumed power, but in diglossic societies L also has highly positive associations for its speakers. It is likely, for instance, that a local person who used H with his contemporaries, whether he was intimate with them or not, would find himself considered at the very least deeply unpopular and might end up being ostracised. In Shetland, for instance, an archipelago some 150km north of the Scottish mainland, a relationship of equality exists between all the native inhabitants, associated strongly with the local dialect of Scots (see Millar 2007a and 2008). If someone chooses to use Scottish Standard English in these communities (which may not now include the capital, Lerwick: Sundkvist 2007; Smith and Durham 2011), the activity will be considered offensive by others. There is even a word, *knappin*, to describe the act of a Shetlander speaking English in a situation where everyone speaks a Shetland variety. On the other hand, if I were a Shetlander giving a talk to school or college students in Shetland on a formal subject such as meteorology, I would use H almost all the time, although possibly not when answering questions or, on this occasion, when referring to different kinds of weather or cloud formations. To almost everyone within a community where diglossia exists relationships of this type seem absolutely normal. Ferguson points out that the relationships involved are highly stable, although they can break down and, as I have pointed out elsewhere (Millar 2005: Chapter 1), extended literacy and mass education may encourage this (although sociological processes of this sort do not *demand* it).

Ferguson suggested that diglossia could only really exist where H and L were variants of the same language (as is the case – at a push – with Scottish Standard English and Shetland Scots). Fishman (1967), however, believes that H and L could actually be entirely separate linguistically. For instance, in the Flanders of the eighteenth and early nineteenth century, the H variety, the language of culture and administration, was Standard French; the language of the great mass of the people was Dutch, spoken in a range of Flemish dialects. If you were literate, you would be so primarily in French; even if you were not, you would still inhabit this Francophile environment, whether you could speak French or not. But with the exception of some members of the urban, particularly Brussels, haute bourgeoisie, almost all Flemish people spoke their local language as a badge of pride and identity. Until the beginning of mainstream Flemish activism in the later nineteenth century, most people would not have questioned this relationship (see Strikwerda 1997: Chapter 2). This by any accepted analysis represents a diglossic environment.

With a concept like diglossia we can perceive a form of sociolinguistics which does not (directly) refer to linguistic variants, instead seeing language as being among the features which are used to define identity, position in the hierarchy, occupation, and so on. Naturally, macrosociolinguistics and microsociolinguistics can rarely be fully separated; instead, the one informs the other. One of this book's primary objectives is to demonstrate how this interaction can be played back into the history of the English language.

1.3 Conclusions

We can therefore say that sociolinguistics in all its forms has gone a long way towards explaining linguistic variation. If, as seems highly likely, an explanation for linguistic variation has inherent in it the basis for an explanation for contemporary linguistic change, then, as has already been suggested, we should be able to extrapolate these features into the past.

Further reading

Good one-volume accounts of microsociolinguistic theory and practice are Chambers (2009) and Milroy and Gordon (2003). There is no equivalent volume for macrosociolinguistics, although Millar (2005) covers a number of issues.

Some issues to consider

1. With your family and friends, can you trace linguistic change across the generations? Where is this easiest to see: with lexis, phonology or structure?
2. Identify a characteristic variable in the variety spoken where you come from. Is its use seen positively by (a) insiders and (b) outsiders?
3. In the riots in England in Summer 2011, those involved used social media such as Twitter or Facebook to discuss what was going on. Often the police were referred to as the *Feds*. Given that this is the name given to the FBI in the United States and would never normally be used for police officers in England, what (a) caused people to use the term and (b) what age group (if you had no other evidence) would use this phrase?

2 Language change and sociolinguistic processes in the past

2.1 Sociolinguistic change in the recent past: /r/ in New York City

As has already been mentioned, probably the most famous sociolinguistic research ever carried out – certainly the one students learn about first – concerns Labov's rapid investigation into the use of /r/ by assistants in three socially differentiated department stores in New York City (Labov 1966). Its fame derives both from its clearness and its apparent simplicity (which actually masks brilliant insight).

Labov was puzzled over what appeared to be an entirely illogical change. In the first half of the twentieth century, the speech of all natives of New York City, no matter their social background, was non-rhotic: /r/ was pronounced only initially or preceding vowels. Words such as *card* or *car* were never pronounced with /r/. By the 1960s, however, some natives of the city were starting to use /r/ in its historical positions, albeit not on all occasions (linguists believe that even if you pronounce /r/ only occasionally in all positions, you are still rhotic because you are able to produce the historical pattern: see Trudgill 2010: 148–9), no matter how intermittent. This kind of resurrection is very unusual.

Labov postulated that people from more prestigious social backgrounds would be more likely to show this re-adoption in their speech, while working class people would generally avoid it (or at least not succumb to prestige pressure). With this in mind, he chose to analyse the language use of shop assistants at three department stores on Manhattan – Saks, Macy's and S. Klein – whose target clientele were, roughly, upper middle class, lower middle class and working class. In each store, Labov asked for directions to a section which he already knew was on the Fourth Floor, a phrase which had both a medial and final *r*, two positions which, Labov postulated, could have different /r/ use. When he had asked for assistance, he then feigned difficulty in hearing the first answer, thus encouraging a second response which, again he assumed, would involve a more emphatic pronunciation of *Fourth Floor* (these final

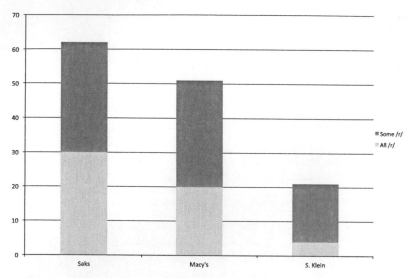

Figure 2.1 Percentage overall stratification of /r/ by store use (Labov 1966)

two points will not be dealt with any further in this discussion, although they are of some importance to Labov's interpretation).

It quickly became apparent that his assumptions were, by and large, correct. Both middle class-associated stores had considerable rhoticity (with a majority of utterances showing variable /r/ use). As suggested by the hypothesis, the more upmarket store, Saks, had assistants who were more rhotic in comparison to those employed by Macy's, although this was a matter of degree, rather than absolute distinction. Equally interesting was the fact that the assistants in S. Klein were also sometimes rhotic (although at a rather lower level: 21% of utterances, in comparison with 51% and 62% for Macy's and Saks respectively). If the social assumptions made about the stores and their employees is correct, these figures suggest that, while the change to full rhoticity is less advanced in working class communities than in middle class ones, the change is nonetheless of considerable prestige in the former communities.

In support of this view, analysis was also made of the divergent rhoticity of people with different jobs within a department store, no matter its intended clientele. Again, the expected results made themselves apparent as Figure 2.2 demonstrates.

Again we see that floorwalkers, ranked higher than sales clerks on the shop floor, are more prestigious in their speech, a phenomenon which can be associated with their greater authority and prestige when dealing

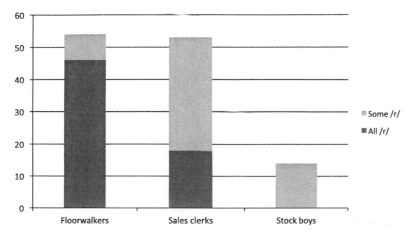

Figure 2.2 Percentage stratification of /r/ by occupational groups

with the public. What is interesting, however, is that both 'classes' have almost the same proportion of rhoticity in their speech; it is just that the sales clerks evince more examples of partial rhoticity. Moreover, as we might expect, stock boys, who are present in stores but whose work is considered menial, rarely involving much interaction with customers, have limited rhoticity, including no examples of full rhoticity. Strikingly, however, they do realise some partial rhoticity. It has to be recognised, of course, that the numbers of floor walkers and stock boys who provided evidence are much smaller than that of sales clerks. It is quite possible that a few unusual pronunciations could affect our interpretation. But the results are indicative. Again this all points to the conclusion that /r/ is highly prestigious in New York City.

There are, of course, a number of problems with this survey, ones which Labov recognised from the beginning of his work. For our purposes, as we discussed in Chapter 1, the most important of these is the assumption that the shop assistants in the various department stores would be of the same social background as the intended clientele. This is particularly problematical with Saks since, we can assume, most upper middle class women and men would not have taken jobs of this type in the early 1960s, except perhaps while students. By the same token, assistants in S. Klein may have been more middle class than the intended clientele. It might be assumed, in fact, that S. Klein could have employed people from more prestigious backgrounds in order to appear 'classy'. There is, of course, only so far that this can go: too great a social (and therefore linguistic) separation between assistants and clienteles might put the latter off by making them feel unwelcome. While it is true that patterns of behaviour associated with linguistic accommodation rules may make assistants more likely to assume elements of the linguistic behaviour of their clientele, in a desire to fit in and give a sense of closeness (perhaps the central discussion of phenomena of this type is Giles, Coupland and Coupland 1991), we cannot assume that this would be complete or nearly 100% accurate. With this in mind, therefore, Labov carried out more controlled tests on /r/ use in the city.

In the first instance, Labov concentrated on the different contexts in which /r/ could be found in speech, moving from casual conversation through to levels of considerable formality and concentration on the speech act. These he defined as *casual speech, careful speech, reading style, word lists* and *minimal pairs*. At the same time he employed a far more nuanced analysis of social background for his informants, instead of the rather blunt three-way split employed in the preliminary study. He used a ten-way split, with 0–1 representing the 'Lower Class', 2–4 Working Class groups, 4 being Upper Working Class, skilled and often aspirational, 5–8 being the Lower Middle Class and 9 the Upper Middle Class. His primary assumption was that the higher your social background, the more likely you were to possess full rhoticity. This was indeed shown, but only partly and with one major exception, demonstrated in Figure 2.3.

In the less casual speaking styles, the 'social order' expected is maintained, although it is noteworthy that some of the lower middle class groups are more inclined even in 'careful speech' to have rhoticity than are the groupings 'below' them. But in the highly formal circumstances of word lists and minimal pairs, something rather remarkable happens. All social groupings realise more use of /r/ in these contexts. But a large part of the lower middle classes actually 'jump' the upper middle class informants. This suggests both that the lower middle classes may be central to the variation in use which is encouraging the re-adoption of the original /r/ use pattern and that what is driving the change is a perception on their part that, insecure of their status in comparison with the upper middle classes, /r/-fulness is therefore prestigious and to be strived for. It could well be argued that the lower middle classes are more inclined towards having loose social networks, thereby encouraging rapid spread of change across space in ways dense networks cannot achieve. But although their evidence is particularly marked, all New York City informants accede to the view that full rhoticity is to be welcomed. Yet these findings do not themselves explain where this unusual change originated; social history may well achieve this.

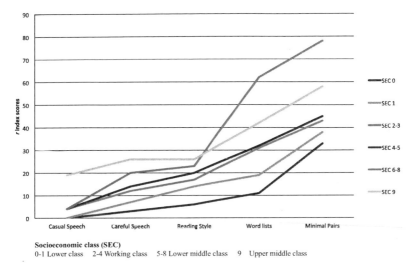

Figure 2.3 /r/ use according to social background and level of formality
(Labov 1966)

2.1.1 The history and ideology of /r/ use in the United States

2.1.1.1 Nativism in the American tradition

From almost the beginning of the settlement of English speakers in
what is now the United States a nativist tradition has existed (Bennett
1988), based upon the idea that those already resident had the right
to make the 'rules' of behaviour and custom for later immigrants,
along with, most importantly, the right to refuse entrance to these
later arrivals, basing these decisions both on numbers of inhabitants
and perceived compatibility of custom. How much these views were
current in everyday experience and discourse is difficult to calculate.
It is true, for instance, that the nativist tradition in American political life, often associated during the period with one form of populism
or another, was deeply suspicious of British intentions. Nevertheless,
the nativist tradition also saw America as being essentially white and
northern European at heart, despite Benjamin Franklin's (1706–1790)
rather odd rant against 'swarthy' [sic] Swedes (Franklin 1961: 234) in
an uncharacteristically racist piece of journalism. Northern Europeans,
Bonfiglio (2002) suggests, were seen as hard-working 'sod-breakers',
associated with the pioneer life still being lived in the American
Midwest in the last decades of the nineteenth century). They were
'not afraid of hard work', were unquestioningly loyal to their country

(with little or no residual loyalty to their ancestors' countries of origin); they lived the American dream even before this was codified. At their heart were people of 'Anglo-Saxon' origin (often including, somewhat surprisingly, people of Scottish and Ulster Scots – 'Scotch-Irish' – background), with other Germanic peoples – the Germans (and Dutch – the two were often conflated) and the Scandinavians (including, sometimes, the Finns) – generally being seen as part of the same group. Protestantism was generally a requirement for entry, although German- and English-speaking Catholics, with the exception of the Irish, might be included. Sects such as the Mennonites were not included, perhaps because of their exclusivity or their communal practices. When the Dutch American Theodore Roosevelt (1858–1919), who came from a well-heeled and largely urban background, chose to move west and become a rancher, hunter and, albeit in a way not entirely unlike Marie Antoinette pretending to be a shepherdess, a pioneer, he was living the ideal of his ethnic identity and destiny as a 'true American'. He was not alone. As Bonfiglio demonstrates, the iconography of this white, northern – often male – European identity can be found in central publications throughout the period when the United States was beginning to take on the role, albeit rather reluctantly, of world power in the late nineteenth century.

As is nearly always the case, an iconography of this type needs an *other*, an opposite to bring the desired ideas and groups into focus. As well as African Americans, who did not enter much into the debate, the largest group which was felt to be different to, and potentially damaging towards, the 'true American' ideal were recent immigrants. As well as the Chinese and Japanese, where racism was codified in legislation in a range of, normally western, states, it was the Irish, southern Europeans and eastern and central Europeans who were considered most 'foreign' and threatening. This was largely due to their religion (many were Catholics or Jews, traditions towards which many Americans felt antagonistic), their ways of life (which often stressed communal over individual virtues and, no matter their 'old country' origins, urban over rural life; many immigrants were also considered to be dirty and 'backward'), their associations with crime (inevitably exaggerated, but real nonetheless, normal among the urban poor), their politics (associated either with ethnic 'bosses' delivering a block vote to a corrupt city government or with far left ideologies) and their language use. With the (partial) exception of the Irish, these immigrants did not have English as their first language. The urban dialects of the northern east coast – Boston and New York in particular, but also to an extent Philadelphia and other smaller centres – along with Chicago, Pittsburgh, St Louis and Detroit further west – came to be associated with these immigrant communities. Although some of the features of these urban vernaculars *were* derived from other languages, such as the loss of /θ/ and /ð/ in New York working class speech, or the sporadic devoicing of final consonants in Chicago speech, most of the features of these varieties are very much part of the dialect mainstream of English. The ideology which considered them foreign was strong and long-lasting, however, and had striking (and in many ways unexpected) effects on the language use of middle class (or aspirational upper working class) speakers. It is in this framework that we must now place the re-adoption of /r/ in the speech of New York City.

2.1.1.2 Rhoticity in the English-speaking world

/r/-loss is an ongoing process in the English-speaking world, whether due to direct influence and diffusion of the change from south-east England or because of a general propensity (*drift* – a concept we will discuss in greater depth later in the book) on the part of many varieties sundered around the world (Trudgill 2010: Chapter 7). As of the beginning of the 2010s, full rhoticity is only found in small pockets in England and Wales – in the south-west of England, central Lancashire and rural Northumberland. Non-rhotic dialects are the norm in South Asian Englishes, most Caribbean varieties (although not Barbados and a few other islands and regions) and all southern hemisphere varieties (with the partial exception of the Scots-influenced Southland varieties of New Zealand). On the eastern seaboard of the United States, loss of rhoticity is widespread, particularly in urbanised areas directly on the coast, all the way from Charleston to Boston. While there is little evidence for the change spreading from these centres much beyond their hinterlands (with the exception of African American Vernacular English speakers in particular), there can be little doubt of its prestige in many places.

New York City therefore bucks this trend. More surprisingly, the change is being reversed in such a way that the prior rhoticity has come again into being in *exactly* the distribution found before the change. The chances of this happening are very low. If, for instance, a non-rhotic person attempts to mimic a rhotic speaker – most English people imitating Scottish accents, for instance – the chances of a completely accurate representation are practically nil, except among talented and highly experienced impressionists and phoneticians. /r/ is used before consonants when it is remembered, of course (although it may be generalised: I have heard English speakers saying /bard/ for *bad* when impersonating Scottish pronunciations), but the 'intrusive' hiatus avoidance /r/, in phrases such as *law and order*, common in the non-rhotic dialects of England, remains. In other words, the temporary rhoticity is only a variation on the normal non-rhotic usage. Regaining a whole system is a much more serious issue.

That is not to say that phenomena of this type are unknown. As readers of Dickens will recognise, and further evidence from the nineteenth century points out, working class people from the south of England during this period appear to have confused /w/ and /v/ words initially, perhaps pronouncing the originally separate sounds at an intermediate place, such as [β]. By the first decades of the twentieth century, however, dialectological surveys demonstrated that this merger had been entirely reversed. With apparently problematical developments of this type, sociolinguists have generally seized upon the concept of *near-merger*. This is a feature whereby pronunciations which divide two sets of words move very close to each other, to the extent that native speakers may not consciously 'hear' a difference, without there being an absolute merger. It could be argued that an intermediate stage in /r/-loss, along the lines of [ʊ], is very similar to the pronunciation of /r/ in the speech of many people (a pronunciation which makes *rawl* appear to be *wall* to some listeners). This similarity (but not merger) allowed the backwards step in New York speech. In other words, merger with zero had not entirely happened; instead, connections between rhotic (or semi-rhotic) pronunciations for one form were maintained at a certain, low attestation, level. But a full reversal implies a considerable alteration in social associations for certain sound patterns across a considerable population.

In his discussion of the southern English /w/ and /v/ merger, however, Trudgill (2010: Chapter 3) suggests that while near-mergers do indeed occur, other explanations might be possible for de-merger, including contact with nearby varieties which did not have the merger. Something like this has obviously happened with the speech of New York City, since most of its immediate hinterland in New York State is rhotic (as of course is most of the United States which all, in a sense, acts as New York City's hinterland). It is likely that non-rhotic New Yorkers heard rhotic varieties every day and had assimilated this alternative system (probably osmotically and at most semi-consciously), particularly given that the size, wealth and excitement of the city would inevitably have drawn immigrants not only from abroad but also from its hinterland. The question therefore is why speakers in an urban area should choose largely to abandon their native system in favour of that of rural districts which we would expect them to consider somewhat backward and conservative.

2.1.1.3 New York rhoticity

The first answer seems to be that the lower middle classes of New York City identified with the external views on non-rhotic pronunciations – including their own – as representing foreign and dangerous ideas rather than merely a local phonological feature. In order to avoid being considered in some senses 'un-American', this highly linguistically sensitive population began to shift towards full /r/ use: an innovation for them, although historically a reversion to an earlier, more conservative, state.

But another sociolinguistic factor needs to be allowed into the discussion, Bonfiglio (2002) argues. For the first hundred years and more of the United States' existence, the eastern elites, generally using non-rhotic varieties, dominated the country, despite the presence of 'backwoods' presidents such as Andrew Jackson (1767–1845; in origin an Appalachian mountaineer of Ulster Scots descent) and Abraham Lincoln (1809–65; born in Kentucky, but came to prominence almost on the contemporary frontier in Illinois). Leaders such as both presidents Roosevelt (Theodore, 1858–1919; Franklin D., 1882–1945) – upper middle class New Yorkers – spoke with accents which, to our ears, may sometimes sound English, primarily because they are non-rhotic. John F. Kennedy (1917–63), a Bostonian, was also non-rhotic; although, as a Catholic of Irish descent, he cannot be said to be of the Establishment, he certainly sounded as if he was. Actors like Bette Davis (1908–89) and Katherine Hepburn (1907–2003) were also phonologically at least part of this apparent mainstream.

Yet the majority of Americans did not come from this kind of background, socially, geographically or linguistically. The populism so closely related to the American tradition, for good *and* bad, has always mistrusted the presence of elites. Throughout the late nineteenth and early twentieth century in particular, much mileage was made of the contrast between the 'honest' toil of farmers and inhabitants of small towns and the moneyed, speculating and decadent elite (under which guise anti-Semitism could sometimes be hinted at without needing to be expressed) who held the former in thrall through their banks and savings and loans companies and fixed exchange rates.

Part of this non-elite image was linguistic: the straight-talking Midwesterner or Westerner has become a commonplace now, but was a product of this age. As the twentieth century grew older, the accents of the Midwest and California became more desirable on radio, films, television and, eventually, in politics, due to this ideological identification and also, it must be recognised, the economic power of Texas and California in particular. Through all of this, rhotic dialects came to be seen by many – including non-rhotic speakers – as being quintessentially American. It might be argued, in fact, that New York middle-class speakers were especially susceptible to this influence because of the city's particular association with immigration and its assumed problems and their desire (often as second or third generation immigrants themselves) to distance themselves from later immigrants, as suggested above.

2.1.2 Discussion

Thus we can see that a modern sociolinguistically induced set of changes, apparently against the flow of language change, can be attributed to the influence of sociohistorical factors reaching back between three to four hundred years which became particularly acute in the middle decades of the twentieth century. In the next section we will consider whether these techniques and concerns can be taken further back in time to societies very different from ours.

2.2 Sociolinguistic change in the more distant past

2.2.1 The sociology of the past

For at least the last 10,000 years or so, it would be reasonable to say that human beings have not changed much. Our mental capacities and our ability to produce language were already in place at the close of the last Ice Age; this meant that our ancestors could teach skills and knowledge about the past, a knowledge transfer passed down the generations. In a sense, while our means of transferring these concepts and skills have expanded considerably, we have not advanced from this vantage point.

But human society has changed greatly. The social structures of a gatherer-hunter society are necessarily casual and highly egalitarian, primarily because there is no benefit to be derived from allowing hierarchical social patterns to develop. Urban centres, however, are inherently hierarchical, no matter their size, since co-ordination of the urban area's defence, production and successful administration practically demands the institution of a top-down model of organisation. Moreover, urban areas encourage occupational specialisation which, of its nature, encourages a sense of separation – geographical and ideological – or even of exclusivity.

Moreover, the ways in which economic systems have worked have altered regularly throughout human history. In the industrialised economies of western Europe and its offshoots from about 1850 to around

1975, manufacturing industries formed the largest single contributor to gross domestic product (Hopkins 2000). Capital which enabled these industries was also largely tied up in them. In order to maintain production, a large class of workers – often termed the proletariat – was necessary; wherever possible, employers attempted to keep wages low to maintain competitiveness. Exploitative though elements of this system undoubtedly were, particularly in its first fifty years or so, there was rarely a lack of acknowledgement that workers – both individually and collectively – were free agents who had a right to withdraw their labour if better deals were available elsewhere. Social mobility was possible as well, even if most people remained in the same essential social class throughout their lives.

This is in marked contrast to the social and economic relationships of ancient Rome (Joshel 2010). From around when Rome utterly crushed its main rival, Carthage, in the second century BCE and became involved in the politics of the eastern Mediterranean basin, the primary economic relationship was slavery. In country districts, large slave-powered estates quickly undercut the traditional smallholdings of free peasants; in cities, the free urban poor's traditional means of earning were gradually rendered obsolete. While the monotony, low pay and poor conditions of modern early capitalist industry may have made members of the proletariat feel themselves to be essentially slaves, their basic liberty at least presented the possibility of bettering their lots, whether through collective bargaining or accession to a higher social class through hard work, education, politicking and good luck, in ways which were not open to those considered the property of their masters.

It is worth noting, moreover, that, even synchronically, people living in different parts of the world, even in similar social situations, may interpret their social relationships and obligations in different ways. Many Americans, for instance, consider the liberty stressed in their constitution to be an abiding difference between their own society and others. Liberty is considered the central factor allowing for social mobility and therefore the fulfilment of the 'American Dream'. Despite the fact that civil liberties in the United States may not actually be any more enabling than in similar countries in Europe, the American ideology leads to a somewhat different view of how society should be organised than is the case elsewhere. Despite the American governmental bureaucracy's size and considerable power, an ideology of self-help and community volunteerism prevails, leading to a rather more personal sense of social relationship than may be prevalent elsewhere (we will return to this point in more detail in Chapter 5). This can be distinguished from other highly developed societies of the modern period where the needs and ambitions of individuals have been essentially sub-ordinated by the 'common good', no matter how interpreted. Modern China, for instance, has tended to emphasise the concept of the rights of the community over the rights of the individual, deriving this view both from interpretations of Communism and the views of early Chinese philosophers (see, for instance, Angle 2002).

We can go beyond political and economic structures to observe other areas of society analysed historically which differ considerably over even quite short periods. In modern, industrialised society it was the norm that only men carried out 'bread-winning' work outside the home (although this view must be modified somewhat by the knowledge that particularly in industries requiring skills in close work, such as weaving, women, whether married or not, were dominant demographi-cally, although rarely in relation to power). In the peasant society of Europe in the Middle Ages, however, while there were specific tasks which were generally associated with one gender, the whole family acted as a team working towards, at least, subsistence and, if possible, surplus. The concept of 'wage-earning' was practically meaningless in any event because country people of that period formed part of an informal economy whose relationship to the money supply was by no means straightforward. Gender as a category obviously existed, but its sociolinguistic associations may well have been different from those it has now.

This may even have been the case in contexts closer in time and cultural associations to our own. As discussed in Chapter 1, in the Sociolinguistic Gender Pattern codified by Trudgill and others in the 1970s, a general assumption prevailed that women largely opt for a more overtly prestigious and therefore standardised form of language, while men from similar backgrounds will choose to adopt more ver-nacular, covertly prestigious, norms. There is considerable evidence in autograph texts from seventeenth- and early eighteenth-century Scotland, however, that women were generally more likely to use local forms in their writing than were their male equivalents. Since we know a fair bit about the society in which this variation took place, it is quite straightforward to suggest that patterns of this type represent the effects of education, with middle class boys receiving a longer and more rounded form of education than their sisters. Whether this distinction was also represented in their speech is impossible to say. If there is considerable doubt over what gender means in such a well-documented context, what can be made of earlier contexts where our knowledge of extralinguistic contexts is limited?

But if that question causes considerable problems for our interpretation of the spoken and written use of individuals across time and across society, it cannot be implied from this that sociolinguistic analyses of the past are inherently worthless. In the following section, these issues will be assessed in the light of two sets of changes in the early modern period, an era well enough documented to be readily comprehensible sociologically but whose social structures were sufficiently different from our own to make for a useful comparison.

2.2.2 Two case studies

Let us consider, then, two sets of changes from a period where we know a significant amount about the structure of society and where we have a considerable amount of linguistic information, both contained in corpora and also from contemporary commentary. The first will present information in a somewhat impressionistic way, since the information which it requires is by its nature only observable either through commentary or by the interpretation of not entirely straightforward evidence, largely because its concerns are phonological. Although this field is, of course, central to synchronic sociolinguistics, its historical status means that it cannot readily be subjected to the rigorous statistical analysis normal to sociolinguistics. The second, dealing with syntactic and morphological change, can be seen as adhering to the centre of historical microsociolinguistics.

2.2.2.1 The 'Great Vowel Shift'

2.2.2.1.1 The rise of the 'new man'

The early modern period in English history represented an era of considerable social confusion and change (for a discussion, see Hindle 2000). While social mobility was probably rather more possible in medieval England than the theorists of feudalism would have us believe, there can be little doubt that social and political forces at work from the fourteenth century on were responsible for allowing people from what we might begin to term the lower middle classes to rise in society and, indeed, eventually to control that society.

As well as the social mobility engendered by plague and famine in the middle of the fourteenth century and the chronic insecurity engendered by decades of war against France for a large part of both that century and the following (discussed further in Chapter 3), civil war between feuding parts of the royal family flared up regularly throughout the fifteenth century, leading to the seizure of power in 1485 by Henry Tudor (king of England until 1509), a Welsh adventurer whose connection to the House of Lancaster was tenuous but who had both the distinction of being 'last man standing' and the wit and luck to stabilise and normalise his power base. These upheavals inevitably led to social mobility, primarily because the ranks of the nobility, traditionally the source of social coherence, had been winnowed out. Moreover, the social origins of the Tudor dynasty probably encouraged them to view the nobility as rivals and to look to the 'new men' of the middle classes as their natural allies.

At the same time new forms of thought were also coursing through Europe. While scholars may sometimes be guilty of overestimating the extent to which changes in philosophical fashion affect everyday life, the new learning certainly affected the literate middle classes, possibly loosening some of the social ties which maintained and enforced their position in society (although it is worth noting that scholarly endeavour was rarely associated with the nobility, at least in England; the difference is, perhaps, in the level to which scholars could exert themselves within the new order). Connected to these developments to some extent was the spread of schooling within the population. Functional literacy – the ability to read to some degree and to write if necessity demanded – was probably quite widespread; the middle classes definitely had access to a rather deeper literacy which could easily develop into scholarship, which of itself could provide an entrance to clerical work for the powerful – in particular the royal administration – and therefore proximity to power.

Connected to these developments to some degree at least was the spread of Protestantism. Although it is true that, in the middle of the sixteenth century it was possible to find people who leaned towards Protestantism or Catholicism (and a number of positions in between) at all levels of literate society, the lower middle classes were particularly well represented in the Protestant ranks, possibly because the individualism often associated with the reformers appealed to the social aspirations of that class. Whatever the theological debate, these changes again encouraged literacy, in particular in the vernacular. But does knowledge of these matters help us to understand central linguistic change during the period?

2.2.2.1.2 The shift

In the late medieval and early modern period in all of the West Germanic languages a series of changes took place in relation to the pronunciation of long vowels and (to some extent) diphthongs. These changes did not, however, take place in the North Germanic languages. Thus Modern Norwegian *skrive* /ˈskriːvə/ 'to write' can be compared to German *schreiben* /'ʃraibən/ (or, for that matter, the rare English word *shrive* 'to be given absolution', /ʃraev/ in my pronunciation); Norwegian *hus* /hus/ 'house' can be compared with German *Haus* / haus/ and English (/həus/ in my pronunciation; the monophthongal pronunciations found with Scots and northern English varieties are due to a separate set of developments in those varieties). In its most extensive form, found in English, these sets of changes are referred to as the *Great Vowel Shift* (although it should be noted that a number of scholars would baulk at seeing all the changes as being part of one unit; this debate does not materially affect what follows).

2.2.2.1.3 The evidence

Before we consider the trajectory of the Great Vowel Shift, however, we need to discuss the evidence upon which our discussion is based. This is particularly striking with this set of changes because there is a considerable amount of documentation related to English pronunciation during the period available and, in Dobson (1968), a considerable, although not infallible, treatment of the issues involved. This level of information is not without its problems, however: the interpretation of some evidence can itself lead to many more questions than answers. Nevertheless, the evidence can be broken down into a range of resources.

In the first instance is the evidence derived from rhymes and puns in poetry and drama, although, given the possibility of eye-rhymes, this evidence needs to be carefully and critically analysed. Secondly, there is evidence from bilingual dictionaries – a largely new phenomenon made possible by movable type's facilitating of alphabetical order. If a dictionary says that French *x* is pronounced with the same vowel as English *y*, and this connection is no longer viable in either present-day language, we may be in the presence of evidence of changing pronunciation. The problem is, of course, that we need to know something about the historical phonology of the other language and that therefore there is a danger that argumentation becomes circular. Perhaps more trustworthy are those occasions where English has been written according to the spelling system of another language – most notably, Welsh. While these rare documents are fascinating, however, we have to recognise that, again, our knowledge of historical Welsh phonology may well be based upon less than sure foundations.

The lower middle classes are famously insecure, probably because their status in relation to the working classes and other middle class groups is fragile and open to change not beneficial to the group or individuals. In the modern age at least this has often been represented in the use of language with, as we saw in the last chapter, a tendency towards 'careful' pronunciations and hypercorrection. The early modern era was, of course, an era in which the lower middle classes were growing in numbers and, to an extent, in power; it is unsurprising, therefore, that an industry intended to teach individuals the 'correct' way to pronounce English should have developed. The people behind these publications are generally termed *orthoepists*. As is still the case today, the quality of these publications in terms of accuracy varies from the truly terrible (descriptions of pronunciations which are so unlikely as to be impossible) to the apparently highly accurate. Interpretation is also hampered by there being no agreed ways to describe sound at the time (leading again on occasion to circular descriptions along the lines of '*x* is pronounced like *y* in Italian'), meaning that interpretation of evidence can be highly subjective. Because they are designed to teach 'correct' pronunciations, however, the work of the orthoepists can give us a sense of contemporary social variation: pronunciations which are criticised are likely to be less prestigious (or more novel) at the time, but may develop into the prestige pronunciation in the next generation (possibly through covert prestige in the present one).

2.2.2.1.4 The processes

The processes generally associated with the Great Vowel Shift can in broad terms be described in the following way. At the time of Geoffrey Chaucer (died 1400), London English had, we think, the following long vowels and diphthongs (laid out roughly according to place of pronunciation within a notional vowel quadrilateral). As is the case with all of the discussions on this matter, what follows is a schematisation, albeit based closely upon the evidence:

A number of observations can be made about this system as it stands. Phonologists tend to speak almost in aesthetic terms about vowel systems. Essentially, symmetry is prized. This later Middle English system is in a sense symmetrical, since the vowels associated with *ride*, *been* and *bean* in the front of the mouth and *house*, *tool* and *road* in the back all fall in essentially the same 'slot' in terms of vowel height as do their equivalents. The same is also true for the two diphthongs. Even the fact that back vowels are all rounded and front vowels all unrounded is in a sense symmetrical. What stands out as different is the vowel associated with *made*, which makes the whole system asymmetrical, with four long front vowels being matched with only three long back vowels. Some scholars (notably Smith, J. J. 1996) have claimed from this that it is this asymmetricality which acted as catalyst to the shift (the *made* vowel had been lengthened through the loss of final -*e* only in the late fourteenth century in London English). Connected to these developments are the

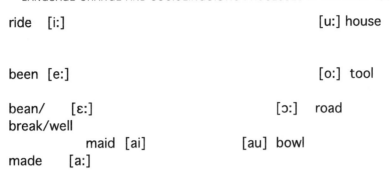

ride   [iː]   [uː] house

been [eː]   [oː] tool

bean/   [ɛː]   [ɔː]   road
break/well
            maid [ai]   [au] bowl
made   [aː]

Figure 2.4 Before the Great Vowel Shift

views put forward by Labov (1994: 176–7) that long ('tense') vowels tend to rise peripherally until there is no further to go (in which case, diphthongisation takes place. It should be noted, however, that, as other scholars have pointed out, this 'rule' is opposed by a considerable number of counter-tendencies)

In the period from around 1425 on, the sounds associated with particular word classes changed. The *ride* class and *house* class moved from being associated with very close vowels to being diphthongs probably pronounced quite high in the mouth. The *been* and *tool* classes moved from being associated with close mid pronunciations to having close pronunciation near the top of the mouth.[1]

What is striking about this stage (Stage 1 in my typology) is that the symmetry which was *almost* present in the Chaucerian system has actually lessened because of the changes. In the first instance, and probably most importantly, a major gap has developed in the front and back of the mouth between the high vowel – *been* and *tool* – and the open vowels – *bean/break/well* and *made* in the front and *road* in the back. Furthermore, instead of there being one front and one back diphthong, there are now two, both front and back. Although the diphthongs are portrayed as quite far apart in this diagram, it is likely that they were actually significantly closer than this appears, meaning that ambiguity (and potential merger) was a major issue. Many phonologists would consider this system to be uneven and would predict that (1) the lower vowels would rise somewhat, thus achieving a more harmonious and symmetrical system and (2) that either the two diphthongs would merge or that one of them would monophthongise. This does indeed seem to have happened, although how it happened depended upon who you were and where you lived.

Sifting through the evidence, we can surmise that, in around 1600, the

been   [iː]   [uː]   tool
     ride   [əi]   [əu]   house

bean/   [ɛː]   [ɔː]   road
break/well
          maid   [ai]   [au] bowl
made   [aː]

Figure 2.5 Great Vowel Shift Stage 1

    been   [iː]   [uː]   tool

    bean/   [eː]   [oː]   road, bowl
    break/well
    made, maid

         ride   [ai]   [au]   house

Figure 2.6 Great Vowel Shift Stage 2a

system shown in Figure 2.6 was most commonly represented in London documents and appears to have been considered most prestigious:

The following appears to have happened (again with no sense of which development came first). In the back of the mouth the *bowl* class merged with *road*. Both rose to a close mid level. In the front of the mouth something similar, but more complex (because of the extra set) happened. The *maid* class (words spelled <ai> or <ay>) monophthongised. A merger of the *bean/ break/well*, *made* (words spelled <aCe>, where C stands for any consonant) and *maid* classes took place. There is a good chance that *made* and *maid* merged before rising to combine with *bean/break/well*, possibly at a close mid level. The *ride* and *house* diphthongs, no longer in competition with lower diphthongs, themselves lowered.

This system, unlike Stage 1, is symmetrical and therefore, if a fully aesthetic point of view is taken, highly viable. The only problem is that, with a few geographical exceptions, such as parts of the north of Scotland and large parts of Ireland, this is not the same system as is used today. That system is much more like the minority system found around 1600, which can be laid out as in Figure 2.7.

been, bean/ [iː]   [uː] tool
break/well
made, maid   [eː]   [oː] road/bowl

          ride [ai]   [au] house

Figure 2.7 Great Vowel Shift Stage 2b

At the back of the mouth, the shifts and mergers are exactly the same as those in stage 2a. In the front, however, a similar, but different, set of changes has taken place. The *made* and *maid* classes have merged and have risen to a close mid position, but they have not merged with *bean/ break/well*, which has instead merged with *been*.

This is not entirely the system we have today in Standard English, of course, primarily because of the distribution of the *bean/break/well* class. The <ea> spelling, orthoepist evidence from the eighteenth century and dialectal realisation suggests, was for many speakers *always* /iː/, so that *break* should be /briːk/ and *well* /wiːl/. With the *break* class – a relatively small class of words which are regularly used, such as *steak* and *great* – a number of intriguing suggestions for the survival of Stage 2a have been put forward (for instance by Samuels 1972: 144–53), although all of them do smack a little of after the fact argumentation (in other words, it would be difficult, to put it mildly, to predict from the evidence in, say, 1700, which of the <ea> words would be pronounced as Stage 2b and which Stage 2a). The variation between /iː / and /ɛ/ in words like *head* and *well* is rather more readily explicable. It seems likely that a considerable number of words had variable length in their central vowel in early Modern English. We can see this in the variations between *black* and *Blake* and *smith* and *Smythe* still perpetuated in names today. With a word like *head*, therefore, we can say that the spelling comes from a long vowel using community, while the pronunciation comes from a short vowel using community. In traditional English style (as shown with *colonel*, with its <l> from Italian, but its /r/ (or non-rhotic equivalent) from Spanish), spelling and pronunciation do not always coincide.[2]

2.2.2.2 A sociolinguistic explanation?

There is a striking problem inherent in this evidence: why did the two systems exist and why could one be replaced by the other? Moreover, do we actually have to speak in terms of one system replacing another?

Taking the last question first, is it possible for mergers to be taken apart in exactly the distribution in which the constituent parts of the merger were found prior to it? As we saw earlier in this chapter in our discussion of the resumption of full rhoticity in the speech of New York City after an apparent full merger of /r/ and nothing, *near-mergers*, where a difference in pronunciation exists even when native speakers do not hear it, are possible. Since they are near-mergers, the problem of reconstitution along previously existing lines may not be as worrying as was previously thought. But such an explanation ignores the facts of this case: social significance appears to have been given to the merger in which the <ea> words took place.

Since social significance was attributed to the distribution of <ea>, it is likely that Stage 2a represents the dialects of (upper) middle class and upper class London. Stage 2b, on the other hand, might be seen as representing the pronunciation of the 'lower orders' of London and, evidence suggests, that of Essex and other areas to the east and north of the city. It is very likely that some users of Stage 2a 'flirted' with the higher pronunciation of <ea>, in a similar way to the use of 'Estuary' pronunciations in the contemporary London area – glottalisation, TH-fronting, and so on – by (normally younger) speakers of RP, perhaps as a form of 'slumming'. Yet of itself this type of variation would have been unlikely to encourage a switch in preference from one (sub-)system to another.

One piece of evidence, in Alexander Gil's *Logonomia Anglica* of 1619, describes the higher <ea> pronunciation among the *Mopsae*, whom he associated with the area to the east of London. Who the Mopsae were has caused considerable discussion among specialists. *Mopsy* is a relatively common word in early Modern English, meaning, according to the *Oxford English Dictionary*, anything from 'beautiful child' to 'frivolous woman'. This does not seem entirely accurate for what Gil is referring to here. Instead, 'social climber' might be closer to the truth (although elements of disapproval carried across from the meaning of *mopsy* probably suited Gil's purposes). These are young women who wish to marry well and thereby climb further up the social ladder.

Again we must therefore return to the New Men briefly mentioned at the beginning of this section. It is likely that many of them came from the same social background as the Mopsae. Throughout the early modern period, moreover, many people of relatively humble backgrounds who gained power in England came from the region to the east and north of London. These include figures such as Thomas Wolsey (died 1530), Chancellor of England and Oliver Cromwell (1599–1658), Protector of the English Republic. The same region was also a centre of radicalism – religious and political – in the seventeenth century; many of the leaders of the Parliamentary army – and many of the foot soldiers – were from this regional and social background. There were also some who gained considerable power in that century – John Churchill, first Duke of Marlborough (1650–1722), springs to mind – who were not from that area, but still came from similar backgrounds. It could be argued that, because of the radical changes in who governed and how they governed during this period, those who had previously lacked in prestige were now highly prestigious; their linguistic patterns would have attracted the same interest.

Thus the present vowel pattern of Standard English (bearing in mind the diphthongisation which affected the long vowels in most, but not all, varieties from the eighteenth century on) was caused by changes in the social structure of England during the early modern period. Previously lowly individuals (and, indeed, groups) had risen to assume considerable power, even if the monarchical system (under a more pliant dynasty) had been maintained. Indeed, among the last users of the Stage 2a system among prestigious inhabitants of London and the surrounding area was the poet Alexander Pope (1688–1744), a Catholic and a Tory, and therefore out of step with the new Protestant and Whig establishment. But while the sociolinguistic patterns underlying these changes appear clear, it must be recognised that the rigour expected for synchronic sociolinguistics, in particular in relation to the dependence on statistical significance, cannot be achieved. In the following example, referring to the same basic period, something like this rigour can be observed, however.

2.2.2.3 Microsociolinguistic change and the spread of the do-periphrasis

A central set of changes in the early Modern English period is the spread and then specialisation of the *do-periphrasis*. In earlier varieties of English, simple present and past tense realisations were represented in their base form in relation to negative adverbs (for instance, *Merchant of Venice*, I, i: 'In sooth I *know not* why I am so sad') and questions (for instance, *As You Like It*, III, ii: 'How *looked* he? Wherein *went* he? What *makes* him here?'; it is worth noting, however, that the next clause is '*Did* he *aske* for me?'). In Present-Day English, of course, we use *do* in these positions as an auxiliary, so that *I laughed* becomes *I did not laugh* and *Did I laugh?* We also use this auxiliary *do* when special emphasis is needed, as, for instance, in *I did laugh*, on an occasion where someone has claimed that you had not done so. In the early Modern period it is actually possible to watch the auxiliary forms spread, possibly from western varieties of English, perhaps under Welsh (or other Celtic)

English influence (see, for instance, Filppula, Klemola and Paulasto 2008 for a recent survey of this issue). At that time, however, auxiliary *do* was not much used in its present pattern. Instead, it seems to have been employed primarily as a means by which inflectional material was carried. The morphological and syntactic routes by which this change took place have been much discussed (see, for instance, Denison 1993, in particular Chapter 10; Langer 2001 presents a discussion of similar changes in other Germanic languages at the same time which were not brought into the standard languages). But how exactly it moved through the social networks of south-eastern England – in particular, London – was only surmised until the development of a major historical corpus of English at the University of Helsinki and a spin-off, concerned largely with correspondence, was created by, among others, Nevalainen and Raumolin-Brunberg (2003). In order to do so, however, they had to rethink and develop synchronic sociolinguistic theory.

As we have seen, a modern class-based analysis of early modern social networks is not particularly helpful. With this in mind, Nevalainen and Raumolin-Brunberg (2003: 136) developed four models of how to analyse the society of the time:

Each of these models has considerable advantages, ranging from coverage (Model 1) through to contemporary awareness of societal ranking (Model 4). After considerable thought, Nevalainen and Raumolin-Brunberg decided on Model 3, primarily because there would not always be sufficient material to represent all the social gradations found in Models 2 and in particular 1, so that any result would inevitably become impressionistic. By the same token, however, Model 4's three-way split probably ignores a feature of the time we have already touched upon: the 'New Men' or, as Nevalainen and Raumolin-Brunberg put it, *social aspirers*, a class whose linguistic behaviour is much more complex than any of the other contemporary groupings. It is necessary to note, however, that there is a potential problem with the evidence. It is much more difficult to establish that what we have is representative (mere chance could come into play in relation to what has survived). Moreover, unlike a modern sociolinguist, builders of a corpus of this type cannot, before taking a sample, ensure that it is socially representative. Inevitably, there will be more writing available from the middle and upper groupings of society since they are more likely to be (fully) literate, better able to afford quite costly items like paper and ink and capable of storing written material they have received. Equally, (full) literacy was probably not as prevalent among women as men at the time. Geographical differences, on the other hand, might have been considerably greater and less easy to bridge, since travel, particu-

Model 1	Model 2	Model 3	Model 4
Royalty	Royalty	Upper ranks	'Better sort'
Nobility	Nobility		
Gentry	Gentry		
- Upper/Prof			
- Lower/Prof			
Clergy	Clergy		
- Upper			
- Lower			
Social Aspirers	Social Aspirers	Social Aspirers	
Professionals	Professionals	Middle ranks	'Middling sort'
Merchants	Merchants		
Other non-gentry	Other non-gentry	Lower ranks	'Poorest sort'

Figure 2.8 models for social distinctions in early modern England
(Nevalainen and Raumolin-Brunberg 2003)

larly perhaps land travel, was significantly more difficult than it later became. Nevertheless, there is every reason to suspect that the evidence Nevalainen and Raumolin-Brunberg present is genuine.

Although analysis of the *do*-periphrasis is possible according to a range of topics – social background, gender, regional origin, and so on – it is at its most revealing in relation to gender. In affirmative statements, such as *I* do *love him*, without necessarily having an emphatic intention, male use was, as the Figure 2.9 demonstrates, initially greater than female. Both then appear to fall and almost meet in the period 1600–1619 (possibly, Nurmi 1999: 179–81, suggests, because of the arrival of the Scottish court in 1603, bearing with them a different pattern of *do* use). After this, male use remains essentially the same through the next six decades. In the middle decades of the seventeenth century, however, female use rises significantly: Nurmi (1999: 177) proposes that this is a common feature in the writing of the East Anglian gentry, a group which, as we saw above, was associated with linguistic innovation at the time), which affects England-wide evidence because so many East Anglian women were writing at this time.

With the negative use of *do*-periphrasis, as found in constructions such as *don't know*, we can be more certain that women are leading the change, as the following diagram shows:

At the beginning of the era it appears that men are leading the change, but usage in general quickly falls off, perhaps due to social constraints. From the early seventeenth century both genders begin to use

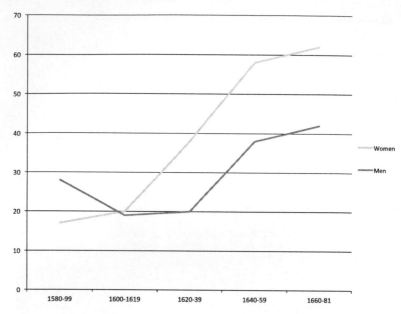

Figure 2.9 Periphrastic DO in negative statements. Percentage gender distribution of DO, excluding Dorothy Osborne (Nevalainen and Raumolin-Brunberg 2003: 126)

the construction; by its last few decades we can say that it is on the cusp of entering its modern pattern as a required feature with most verbs. Yet it is women, not men, who have led this change, demonstrating a more advanced pattern of usage across the century.

As is often the case, it is quite difficult to say exactly *why* these gender patterns should be favoured with these variables. The variation is not random, however, and sociolinguistic forces of some sort are at work on the writers of the time.

In a study developed from the same corpus as that used by Nevalainen and Raumolin-Brunberg, Nurmi (1999: 158) demonstrates that social aspirers initially stayed behind in the change – possibly due to their social insecurity – but later were in the lead in the spread, perhaps because of awareness that it was prestigious or fashionable:

2.3 Discussion

It can therefore be argued that microsociolinguistic theory and techniques of analysis can be applied to historical linguistic change, so long

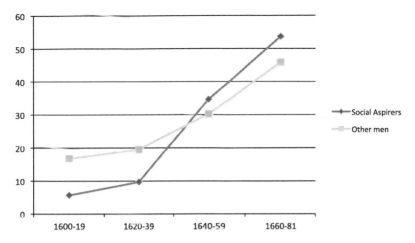

Figure 2.10 Percentage use of DO: social aspirers versus other men (Nurmi 1999)

as there is a generous and trustworthy source of data. Equally important is sufficient knowledge of the society in which a particular change or set of changes took place. Naturally these provisos make employment of microsociolinguistic techniques rather more straightforward in the recent past, where copious sociohistorical evidence and analysis is available, rather than those periods – the European Dark Ages being a good example – where information is limited and surmise can wander freely.

In this book, while change in the last 500 years will be discussed more than that which came before, attempts at an historical sociolinguistic analysis of linguistic change before this date will also be made. It is to be hoped that the *macrosociolinguistic* patterns associated with societal views on, and treatment of, language, will aid these investigations and deepen their findings.

Further reading

The classic text on historical microsociolinguistics is Nevalainen and Raumolin-Brunberg (2003). J. Milroy (1992) also provides a great many thoughtful theoretical and methodological insights into the way English (or any other language) changes sociolinguistically and linguistically across time.

Some issues to consider

1. What *linguistic* (rather than *sociolinguistic*) factors might underlie the development and spread of the *do*-periphrasis?
2. Compare the linguistic changes in relatively recent times discussed at the beginning of the chapter and the changes in the early modern period looked at towards the end. Do you think that different kinds of social relationships can affect how change takes place?
3. Consider reversal of merger again, as discussed in this chapter. Is it possible to explain changes of this type without turning to sociolinguistics?

Notes

1. There is a longstanding (and often bitter) debate among historical linguists over whether this initial stage represents a *pull chain*, where *ride* and *house* changed position, pulling *been* and *tool* into their former positions, or a *drag chain*, where *been* and *tool* rose in pronunciation, forcing *ride* and *house* to diphthongise, since they could not rise any further. This disagreement has no real bearing on our discussion here, so I have chosen to ignore it.
2. It would, of course, be impossible to define *well* as an <ea> word if it were not for the pronunciation evidence we have from the early Modern era of words like *Commonweal* 'commonwealth, republic' and Modern Scots /wil/.

3 Standardisation

3.1 Theories of linguistic dominance, subordination and standardisation

In literate (and quite possibly in non-literate) societies, the status of language varieties is rarely equal. Inevitably, one of the varieties will be associated with cultural and political prestige; put more bluntly, with economic and political power (see, for instance, the discussion of sequential linguistic hegemonies in Millar 2010c). In ancient Greece, for instance, a myriad of – often highly divergent – dialects were spoken. Many of these had some written expression; indeed, the use of dialects in writing became stylistically conditioned. The chorus in a tragedy, for instance, employed Doric dialect, even though the overwhelming majority of tragedies which survive were written in areas – such as Athens – where other dialects were used; by the same token, many poets who came from other dialect areas attempted to use Ionian dialect – the primary dialect of the Homeric epics – in their writing. But this diversity was eventually replaced in the last pre-Christian centuries by a homogenous variety – the *koine glossa* 'common language'; so successful was this takeover that only one contemporary Greek dialect not wholly descended from the *koine* survives (Tsakonian, spoken in the Peloponnese). The *koine* is essentially an Attic variety – based upon the dialect of Athens – although there are features which seem derived from the closely related Ionian varieties. Interestingly, these features often represent occasions where specifically Attic features are out of step with constructions found in most Greek dialects.

The initial impetus behind the use of an essentially Attic variety as the basis for a standard Greek was the cultural prestige of Athens. I do not need to rehearse here the contributions citizens of Athens made to the development of theoretical and applied science, philosophy (if that can be separated from science) and the writing of literature and history, among other literate activities. The prestige of these developments continued to affect other Greeks long after Athens had been eclipsed politically. All literate Greeks looked towards Attic writing as a model; their Greek (initially written but eventually spoken) was inevitably affected by this adulation. But the primary spur for homogenisation was not this elite appreciation of cultural prestige.

Instead, it was the expansion of Hellenistic rule under Alexander of Macedon and his successors which spread the *koine* as a lingua franca among speakers of a range of different dialects and, eventually, different languages. The usefulness of the dialect was obvious to almost everyone; the political and economic clout of the Hellenistic world and its rulers lay at the heart of the variety's ubiquity, however.

These observations can be applied almost anywhere where literacy is present. One variety of a language becomes associated with power and prestige; eventually use of other varieties, particularly in writing, becomes highly marked. Their use may even be frowned upon. Indeed, eventually use of that language will lessen to the point where language shift has taken place, a point to which we will return. Joseph (1987) suggests that, at least since the first literacies in south-west Asia over 4,000 years ago, this assumed superiority on the part of a privileged variety has always existed, even if, as is often the case, most people do not speak that variety as their birth variety. Most of the time, nearly everyone accepts this state of affairs as normal. On occasion, however, a *linguistic avant-garde* develops within the less-valued speech community. Their primary purpose is to attempt to improve the status of their variety: often this implies the planned assumption of the linguistic domains – the contexts in which a particular variety is likely to be used – presently associated with the prestige variety. Normally inherent in this is the planned obsolescence of the previously prestigious variety.

Naturally, this is not a straightforward exercise. In modern times large-scale status raising is generally planned, as is the orthography, grammatical and lexical structure of the variety, Joseph's term being *engineered standardisation*. Individuals or, more often, groups consciously decide which forms of a variety are to be preferred, for whatever reason. Much more common in the past, however, was what Joseph terms *circumstantial standardisation*. On these occasions, practically no-one in the avant-garde is consciously planning to raise the status of their variety, although the intention of using that variety in places where the present high variety (H) is normal must have been present at some level (the resemblance to diglossia is intentional and considerable). The developments which make up this process are therefore often semi-conscious and certainly improvised (albeit with weighting towards the language of those with economic or cultural power in a community). The standardisations described in this chapter are all essentially of the circumstantial type; many features of the changes described in the next chapter are engineered, however.

Essentially, the Low variety (L) always labours under a considerable handicap in relation to H: years of development and enforcement for H have meant that L is perceived as lacking that variety's range and appropriateness. This is particularly the case where L has rarely, if ever, been used in writing. Many of the functional domains inhabited by H – political debate, literary exposition, and so on – might not exist for L, or might be of a strikingly different type from H, interpreted as lacking in prestige. With this in mind, the linguistic avant-garde will normally develop features within L which make it more like H, the model, even when it is despised; Joseph terms this process *elaboration* and *acculturation*.

An example of this process can be found in the development of Turkish in the medieval and early modern periods. During this period, Turks, previously a largely non-literate Central Asian people, infiltrated and eventually politically, linguistically and demographically dominated large parts of south-west Asia. This hegemony did not erase the 'cultural cringe' which many literate Turks felt, particularly in relation to the two highly developed Moslem languages of the area – Arabic and Persian – and their speakers. Written Turkish – often termed *Osmanlı*, 'Ottoman', after the ruling house – was made to take on many words and phrases from Arabic and Persian, in an attempt to achieve the same prestige as these languages. This elaboration and acculturation led to tensions between the spoken Turkish of the masses and the elaborated Ottoman of the literate few, eventually decided in favour of the former during the Kemalist revolution in Turkey in the period following the First World War. Many elements of the initial elaboration remained, however, because they suited literate expression, or were at least what people had been taught to consider admirable (for a discussion of these developments, see Lewis 1999).

Kloss (1978) approached the same themes from a somewhat different angle. The heart of his work was concerned with the question: 'what is a *language*?' In short, he proposed, language status is acquired through a combination of two factors: *Abstand* 'linguistic distance' and *Ausbau* 'linguistic development'. Abstand is, in a sense, the more 'natural' means of receiving language status. Albanian, for instance, had little in the way of written use before the nineteenth century; literacy levels were very low until quite recently. The language has borrowed, over a considerable period, from the languages of its neighbours, meaning that there may be more borrowed lexical items than native now present in the language. And yet Albanian remains a language by distance. While we cannot readily reconstruct its history, it is obvious that it is a member of a branch of the Indo-European languages, discrete from its sister languages.

On the other hand, it has become quite normal over the last few centuries for languages to be considered as such because of the contexts in which they are used. Perhaps the best way to think of this, Kloss suggests, is as a process where varieties used only in local contexts in a *volkstumlich* (probably the best English translation of this is 'folksy', although this does not capture all of the German word's nuances) way move towards more general and more abstract contexts. In modern terms, a variety might originally only have been used in slightly jokey guides to the area in which it is spoken; perhaps also in advice for gardening or other 'scientific' domains. Over time, status raising means that the language could be used, for instance, to write a doctoral dissertation on inorganic chemistry (although Kloss notes on a number of occasions that reaching this pinnacle is rarely regularly possible except for around six languages today – English, French, German, Spanish, Russian, Arabic and Mandarin Chinese – both because of speaker numbers and the political, economic and social clout, perhaps also intellectual force, associated with them), as illustrated in the following. *Domain conquest* in modern times has been largely carried out by individuals and groups who are consciously aware of what they are doing – in other words, engineered standardisation. Fully conscious language planning is not the only process by which Ausbau can take place, however, as we will see in this chapter.

Inherent – indeed, often explicit – in both Joseph's and Kloss's models is a sense of dynamics in relation to the status a particular variety possesses at a particular time. As we have seen, the prestige of a particular variety can improve through the acts of a linguistic avant garde; by the same token, this status can gradually be lost. Kloss in particular discusses varieties which he defines as *Ausbaudialekt* ('Ausbau dialects'), varieties which can be used in writing in a range of domains not normally associated with *Normaldialekt*, as he terms them. Thus it would be quite possible for someone to write a novel in an Ausbaudialekt whose subject matter was not primarily comic (the latter would be possible with most dialects). But an Ausbaudialekt would be very unlikely to be used as the default language of a bureaucracy or of government decrees (although it might be used in these contexts for particular reasons and on specific occasions). There are a number of reasons for why these 'halfway house' language varieties have come into being; the one which interests us in particular is *dialectalisation*.

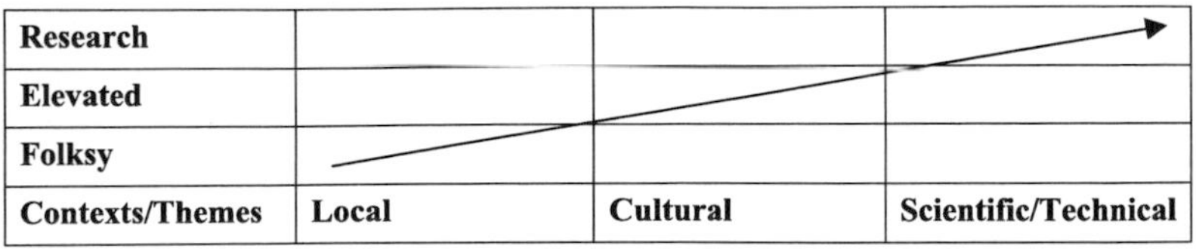

Contexts/Themes	Local	Cultural	Scientific/Technical
Folksy			
Elevated			
Research			

Figure 3.1 The achievement of *Ausbau* (Kloss 1978: 304; my translation)

In high medieval western Europe, one vernacular was culturally dominant: Occitan, the Romance variety (or, more accurately, varieties) of southern France. The most experimental – and most popular – literature of the day was written in this variety by *troubadours*, poets who came from a variety of different social backgrounds, including the highest levels of the aristocracy. The influence of these Occitan models can be found in other Romance varieties, as well as in literature written in the Germanic, Celtic and, to a degree, Slavonic languages (Millar 2010c: Chapter 6). Even more striking is the writing of Occitan verse in Occitan styles in places where, we assume, comprehension would not have been straightforward to most people, such as Spain and northern Italy. Courts in Paris and even London welcomed the arrival of troubadours; particularly in London a considerable part of the audience would not have been able to understand the verse being recited; nevertheless, attendance must have been imbued with sufficient importance (or snob value) to make a long stand listening to something incomprehensible worthwhile. At the same time, the northern French dialects, while certainly recorded in literature, did not have the brilliance and novelty of their southern sister.

And yet Occitan has now become little more than a dialect of French, a standardised northern dialect. Although a considerable number of people still speak a southern dialect – and many more can understand one – this population is ageing and, it seems likely, Occitan as a discrete unit will not survive for much longer. Although this homogenisation is not particularly old – at the time of the Revolution, for instance, most people in southern France could not speak French – its roots are ancient and based upon shifts in the use and importance of varieties at least 500 years before. Northern French dialects, for instance, began to be used in prose – literary to begin with, but later concerned with government at a variety of levels; Occitan never achieved this goal. Moreover, the language of Paris became increasingly associated with Royal power, a power which grew during the rule of the Capets through the maintenance of Royal privilege throughout the kingdom, but particularly in the Ile-de-France, their family heartland. The lack of such an ecologically created centre in southern France meant that no effective resistance could be made against northern encroachment. In other words, the creative use of written language can never succeed against written, functional prose (*Sachprosa* in Kloss's terminology).

This dialectalisation, where a previously discrete language is subsumed within another variety's dialectal variation, is common wherever literacy has achieved a considerable position in a particular place. Low German, for instance, once a discrete language with hundreds of thousands of speakers across a large part of the north European plain, itself a particular influence upon the languages of Scandinavia in the late medieval period (as we will discuss in Chapter 5), has, since around 1500, become an Ausbaudialekt in relation to High German. The language varieties which we will concentrate on in this chapter demonstrate how these processes – expansion and contraction in domain use – are to a degree cyclical and are implicitly and explicitly dynamic.

3.2 The standardisation of early Modern English

3.2.1 The 'submersion' of English

From the point in the late sixth century when Christianity – derived both from the Frankish heartland of Europe and, to a somewhat lesser extent, the potent Celtic traditions of Scotland and Ireland (and quite possibly also Wales and Cornwall) – began to make converts among the ruling classes of the Anglo-Saxons, the written use of English in both poetry and prose was, we think, considerable. In the period from the beginning of the tenth century on in which the West Saxon royal house led a 'reconquest' of England from the Scandinavians, their variety – West Saxon – came to assume something like standard status, even if, in relation to later standardisations, a comparatively low percentage of the population were literate (see Gneuss 1972 and 1996 and Hofstetter 1987 and 1988). Elsewhere (Millar 2005), I have termed this *micro-standardisation*, in reference to a variety which shares many of the features of full standardisation without the demographic groundswell of the processes discussed in this chapter for early Modern English, for instance. Although the final decades of Anglo-Saxon England were deeply unstable in terms of government, this tradition of vernacular use in a range of literary and non-literary genres, in particular in prose, persisted even after the Norman Conquest of 1066–7, with one manuscript of the *Anglo-Saxon Chronicle* continuing to be written until the middle of the twelfth century (of which more will be said in Chapter 5) and Old

English religious homilies and other materials continuing to be copied until the end of that century (Millar and Nichols 1997; Franzen 1991). Nevertheless, 1066–7 marked the effective end to the precocious vernacularisation programme for English for a number of centuries. Thus standardisation was followed by the imposition of an external Abstand variety, French. The original native variety became, in a sense, dialectalised (although the fact that the two languages involved are only distant relatives meant that Abstand prevented full dialectalisation, thus allowing greater possibilities for the further development of the L variety).

The reasons for the eventual new standardisation seem straightforward. Simplifying somewhat, the new ruling classes were uninterested in the previous vernacular tradition. This was, perhaps, most marked in the royal family: it should be noted that the first post-conquest king of England actually to be born there was Henry IV (who became king in 1400); interestingly, Henry was a usurper: his cousin, Richard II (reigned 1377–99), whom he overthrew, was born in Bordeaux. This does not mean that these upper echelons did not speak English. Common sense would dictate that, at least within the first few decades of Norman rule, most French-speakers would also have been able to speak English. It is likely, however, that this knowledge would have been, at least to begin with, concerned with the mundane and everyday; indeed, it is likely that it would represent something like the 'kitchen Spanish' or 'kitchen Hindustani' of later imperialisms. Again this observation needs to be revised in relation to the Royal family, where (monolingual) French appears to have continued for a considerable period. This naturally depended upon the king. Henry II (reigned 1154–89) apparently spoke English well, although he did not settle in England until adulthood, while his son, Richard I (reigned 1189–99), was neither so gifted nor interested.

In terms of literature, French had replaced English as the vernacular medium of choice. Indeed a number of the greatest Old French poems, including the *Song of Roland* and Robert Wace's *Brut*, appear to have been written in England (Howlett 1996). Latin, already important administratively in Anglo-Saxon England, became central to the post-conquest administration, with French being used in certain semi-formal contexts and, no doubt, the working spoken language of the administration until at least the thirteenth century. Indeed, so embedded did French become in England that a separate English variety of the language – based upon the Norman dialects brought over during the conquest and in the years immediately after it – developed: Anglo-Norman. Although not closely related, English was effectively dialectalised under French.

But throughout this period, writers continued to use English. This became particularly true after around 1200 when, as we will see, the knowledge and use of Anglo-Norman began to decline. Many of these English writers knew something of the Anglo-Saxon tradition: Laȝamon (active in the first part of the thirteenth century), the author of the first English Arthurian poem, *Brut*, for instance, appears to have been aware of Old English poetic structures and models (Stanley 1969); the rather less eccentric productions associated with the 'AB language' of the south-west midlands of England (Tolkien 1929) also demonstrates considerable awareness of earlier prose traditions (Jack 1979; see also Chambers 1957). Nevertheless, the speed with which English developed during this period (Millar 2000a; see also Chapter 5) away from its Old English structures towards an analytic syntax meant that it became impossible for writers to replicate late West Saxon Old English. Moreover, while it would be wrong to say, as the great nineteenth-century philologist Luick did, that *man schrieb wie man sprach* 'you wrote as you spoke' (Stanley 1988), it is certainly the case that, in the absence of centralised models, more small-scale centres began to exert pressures on the written language of people in the surrounding area, no doubt due to the prestige which certain literate individuals and units held within the community.

3.2.2 The 'rise' of English

As time ran on, however, the English language – always the majority language and with a large monolingual population – began to reassert itself. To a large extent this was due not to any newly perceived virtue on the part of English, but rather through the decay of the French of England. When Normandy was lost in 1204 to the French crown, the ties between the two Norman-speaking zones, Normandy and England, were severed. Although in the following centuries the English monarchy expanded from its Gascon territories in the south-west of France, including a period in the early fifteenth century where an English king was declared the heir to the French crown, these connections were not as strong or as widespread as the old Norman ones, and involved far fewer people. The agreement of 1204 – that English landowners who also held land in Normandy had to choose between holding one or the other – in a sense doomed Anglo-Norman to a protracted death, due to its creation of an anomalous French-speaking but English class.

In the course of the thirteenth and fourteenth centuries, French-speaking families, most of whom were, we assume, bilingual, shifted over to English as their primary language. When Anglo-Norman was spoken, as it continued to be in some formal domains, such as in certain parliamentary contexts, the 'French' involved may have been largely lexical – a vocabulary often shared with English by this point, of course – but English in terms of syntax. In the General Prologue of his *Canterbury Tales* (written in the last decades of the fourteenth century), Chaucer pokes gentle fun at the Prioress, obviously someone from a high prestige background:

> And Frenssh she spak ful faire and fetisly,
> After the scole of Stratford-atte-Bowe,
> For Frenssh of Parys was to hir unknowe.
> 'And she spoke French very beautifully and accurately after the school of Stratford-at-Bow [in London's East End], for the French of Paris was unknown to her'.

The awareness of provinciality in relation to the French of Paris must have sped the demise of Anglo-Norman as a genuinely living language, particularly since, unlike earlier times, the French spoken by the English king would not have been Norman; rather, Gascon varieties may have been dominant, along with the usage of Paris.

3.3 The development of an English standard

As has already been noted, English continued to be written in a considerable range of regional varieties. Literate users of English were very much aware of the diversity. John of Trevisa, for instance, a late fourteenth-century translator and writer, demonstrates knowledge of the major English dialect groupings – Northern, Midland and Southern – while at the same time suggesting that the dialects of the English midlands were the best possibility for a *lingua franca* English speakers had: an Anglian dialect like that of the north, but without the phonological 'peculiarities' of either that region or the Saxon and Kentish dialects of the south (for a discussion, see Lass 1999a: 7). This represents a sound interpretation; interestingly, however, just as with Dante's early fourteenth-century *De Vulgari Eloquentia* for Italian, an attempt to show which 'Latin' (Italian) Romance variety was the most appropriate for use in writing, no-one, at least consciously, took up these suggestions for engineering; instead, social forces were already beginning to push towards a single written form for the language for reasons which need not be fully associated with appropriateness.

Two further points can be made about fourteenth-century written diversity. In the first instance, as Trevisa's comments suggest, there was tangible passive knowledge of other dialects; this could easily slip into parody. In Chaucer's 'Reeve's Tale', for instance, the northern dialect of the students who take revenge upon the corrupt miller is part of their character. It is very typical of Chaucer, however, that he does not represent the students as 'country bumpkins'; they are, in fact, the sharpest characters in the action. This awareness of how distant dialects sounded can also be found in the second 'Shepherds' Play' in the York Cycle of Mystery Plays. One character – a dubious shepherd-cum-sheep-thief named Mak – uses southern dialect in an attempt to cover up his geographical and personal identity. His fellow shepherds quickly work out who he is, criticising him for his 'sothren tothe'.

On the other hand, there is considerable evidence of scribes 'translating' the dialect of a text to make it more acceptable to his local audience. Of course, normal transcription inevitably involves a degree of translation interference as clauses pass through the scribe's head on their way to the blank page. This goes considerably further, however: it must be assumed that local tastes *demanded*, wherever possible, works which represented local speech. It is often only in the rhymes of a poem, for instance – where different local pronunciations might affect the appropriateness of the word choice – that we find original spellings remaining (although even this is not always the case). This tradition does suggest a largely egalitarian relationship between the dialects. This, however, is only really possible when the central authorities rarely, if ever, used any variety of English.

3.3.1 The move towards standardisation

3.3.1.1 A 'Chancery Standard'?
Over time, however, this ceased to be the case. The standard account of the early standardisation, associated in particular with the work of Samuels (1989a and elsewhere), has it that, from the 1370s on, boys from the upper social strata in London began to be taught in English (rather than French) as a preliminary to the learning of Latin. Inevitably, like the scriptoria before them, these schools developed, whether consciously or not, house styles for writing the local English. By around 1420, boys educated in this way were beginning to ascend to the uppermost echelons of governmental service. Because of their elevated status, their English became the English of the administration as a whole. This dominance and acquired status also explains why people from elsewhere in England were willing to learn how to write in the 'Chancery Standard': they wanted to demonstrate that they were part of the same 'club', with assumed shared values and needs, in a sense a *community of practice*. Fisher (1996) even goes so far as to suggest that this promi-

nence represented a statement of national identity by the usurping Lancastrian monarchy and its governmental apparatus.

New technologies also assisted this spread. The arrival of move-able-type press printing in England in the middle of the 1470s led to 'Chancery Standard', the most prestigious in London and, effectively, in England as a whole, becoming the primary variety produced in that medium. Printing's mass production possibilities made this connection much more effective than was the case with manuscript culture. While there were inevitably many more scribes at work in London than anywhere else in the country, each scribe could only produce a certain number of pages a day, so that this preponderance was to a degree neutralised. Printing produced a very different linguistic situation.

Nevertheless, it should be noted that while 'Chancery Standard' may have had the position of *primus inter pares* in terms of constructing the written English of the late fifteenth century, thereby fitting our image of a synecdochic dialect, if not actually an incipient standard, other written forms of English – not purely regional in nature – were to be found in England at the time (of which more in the following sections). Moreover, codification and elaboration were at best only starting at this point – a great deal of variation in orthography and morphosyntactic usage was present into the seventeenth century which would not be acceptable in Standard English today.

Taking this further, it should be noted that the standard has been analysed as having commercial antecedents (see, for instance, Wright 1994 and 1996); equally significant, perhaps, is the near-standardising process analysed by Taavitsainen (2004) in translations of scientific and medical texts in the fifteenth century. The debate over these matters has become heated, polemical and, unfortunately, on occasion strident (see, for instance, Hope 2000 and Benskin 1997). Wright (in particular 1994) makes much of these issues in her attempts to debunk 'Chancery Standard'. But while some issues with the Chancery model are worrying and will be dealt with in more detail in the following, many of the points Wright makes work better as rhetoric than as actual evidence. She makes, for instance, a comparison between English standardisation and Norwegian Nynorsk, an *engineered* standardisation rather than circumstantial. Making such a connection means that the conscious agency Wright appears to suggest that her 'opponents' believe to be present in the creation of 'Chancery Standard' is based upon a false analogy. There is no-one remotely like Ivar Aasen in the history of English. No-one who wrote 'Chancery Standard' would have analysed it in these terms (although there might have been some awareness of an elite house style). It should be noted, however, that Nevalainen and

Raumolin-Brunberg (2003: 161) also question the unitary derivation of the incipient standard from 'Chancery Standard' alone, pointing out its likely commercial connections, although in a rather less confrontational way.

Wright also makes much of the comparative lack of Chancery documents using the 'Standard'. This is certainly true, although it need not make them unusual or distant from the centre of literate use at the time. It is most unlikely that documents of this type would not have had a privileged and prestigious position in literate circles both within London and beyond. While we cannot point at the exact moment written standardisation takes place we *can* see its fruits, even if full focusing of orthography and morphosyntactic practice did not take place until considerably later. What can be said is that it is possible, indeed probable, that political, cultural and economic power helped to move the set of developments in a particular direction, and it is this which we will now investigate.

3.3.1.2 Sociohistorical background: the 'long fourteenth century' and the population of London

What we have just discussed is by no means the only way in which the standardisation of English is interesting. We need also to look at what London English (and, indeed, other varieties of English) was like in the build-up to standardisation. At the same time, we have to recognise the social, economic and political forces which rendered standardisation both possible and necessary, along with the evidence for who lived in London in the fourteenth and fifteenth centuries.

The hundred years before 1425, while in retrospect formative for much that was to come in English cultural and political development, must at the time have seemed like a series of crises, most of which were beyond anyone's control or remedy (for a discussion of many of the points raised here, see Sherborne 1994 and Pollard 2000). The European population, which had been steadily growing for some time, had reached a level the inefficient agricultural practices of the period could barely support. In less fruitful years, often associated with poor weather conditions, want became a very real presence in most parts of Europe; in particular those where agriculture was already marginal. In even worse years (or successions of years), dearth and eventually famine became possible. In mid-century, plague, which had been unknown in western Europe for half a millennium, was spread across the continent. The death toll varied from place to place (and is contested between scholars), but it is likely that the loss of a tenth of the population was the very least that happened; in some places a third – perhaps a half – of the population were killed in the matter of a year. In the following two to three centuries plague returned roughly every generation, which meant that even if you survived one visitation you or, more importantly for the perpetuation of your genetic line, your offspring might be wiped out in the next.

As well as the terrible personal trauma that these events must have caused, they all also altered the way that individuals (and units) related to each other economically and politically. Although feudalism in the theoretical sense outlined by historians was probably never entirely in place in England, there can be little doubt that, in the early fourteenth century, most agricultural workers owed a degree of service through labour to their 'superiors' in return for holding land from them for their own cultivation. While some lords were already reinterpreting these relationships as ones in which tenants paid rent either in money or, doubtless more often, in kind, the landlord still expected to be paid for his permission for a peasant to reside on and cultivate his land. This relationship became increasingly difficult to enforce as the population dropped and new possibilities opened up for the survivors.

It was not long before workers began to organise to demand wages. The prior economic relationship was turned on its head: those who had previously paid were now to be paid. Given the difficult circumstances, it was also problematical to enforce serfdom. Those who wished to could 'escape' to the developing urban centres (or even to a better 'master'); while actions of this type had probably always been common, the chances of being traced and returned dropped with the population. Naturally the ruling classes did not welcome these changes, as the draconian wage-capping legislation regularly ratified by the English Parliament demonstrates. The fact that legislation was so draconian, however, strongly suggests frustration on the part of the rulers: it is likely that the laws involved were rarely effective (for a discussion of the long-term impact of these changes, see Britnell 1993).

In urban areas, population was again growing. While there is some evidence that the unhygienic environments in which urban dwellers, both rich and poor, lived until relatively recent times encouraged a net decline in resident population, the new mobility of the poor (as well as, as we will see, the rich and the 'middling sort') led to a perpetual source of growing population (Keene 2000: 104–5). Since this new population was derived from a range of different origins, linguistic *koineisation* was likely to be prevalent. *Koineisation*, of which we will have more to say in Chapters 5 and 6, is a process where users of different varieties of the same language accommodate towards each other in an attempt to decrease both incomprehension and the use of linguistically marked features, features which may seem strange or even incomprehensible to other speakers.

Population centres – particularly London, England's only true metropolis at the time, but also smaller centres such as Norwich in East Anglia – also attracted considerable numbers of richer and (potentially) more powerful immigrants. Keene (2000: 105) states that:

> These two types of migration, sometimes characterised as subsistence migration and betterment migration, presumably could have very different outcomes, since their practitioners differed sharply in their status within London and interacted with the mass of Londoners in very different ways.

The cash-based economy meant that certain staples – most notably wool, but also grain and other foodstuffs – assumed considerable importance in the life of the whole kingdom (they already had great regional significance). Control over these staples became a major stepping-stone to economic and political power (which explains why the royal family attempted, by law and by action, to maintain monopoly rights over them). A considerable number of people (or family groups) who had become wealthy in provincial centres were tempted to continue their rise in the capital; as we saw in Chapter 2, the *new man* was a feature of late medieval and early modern English life.

Good examples of this tendency were the Pastons (their lives discussed in a now venerable work, Bennett 1932), an increasingly rich and powerful Norwich family who, in the middle of the fifteenth century, began to develop business and political interests in London, often highly successfully. Their rise (with an occasional hiatus brought about by shifting political power at the centre) is catalogued in a large collection of letters. Interestingly, this move in focus of interests is matched by a change in language use among the younger members of the family, at least when not writing to older members of the family permanently resident in Norwich, where East Anglian English features remained prevalent (Davis 1952). This change can be taken as representing a move towards the standard; such an interpretation, while correct in the long term, is probably not a fair representation of the sociolinguistic processes through which a writer passed when producing more standardised forms of writing, however. The Milroys' concept of loose network ties can also be applied to an analysis of variation of this sort: the London-based Pastons are replicating the language use of a large number of their acquaintances rather than making a self-conscious decision to use the standard.

Table 3.1 Orthographic and lexical patterns in Samuels Types 2–4

Type 2	Type 3	
nou3t, no	nat	negative adverbial
eld(e)	old(e)	'old'
þai, hij	they	'they'
þei(3)	though	'though'
-ande, -ende, -inde	-yng	present participle
werld, warld	world	'world'

Type 3	Type 4	
nat	not	negative adverbial
yaf	gaf	'gave'
hir(e)	theyre, þeir(e), þaire, her	'their'
swich(e)	such(e)	'such'

3.3.1.3 Late medieval London English in its sociolinguistic context

We may also be able to employ the evidence of inward migration to understand the evolution of London English in the period before, and during, standardisation. Basing his work on the findings of Ekwall (1956), Samuels (1989a) put forward the following model for influential varieties of written late Middle English – written varieties which were not only written by people from their original focal areas. The first of these he terms Type 1, derived primarily from the writings of the followers of the religious reformer John Wyclif (died 1384), although it was also employed by their orthodox opponents and in fields which had no connection to the religious debates of the time (Taavitsainen 2004).

The other types he recognises are largely, although not exclusively, associated with London.[1] Type 2 is associated with a range of manuscripts copied in the mid-fourteenth century and is markedly different from Type 3, associated with London documents of the late fourteenth century, including some of the earliest manuscripts of Chaucer's works. The orthographic and lexical distinctions between these types can be illustrated thus:

A startling morphological difference between the two types (discussed by Samuels in 1989b, despite Wright's criticism that his focus is wholly orthographic) is that Type 2 is more 'modern' in its treatment of -e than is Type 3, the latter maintaining its ability to mark for plurality and the strong/weak distinction in adjectives, the different morphological realisation of adjectives preceded by a definer and those which are not (Horobin 2007: 105–7). This is an unusual set of changes, since the more modern usage (in relation to the history of the English language as a whole) seems to have been replaced by the less modern.

There are considerable differences, as can be seen, at all levels of the language, between Type 2 and Type 3. Type 4, on the other hand, is different from, but along the same lines linguistically as, Type 3. Samuels associates this final type with high prestige writing in London beginning in the first quarter of the fourteenth century and thus with 'Chancery Standard'. Despite these dates, however, it should not be assumed that one type necessarily replaced another immediately. Types 1, 3 and 4 (or any two of these) co-existed in some places for some time, before a descendant of Type 4 became the norm.

Samuels then constructs an argument based upon these different types, associating them with different migration patterns. Before this, however, he makes the reasonable claim that a major settlement like London would inevitably have had a mixture of dialects – native and immigrant – spoken. London proper was historically part of the territory of the East Saxons, while Westminster, for all that there is no more than three kilometres between the two cities, was historically a part of the kingdom of the Middle Saxons and, as West Saxon power spread across southern England in the tenth century, elements of the royal administration were established there, leaving the local written (and quite possibly spoken) form more open to western influences. The counties of Surrey and, in particular, Kent, with its ecclesiastical associations, must have injected undoubtedly southern features (albeit of rather different sorts) into London dialect; at the same time, London had a strong connection to the Danelaw and with the South Midlands varieties spoken in the 'northern Home Counties' to the city's north and west. In the few English documents from London and Westminster which survive from the twelfth century, we can find (*pace* Keene 2000: 106) considerable evidence for mixed language deriving from these sources. Written London language is therefore already exhibiting compromises between different sources of different status even before the political, economic and demographic shifts of the fourteenth century.

Samuels' case is as follows. Type 2 exhibits characteristics which it shares with the language of East Anglia; in particular, that of Norfolk. This he connects to the movement into London of well-heeled East Anglians in the first half of the fourteenth century. The vogue for this style of writing was replaced relatively quickly from mid-century on by use of Type 3, the 'Chaucerian' variety. This variety he associates with the movement of speakers from the central midlands into London immediately following the apparent East Anglian hegemony. Type

4, which he associates with 'Chancery standard', was an evolution from Type 3, rather than representative of a radical shift. The Central Midlands influence became greater and more 'northern' forms, such as *them* and *their*, were employed (alternatively, it could be argued – see Chapter 5 of this book, for example – that these Midlands dialects were becoming more 'northern' themselves because of the southward spread of features which could be analysed as representative of 'repair' measures within the language).

A number of reservations have been aired for this model. Wright (1994), for instance, makes the point that Samuels bases his typology on a reading of Ekwall's findings which cannot be supported by the evidence. The East Anglian and southern midlands demographic dominances he suggests as underlying his types are illusory, Wright suggests. In the fourteenth century, as many, if not more, of the immigrants into London came from southern areas. Her argument is somewhat lessened in effect, however, by her analysis of the northern Home Counties as 'southern', when historically they were part of the midlands. Moreover, as we will find when considering Mufwene's *founder effect* in Chapter 6, it need not always be the most numerous whose language is considered local or representative. This distinction would be even more the case in an environment, like the later Middle Ages, where society was hierarchical, but elements of the hierarchy were beginning to break down and, precisely for that reason, elites may have been particularly prone to preserving and broadcasting their hegemony. This might especially have been true when dealing with the artificiality of the written (as against the spoken) form. The fact that Samuels can demonstrate where certain forms originated, due to his central role in the creation of the *Linguistic Atlas of Late Mediaeval English* (McIntosh, Samuels and Benskin 1986), is not something which Wright truly addresses. Indeed, no model of the development of the standard, no matter how tentative, is offered, only dubiety about a previously existing model.

It can be said, therefore, that, while the specific details of Samuels' model can be questioned, his analysis of change in the written London dialect as being due at least partly to the influence of written forms brought in by prestige immigrants and their attendant scribes appears to suit our understanding of how an urban koine, a new variety of a language, influenced by the written and spoken forms used around it (as we will discuss further in Chapter 5) develops. Moreover, the 'northernising' tendencies of Type 4 made written London English better suited (entirely unconsciously) to being a 'national standard'. This begs the question, however: did well-heeled Londoners know that standardisation was taking place through their actions?

3.3.1.4 Economic paths to standardisation

To answer this, we have to consider the extent that native speakers are aware that they are writing a standardised version of their language after the achievement of what Joseph (1987) terms a *mature standard*. Of course, since the institution of free and compulsory education in Britain in the 1870s, many people have had to learn a written dialect very different from their spoken variety. Although the word *standard* was rarely, if ever, used, it was still the case that overt and covert prompting led to the reification of the written form as *English*, not merely a form of that language. But while it is likely that elements of this identity construction date back to the completion of the standardisation process in the fifteenth century, we cannot assume such a centralised view of the language in its first centuries (indeed we will be dealing with aspects of what happened when this conscious awareness began to spread in the next chapter).

Instead we should envisage a situation where those with (cultural, economic or political) power and influence acted as a potent pole of attraction towards which speakers (and originally writers) of English were pulled on sociolinguistic grounds. A willing submission to prestige was undoubtedly conjoined with something like coercion: carrot and stick. In a famous passage from the introduction to his translation of the *Eneydos*, itself a French reworking of Virgil's *Aeneid*, William Caxton (died 1492), who introduced movable-type printing to England, remarks:

> After diverse werkes made, translated, and achieved, having noo werke in hande, I, sitting in my studye where as laye many diverse paunflettis and bookys, happened that to my hande cam a lytlyl booke in frenshe, whiche late was translated oute of latyn by some noble clerke of fraunce, whiche booke is named Eneydos ... And when I had advised me in this sayd booke, I delybered and concluded to translate it into englysshe, and forthwith toke a penne & ynke, and wrote a leef or tweyne, whyche I oversawe again to corecte it. And whan I sawe the fayr & straunge termes therin I doubted that it sholde not please some gentylmen whiche late blamed me, saying that in my translacyons I had over curious termes which coude not be understande of comyn peple, and desired me to use olde and homely termes in my translacyons. And fayn wolde I satysfye every man, and so to doo, toke an olde boke and redde therin; and certainly the englysshe was so rude and brood that I coude not wele understande it. And also my lorde abbot of westmynster ded do shewe to me late, certain evidences wryton in olde englysshe, for to reduce it in-to our englysshe now usid. And certainly it was wreton in suche wyse that it was more lyke to dutche than englysshe; I coude not reduce ne brynge it to

be understonden. And certainly our langage now used varyeth ferre from that whiche was used and spoken when I was borne. For we englysshe men ben borne under the domynacyon of the mone, whiche is never stedfaste, but ever waverynge, wexynge one season, and waneth & dyscreaseth another season. And that comyn englysshe that is spoken in one shyre varyeth from a nother. In so moche that in my dayes happened that certain marchauntes were in a shippe in tamyse, for to have sayled over the see into zelande, and for lacke of wynde, thei taryed ate forlond, and wente to lande for to refreshe them. And one of theym named Sheffelde, a mercer, cam in to an hows and axed for mete; and specially he axyd after eggys. And the goode wyf answered, that she coude speke no frenshe. And the marchaunt was angry, for he also coude speke no frenshe, but wolde have hadde egges, and she understode hym not. And thenne at laste a nother sayd that he wolde have eyren. Then the good wyf sayd that she understood hym wel. Loo, what sholde a man in thyse dayes now wryte, egges or eyren? Certaynly it is hard to playse every man by cause of dyversite & change of langage. For in these dayes every man that is in ony reputacyon in his counter, wyll utter his commynycacyon and maters in such maners & termes that fewe men shall understonde theym. And som honest and grete clerkes have ben with me, and desired me to wryte the moste curious termes that I coude fynde. And thus bytwene playn, rude & curious, I stande abasshed. But in my judgemente the comyn termes that be dayli used be lighter to be understonde than the olde and auncient englysshe. And for as moche as this present booke is not for a rude uplondyssh man to laboure therin, ne rede it, but onely for a clerke & a noble gentylman that feleth and understondeth in faytes of armes, in love, & in noble chyvalrye, therfor in a meane bytwene bothe I have reduced & translated this sayd booke in to our englysshe, not ouer rude ne curious, but in suche termes as shall be understanden, by goddys grace, accordynge to my copye. (Baugh and Cable 1993: 191–2)

Despite the fact that Caxton is probably overegging the pudding somewhat (genuine incomprehension must have been relatively unusual under most circumstances – the *eggs* story is quite possibly an anecdote of indeterminate origin – a very early urban myth – rather than an actual recent event), the commentary as a whole foregrounds a central point encouraging standardisation in the modern era. Caxton was a businessman, first and foremost. He certainly had an interest in creative literature; it is for this interest we remember him now. But his primary aim was to sell as much printed (and thus replicated) material as possible. From that point of view, as he suggests, the less variation in spelling, grammatical structure and word meaning there was, the better.

Otherwise the effort involved would be considerable; far easier to be able to set up common words in the same spelling, thus making the job of typesetting much more straightforward.

Interestingly, Caxton never claims to make large-scale decisions about the nature of written English. With a few (small-scale) exceptions, a prestigious variety of the language already exists, which he was happy to broadcast through his press (indeed the fact that his work is amongst the earliest in this book I do not need to translate suggests that what he is writing is essentially Standard English, albeit of a very early type). Because he came from Kent, there is every reason to suspect that his native dialect would have been rather different from (Chancery) Standard; he has obviously taken the decision to use only the relatively new prestigious variety in his business. This may well have included the work of other writers, in fact, including, to some degree, the printed version of Sir Thomas Malory's Arthurian works, where the level of northern and North Midlands dialect material, deriving from Malory's origin and upbringing, is considerably greater in the Winchester original than in Caxton's printed version (Hellinga 1977; Lumiansky 1987).

Over the same period, what teaching there was of English (rather than *in* English, which must have been the norm) was increasingly likely to be in the new 'English', the prestige of which spread quickly into the usage of all English writers (albeit at times through a 'colourless regional' stage and, on occasion, temporarily in competition with an English heavily influenced by the usage of Chaucer's generation of cultured Londoners – possibly under the influence of the poet himself – and surviving examples of Samuels Type 1, the 'Wycliffite Standard' (Samuels 1989c; Sandved 1981; Lucas 1994; Taavitsainen 2004). Nevalainen and Raumolin-Brunberg (2003: 168), following the findings of Hernández-Campoy and Conde-Silvestre (1999), demonstrate that, in the course of the early sixteenth century, figures central to the royal administration, such as Thomas Wolsey (originally from Suffolk) and Thomas More (a Londoner), negotiated an ongoing compromise – an accommodation – between their native writing styles and the standard. Probably more common, however, since formal schooling beyond a certain level may not have been prevalent well into the nineteenth century, was the process whereby people independently altered through practice their written English – whether consciously or not – towards the new norms, quite probably through the loose networks opening up through social change and mobility. At the same time, doubtless in part fanned by the Protestant Reformation, English cultural nationalism was expressed through the use of an English of some standing; essentially, a modernised development of earlier standardising variants. The increasing prestige of the standard and its association with the nation cannot be downplayed. This association would only become stronger in the early years of the seventeenth century, where a particular summit of literary achievement was reached, including, obviously, the works of Shakespeare (who would not have been a native speakers of London English, but who produced nothing but the prestige variety – and stereotypical dialect, of Kentish men, Irishmen or Welshmen, for instance), along with the first wholly satisfactory translation of the Bible into English – the *Authorised Version* of 1611.

3.3.1.5 Before focusing

The prestige variety which Caxton, education and literature helped to spread was not fully standardised (or, rather, not fully *focused*), however. Variation in usage had decreased, but was by no means outlawed. From another point of view, the pool of variants had ceased to have a fully geographical focus, but continued to allow variation at all levels within what was essentially one variety, based on a prestigious form of London English. Indeed the linguistic creativity of writers like Shakespeare is a sign of a developing standard; nothing like it has been seen since in the mainstream, primarily because English is now a mature standard. It is likely that every user of the prestige variety would have had a set of spellings for most words, a set of spellings shared with most other users of the written form. They also, obviously, had access to a wider set of morphosyntactic variants than is now available in Standard English. This coincidence in usage would increase over time, with the seventeenth century acting as something like a tipping point towards an authoritative (or, following Joseph's analysis, fully *mature*) standard. And yet even at the end of the century, it was still possible for Nahum Tate (1652–1715), later to be poet laureate, to produce the couplet 'Our plot is took:/ The Queen's forsook', primarily for metrical purposes, for Henry Purcell's opera *Dido and Aeneas* (first performed in 1689). While the use of *took* and *forsook* as past participles is still common in non-standard varieties, it would have been unacceptable even fifty years later in such a high culture domain, except ironically or comically (which is not what is intended here). Other forces were at work on English in the late seventeenth and early eighteenth centuries, as we will see in the next chapter.

3.3.2 A spoken standard?

Up to this point we have been primarily concerned with written standardisation. A secondary concern which has caused many scholars considerable worry is whether a standard spoken form existed, since, in a variety of ways, such a spoken standard has existed in English for at least the last two centuries, and probably considerably longer.

This issue needs, I think, to be broken down into two units. The first is the active use of a code similar or identical to the written standard, employed with the speaker's native accent. This is the norm in Scotland. When I am lecturing, for instance, I may well be aware of features native to my speech which I do not use in such a formal context (the assimilation of /d/ to /n/ in words like *hand* being a good example), particularly since many of our students are not from Scotland (and a considerable number are not native speakers of English), avoiding them when necessary. But otherwise my accent remains the same in my native dialect and in Scottish Standard English. Rather, an alternation in dialect has taken place – in relation to morphology, syntax, phonology and lexis. Because I have been in contact with Scottish Standard English at least since when I went to school at five, this switch is barely conscious if at all and is certainly not an effort to carry out.

The second interpretation of the concept of spoken standard is rather more all-encompassing. In some parts of the world, a single accent is dominant. In England, for instance, Received Pronunciation remains the accent associated with power and prestige. Most politicians, upper level civil servants, bishops of the Church of England, higher ranking officers in the Forces (in particular, perhaps, the Army) and academics use RP as their native variety. Until recently, practically everyone who reported on the BBC news or in current affairs programmes also used this accent (unless they were Scottish, in which case somewhat Anglicised local accents were acceptable); they are still the most common. RP is generally associated with Oxford and Cambridge Universities and a circumscribed number of fee-paying schools (the 'Public Schools'), although many of the people who use that accent would not come from that kind of background: in the south-east of England in particular many middle class people who have attended state schools will use a variety of RP (often nowadays in particular veering towards the intangible 'classless Cockney' *Estuary* accent, much copied in the speech of even upper class young people, including younger members of the Royal Family). Most English people, while perfectly capable of using Standard English in their native accent, do not use RP. There can be little doubt that a degree of social snobbery flows from these distinctions. What is interesting, however, is that almost everyone from England, no matter their native accent, will accept that RP is the 'proper' way to speak English, even when they dislike the situation as it stands (a point demonstrated by Przedlacka

2002, even though she is herself discussing the rise of a potential replacement, 'Estuary English').

Much of the debate about this issue will be investigated in the next chapter. But it is pertinent now to ask how far back an accent like RP was associated with power and prestige. In the sixteenth century, for instance, there was some awareness that the 'best' accents of English were to be found in London (often in association with the two universities of Cambridge and Oxford) and its surroundings. The author of *The Arte of English Poesie* (1588) advises the poet: 'ye shall therefore take the usuall speach of the Court, and that of London and the shires lying about London within lx. myles, and not much above' (Baugh and Cable 1993: 190). What is actually meant by this is, of course, difficult to tell. What is likely, however, is that, even before standardisation, some varieties of South-East English were considered preferable to others. As the Standard replaced all other prestige varieties a set of prestige pronunciations, similar but not exactly the same, perhaps, continued to be used by the upper and upper middle classes of the region. That prestige accents of this type existed can be readily demonstrated through the rise of orthoepism in the sixteenth century, as we saw in Chapter 3. The desire to use your accent as a form of social climbing implies strongly embedded views on appropriateness and acceptability.

And yet these patterns were relatively circumscribed in comparison with the hegemonic nature of RP in later times. Some members of the ruling class did not use the south-east prestige accent in their everyday discourse. Sir Walter Raleigh (died 1618) apparently used his native Devon accent at court and possibly his native dialect (for a recent discussion, see Claridge and Kytö 2010: 20). The fact that he came from outside the south-east of England may be of some importance, although we also have to recognise that Raleigh had lived in the south-east for a fair part of his adult life and that he might have cultivated an image of himself as a 'diamond in the rough'. Equally, the fact that other courtiers bothered commenting on his speech does suggest that such dialect use was uncommon at court.

As we will see in the next chapter, rising levels of literacy inevitably meant that knowledge of the Standard – promoted normally as the *only* written form of English if not the only English – spread; carrying on from this, ability to speak the Standard also would have become common. Among the middle classes, social attitudes were undoubtedly related to this ability to use Standard; it is likely that monodialectalism would have been perceived as prestigious. These views are played out in fiction across the nineteenth century, in particular in the works of Dickens and George Eliot, although in both it needs to be stressed that a Romantic ideology is already present. In *Great Expectations* (published 1860–1), for instance, Pip's ascent into the middle classes is represented, even when he is a child, by his use of Standard English; his brother-in-law, however, the almost saintly Joe Gargery, speaks in Kentish dialect throughout the novel, something which undoubtedly contributes to our perception of him as pure hearted. In *David Copperfield* (published 1849–50) similar associations are made; interestingly, however, the only true villain in the novel, Uriah Heep, is neither a working class dialect speaker nor an assured middle class Standard user; instead, he speaks what is essentially Standard English, but 'drops' /h/. He is therefore neither a 'pure' dialect speaker nor a gentleman (albeit on a small scale); instead, he is a social climber and to be mistrusted.

What is left out in this discussion is what accent was used. While it is likely that an educated London dialect existed at this time (and considerably before), not everyone picked this up, despite going to the 'best' schools or attending university (or, indeed, residing in London for considerable periods). Neither Sir Robert Peel (1788–1850) nor William Ewart Gladstone (1809–98), Prime Ministers of Great Britain and Ireland who attended prestige educational establishments in southern England, ever used anything other than their native, undoubtedly middle class, Cheshire and (southern) Lancashire accents respectively. How this diversity was gradually ironed out will be a main concern of the next chapter.

It should not be assumed from the above, however, that Ausbau of this sort is always successful, or that a developing standard necessarily will become a fully fledged mature standard. Evidence to the contrary can be found in the development of Standard English's closest relative, Scots.

3.4 The dialectalisation of Scots

Standard English is not the only variety of 'English' where standardisation has been attempted. By the late fifteenth century Scots, the descendant of Old English spoken in Scotland, was beginning to develop into a national language, associated with the royal court in Edinburgh. In the following century, some of the greatest literature written in Europe during the period was produced in the language. The administration used the language in a variety of ways which approached what Kloss terms *Sachprosa*, non-literary official prose. The usage of Edinburgh began to be copied elsewhere in Scotland, both by private individuals and institutions. Yet by the century's end, the decline of

Scots as an Ausbau language was already underway; by the end of the seventeenth century this decline had led effectively to dialectalisation under Standard English. Why should this have happened?

3.4.1 Sociohistorical factors in this decline

In the first place, we need to recognise social and cultural reasons for the decline of Scots as a discrete written language. Scotland was a less populous and, more importantly, far less prosperous country than England. Printing, for instance, had a permanent base in England more than a century before this was the case in Scotland. In general, majority usage tends to push out minority, even when the minority language is associated with social, cultural and economic power (as was the case with Norman French in relation to English in the period after 1066). When the majority variety is itself associated with political, economic and cultural power, however, the shift may be more rapid and marked. Although in theory Scotland maintained its political integrity until 1707 (with the exception of the brief Cromwellian annexation), in effect, even when the tensions between Scotland and England were at their most acute, English economic and political conditions and decisions had an immediate effect on their Scottish equivalents. This also meant that many Scots with entrepreneurial ambitions slipped across the border to the assumed rich pickings in the south. The need to have a knowledge of the developing Standard English must have been considerable.

Moreover, the sixteenth and early seventeenth centuries were periods of considerable change. In particular, the Protestant Reformation left its mark on language use in a variety of ways. After centuries of largely monolithic use of Latin as the language of liturgy and Bible, an article of faith among most Protestants was the possession of Bible translations in the vernacular, thus making possible an ability to discuss and interpret the Bible by the 'common man'. This ability was also associated with broadening (male) literacy. Different Protestant traditions stressed this article of faith in different ways and at different levels, so that Anglicanism was perhaps more lukewarm in its vernacularisation programme than were the Calvinist churches, of which the majority Presbyterian tendency in Scotland was a noteworthy example.

The problem with Bible translations is that they require considerable outlays in time and (to some extent indirectly) money. In itself a text of considerable length and complexity, its centrality to Christian life and its textual difficulty and intensity means that considerable care needs to be employed in producing a translation, particularly since questions of orthodoxy must also be addressed. During the Reformation this final concern would have assumed a central importance in the methods of translators, primarily because the production of translations which – intentionally or not – veered away from the orthodox position could have unpleasant consequences for the translator. All of these features require considerable amounts of time and, often, a number of translators, whose work, naturally, has to be coordinated by a responsible individual or individuals. In England, where all of these conditions and resources were available, the process of producing a translation which satisfied all of these criteria took almost one hundred years and included a number of individual translations which were not deemed entirely acceptable or appropriate. The expenditure in time and money must have been considerable. In Scotland these conditions and resources were not available. Some translation activity took place; this was unsuccessful, however (for a discussion, see Tulloch 1989).

As well as these factors, we must also consider the nature and views of a number of the Scottish reformers. The foremost of these was John Knox (died 1572), whose authority lay more in the power of his preaching and writings than in his holding major offices in the church. Because of shifting religious associations in Scotland and elsewhere, Knox spent a considerable amount of his adult life outside Scotland, either in England or, in the case of his Genevan exile, in the company of English speakers. His own written use, while not devoid of Scotticisms, was heavily anglicised. We can make too much of this as an influencing factor on the written use of others reformers, but it is fair to say that, during the seventeenth century, the use of Scots in a written context when dealing with religious matters (and sometimes when not) became associated with the 'conservative' party in Scotland, whether Episcopalian or Catholic. God spoke English in Scotland.

The build-up to, and aftermath of, the Union of the Crowns of Scotland and England of 1603 inevitably had an influence upon written language use in Scotland. It is easy to discern why James VI so coveted the English throne as his cousin Elizabeth grew older while remaining childless. England was, as we have already noted, far richer than Scotland; it also had – or, as events proved, seemed to have – a culture of political subservience to the monarch largely lacking in Scotland. The centralised nature of the English state was in marked contrast to the decentralised reality of power in the northern kingdom. While this union did not make a great deal of everyday difference to the lives of most Scots – with the exception of the cessation of the endemic, albeit largely limited, violence along the border – the upper nobility followed the monarch south, probably for exactly the same reasons which led to James VI's abandonment of his Edinburgh court. This change-over can be seen in James' two versions – one in Scots, the other in English – of his *Basilikon doron*, written in the last years of the sixteenth century for his eldest son, Prince Henry. In cultural terms the loss of the most powerful and richest people in the country meant that poetry in Scots ceased very quickly to have major sponsors as the nobility realigned itself culturally and linguistically. In order to make a living, writers therefore had to follow the same trajectory, as seen perhaps most noticeably in the career of William Drummond of Hawthornden (1585–1649), one of the first Scottish poets to choose to write only in Standard English. While it is possible to make too much of the influence literary writers have on everyday use, there can be little doubt that they do represent a snapshot of written use across the period, and are only a little advanced in comparison with official writings, semi-official correspondence and, as we will see, at the end of this continuum, private correspondence. By the Union of Parliaments of 1707, therefore, few, if any, public writings – including semi-public correspondence – had many Scots elements in them, whether vocabulary, grammar or orthography, although Scotticisms remained in private writings for some time after this.

This process has been extensively covered in the historical sociolinguistic literature (see, for instance, Meurman-Solin 1993 and 1997, and elsewhere, and Devitt 1989). Given that Scots and Standard English are close relatives, it may be that people were not terribly aware that they were moving from one code to another. It was often a matter of gradually changing spellings (preferring <ee> to <ei> for /i(ː)/, for instance, or choosing to write *home* rather than *hame*, even though your own pronunciation was more accurately represented by the latter). For each literate person there was considerable variation which, at that level, appears chaotic. But if we look at the material from a more elevated viewpoint, it becomes apparent that, over time, each generation used fewer Scots features in their writing, so that by the middle of the seventeenth century the process is, for most writers, complete, with the proviso that more public uses of literacy – published sermons, letters which could be expected to be read aloud, and so on – were more 'English' than were intimate writings such as diaries and private letters. This pattern of use has, to some extent, never fully disappeared and certainly remained part of many Scottish writers' repertoire into the eighteenth century. The war had been won by English norms, however. Indeed, when Scots returned as a literary language in the eighteenth century, its spelling system was almost entirely English.

3.4.2 Scottish identity and Scots

There can be little doubt that these changes took place in the ways they did. Discussions of their development leave unanswered an important question, however. Why is it that this process was so rapid and largely uncontroversial when it is self-evident that Scottish identity has for long constructed itself to a considerable extent in reaction to England and English identity? The answer must surely lie with the nature and construction of that identity as much as the external history of the 'rise and fall' of Scots (see Millar 2010d for discussion).

One point stands out in this debate. Scots has never had the absolute identification with the Scottish people and nation which, for instance, English has for England. While the modern French nation has been able to construct a French monolingual identity from the previous linguistic diversity, the French state had the strength, unity and wealth to implement this linguistic settlement (largely through *hegemony*). Scotland, as we have seen, was in nothing like such a happy situation. Moreover, while the association of Standard French with the literacy policies of France throughout much of the nineteenth century acted in favour of that variety's status and longevity, the opposite was true for Scots in the seventeenth century in particular, where the fairly widespread basic literacy fostered by the Protestant Reformation was almost entirely in English, as were the school materials (although there is evidence to suggest that Scots long remained the language of instruction in elementary education: see Williamson 1982 and 1983 for discussion).

In addition, although Gaelic was at best peripheral to the cultural and political leaders' construction of their and the country's identity in the early modern period, there can be little doubt that its existence led to greater doubt over what specifically constituted a Scottish language, its linguistic (and cultural) Abstand emphasising, perhaps, the similarities between Scots and English, where Ausbau was a central feature in the distinction between the two languages.

This leads on to a further point. It is relatively easy to find commentary from the period which emphasises the difference between English and Scots, often treating the latter as a discrete entity. But there are also occasions where commentators equate English and Scots, normally as part of the same cultural and linguistic unit, rather than as absolutely the same variety. One example of this can be found in the writings of William Dunbar, whose finest work dates to the first decades of the sixteenth century. In one of his less aureate ('golden', highly ornate) and more conversational poems – 'When he wes sek', also known as 'Lament for the Makars' – he provides a litany of other *makars*, 'poets', now dead. The first of these is Chaucer, rather than a major early Scottish literary figure such as John Barbour (died 1395). This admiration leaks into Dunbar's high register poetry, where English spelling conventions, based upon southern English phonology, occasionally occur. It is likely, therefore that the English of London and its environs, now developing into an (English) national standard, had profound elitist association for him and, very likely, his audience. That he also embraced full-blown vernacular 'vulgarity' in low register poems such as 'The Flyting of Dunbar and Kennedy', a poetic duel carried out with considerable invective (and ability) on both sides, only demonstrates further that intellectual and lyrical poetry under strong English influence appears to be being opposed by the earthy powers of the vernacular. This conflict lies at the heart of the *schizoglossia* (to misuse Haugen's 1962 term) still present in relation to Scots. This suggests, in fact, that it was not merely external pressures which led to the dialectalisation of Scots. There were, it would appear, forces close to the centre of power which developed (or maintained) a sense that Scots was not a separate entity from its southern sister. Yet, as we will see, this did not represent the end of the use of Scottish features in the written English of Scottish people.

3.4.3 Scottish Standard English

By the early eighteenth century, therefore, little differentiated the writing of the fully literate in Scotland from their equivalent group in England. By the same token, there is considerable evidence for the overwhelming majority of Scottish people who were not Gaelic speakers being Scots speakers – and *dense* Scots (McClure 1979) at that. Almost inevitably this led to a degree of slippage from the spoken variety to the written, which equally inevitably led to great self-consciousness among middle class speakers and, in the middle of the century, a new industry, designed to teach Scots speakers how to use the same 'English' as people from London, came into being. In part, this involved classes in Standard English, particularly in Edinburgh, but also in Glasgow and elsewhere. Perhaps more importantly, a number of writers – including major figures, such as the philosopher David Hume (1711–76) – published lists of *Scotticisms* to be avoided, obviously meeting the needs of a considerable market.

These lists were by their nature attuned towards lexical usage, normally, as Dossena (2005) demonstrates. A somewhat dualistic and absolute view of the differences in usage between the two varieties could be engendered by this portrayal, rather than the continuum-like use of lexis across the island of Britain at the time. Nevertheless, their popularity (and therefore their perceived usefulness) is demonstrated by the number of reprints many pamphlets had. What can be said, therefore, is that self-help brought about a powerful shift towards the Standard English of London in both the writing and, secondarily, the speech of many urban middle class Scots. Many of these views were also carried into every part of the Kingdom by archetypically middle class authority figures such as religious ministers and schoolmasters, whose language attitudes can be deduced from their writings (see, for instance, Millar 2000b and 2003).

There is, however, a problem in this analysis. As we might expect, in particular because of the strong sense of nationhood most Scots have (and had), Scots dialects survive better than most other traditional non-standard varieties of 'English'. But the variety of Standard English employed in Scotland – Scottish Standard English – is distinctive in relation to all other national varieties. There are features in Scottish Standard English which cannot be traced back to the Standard English of London. These differences involve lexis, such as *jigot*, a specific type of pork chop and *the back of*, used in reference to time for the period immediately *after*, rather than *on*, the hour, quarter, half or three quarters of an hour; less common, but still present, are morphosyntactic features, such as the past participle *proven* of the verb *prove*. If the move towards Standard English was so inexorable, why is it that Scottish Standard English is so Scottish?

This is an important point because, in the late eighteenth century and beyond, the specifically Scottish version of Standard English – rather than a form of Standard English used by Scottish people whose Scottishness in language was largely accidental and to be regretted – came into being. Partly this may be due to the fact that the lower middle classes were expanding at this point and were joining the fully literate, but without the exposure to Standard English models which their upper middle class predecessors, half a century before, had had. But this cannot be the only reason for this peculiar nature. Aitken (1979) made a distinction in present-day Scottish Standard English between *covert Scotticisms*, where speakers generally do not know that the lexical item or construction is not mainstream English, such as *popeseye*, a specific cut of steak, used only in Scotland, and *overt Scotticisms*, where users – often not everyday Scots speakers – employ a Scots turn of phrase, such as *kenspeckle*, 'well known', consciously, often for comic effect, but also to express solidarity with others of Scottish background. The latter adds extra features to Scottish Standard English and has a background in the literary use of Scots, I believe.

Dossena (2005: 24–6, following Aitken 1992: 904–5) presents the following schematisation of how words of Scottish origin are used and perceived when used in Standard English:

1. *words of original Scottish provenance used in the language at large for so long that few people think of them as [Scottish Standard English]:*
   caddie, collie, cosy, croon, eerie, forebear, glamour, golf, gumption, lilt, golf links, pony, raid, rampage, scone, uncanny, weird, wizened, wraith.

2. *words widely used or known and generally perceived to be Scottish:*
   bannock 'unleavened, often barley, bread', *cairn* 'heap of stones', *ceilidh* 'traditional dance/story-telling and singing session', *clan, clarsach* 'traditional Scottish harp' . . .

3. *words that have some external currency but are used more in Scotland than elsewhere, many as covert Scotticisms:*
   bairn 'child', *bonnie* 'beautiful, pleasing', *brae* 'steep hill', *burn* 'rivulet, stream', *canny* 'instinctively knowledgeable, witty', *douce* 'gentle, well-behaved', *Hogmanay* 'the Scottish New Year festival; in particular, 31 December' . . .

4. *general words that have uses special to [Scottish Standard English] and Scots:*
   close n 'central corridor in a tenement', *stay* 'inhabit', *tablet* 'very sweet fudge-like confection', *uplift* 'collect' . . .

5. *Scottish technical usages:*
   advocate 'barrister', *convener* 'chairperson of a committee', *janitor, provost* 'mayor' . . .

6. *colloquial words used and understood by all manner of Scots and by the middle class as overt Scotticisms:*
   braw 'good, exciting', *chuckiestane* 'small stone or pebble, used in building' (also *chuckies*), *footer* 'to mess about', *girn* 'to whine', *glaikit* 'stupid', *haar* 'the cold wind and fog which comes in off the North Sea in the summer' . . .

7. *traditional Scots words occasionally introduced into [Standard English] contexts in the media and known to minorities:*
   bogle 'goblin, sprite' *makar* 'poet', *owerset* 'translate', *yestreen* 'yesterday evening' . . .

The amount of cross-over between Scots and Scottish Standard English is striking, demonstrating how great a nationally driven resource the former is for the latter.

It is strange but true that, just as Standard English appears to have conquered written space in Scotland, a new literature in Scots developed, influenced to some extent by the writings of the seventeenth century, but written in a new, largely English-based, orthography. Although Burns is the latest and most famous of this school of poets, it could be argued that its first flowerings came as a result of the unpopularity of the Union of 1707, in particular among artists and other thinkers who might anachronistically be described as left wing (even if they occasionally exhibit Jacobite sentiments). The effects of Burns' work in particular transcended literary circles; in Scotland there remains the tradition of the 'Burns scholar', someone who has developed a profound knowledge of Burns' works, life and times and often criticism of the corpus, despite holding down a job unrelated to the study of literature. Burns' influence also transcends Scotland, making him among the most popular writers of the modern age; in Scotland, however, his writing and language have had a profound effect upon the written and spoken usage. Indeed it has produced a type: the Scottish person who has no active ability in Scots except when for the works of Burns.

All of these features involve a counter-current to the Anglicisation process analysed above, a process connected to Scottish culture and, beyond that, a sense of separateness from the English mainstream. Something of this sea change can be found in middle class writings on language use in the late eighteenth and early nineteenth centuries. Perhaps the most prominent and representative of these resources is the *Original Statistical Account*, a collection of commentaries on all the Church of Scotland parishes of the Kingdom of Scotland, written mainly by the local minister, on many features of local geography, economy and culture, guided in terms of subject matter and the *New Statistical Account*, put together in the same manner in the 1830s and 1840s. While there is great variation in the commentary on local language (in particular outside the *Gaidhealtachd*, the Gaelic-speaking part of Scotland) in both collections, it would be fair to say that, in the *Original Account*, most ministers welcomed what they perceived as the imminent demise of Scots (Millar 2003), while, in the *New Account*, many contributors commented on their regret over local features – linguistic, but also generally cultural – disappearing, especially in rural areas, coupled with an unease about the new urban varieties of speech appearing (Millar 2004).

3.4.4 Discussion

At the same time as cultural nationalism was on the rise in Scotland, full literacy was also spreading, as part of the processes discussed in the next chapter. In Lowland Scotland it is very likely that a fair number of people from relatively humble backgrounds could at least read and probably write – a side effect, perhaps, of the radical Protestantism the majority of Scots had embraced in the sixteenth and seventeenth centuries. With rising prosperity in the late eighteenth century – along with, eventually, new paper making and printing technologies – writing became more attainable for a much larger section of the Scottish population than had previously been the case. This population might only have had a few years of formal teaching, however, meaning that the chance of their having eradicated all Scots features from their ostensibly Standard English writing was low. Unconsciously, therefore, many (perhaps most) literate Scots included Scotticisms in their written – and eventually spoken – 'English' usage.

At some point, at the very end of the eighteenth or beginning of the nineteenth century, therefore, the conscious, 'Romantic', use of Scots vocabulary, often produced by members of a rather Anglicised elite, combined with the relatively unconscious 'interference' use of Scots lexis and structures considered by many to be less prestigious. This produced the earliest version of Scottish Standard English, replacing a rather more Anglocentric version of Standard English used in Scotland. Of course few would have been aware of the process at the time. As has already been pointed out, the larger part of these introductions from Scots were made by people who probably did not know that the forms they were using were not Standard English. Indeed, it is likely that the reason why Scottish Standard English so successfully maintained its Scots features was that, in this crucial, founding, generation, most users were unaware of its presence.

This does not mean that some better educated users of Scottish Standard English were not aware of the Scottish nature of some of the features of the Standard and therefore consciously used these features, which had been unconsciously introduced by other users, as in some way an expression of identity. It would have to be stressed, however, that the majority of users are likely to have been of the latter sort. Moreover, this second group, made up largely, we assume, of members of the lower middle classes and the artisan class at the pinnacle of the skilled working classes, may have had even more influence than their numbers suggest, especially since they were the primary source for authority figures associated with education across Scotland, as teachers, but also religious ministers, thereby ensuring the replication of *their* Standard English by generations of users. Indeed, as traditional Scots dialects have declined in speaker numbers over the last two centuries, there are now a significant number of Scottish people whose only contact with Scots is via their use of Scottish Standard English.

3.5 Conclusions

The history of the standardisation of English appears to support both Joseph's and Kloss's views on how standardisation develops. In the fifteenth century, English developed a synecdochic dialect which eventually emerged as a standard. Understandably, this variety was created from a form of prestige London English. Over time, this variety drove out all other written forms, although the speed and nature of these changes probably differed from place to place and person to person. Kloss's view that the more often the variety could be used in non-local and more abstract contexts, the more likely it would be awarded language status also appears strongly supported. Moreover, the use of the variety in governmental and administrative domains – in non-literary prose – would encourage its greater status, although Standard English's use in high literature is also of some importance.

Our analysis of the history of Scots, however, reminds us that developments of this type are neither universally successful nor unidirectional. Scots *nearly* became a standard language, but elements in the identity associations its speakers had with the language, along with the loss of political and economic independence, led to retrograde effects, including the dialectalisation of a previously autonomous language variety through the loss of Ausbau characteristics. But as our analysis of the birth and development of Scottish Standard English demonstrates, Scottish identity continues to be expressed through language, albeit set in a Standard English framework.

Further reading

The classic works on the theory of standardisation are Joseph (1987) and Kloss (1978). Since the latter is written in German, it may not be very approachable for many readers. Probably the most readily available discussion of his work is Kloss (1967), therefore. The most significant works on the standardisation of English are still those of Samuels (1989a and c), although with the provisos mentioned in this chapter. The best short history of Scots is Macafee (2002). The contributions to Jones (1997) provide much evidence and depth.

Some issues to consider

1. What do you think the primary differences in effect are between *circumstantial* and *engineered* standardisation? Do you think Standard English would have been different if it had been engineered?
2. Popular histories of English often suggest that William Caxton single-handedly standardised English. Why do you think they have come to this conclusion?
3. Choose one poem by Robert Burns where he uses Scots ('To a mouse' is a good example). Does he consistently use Scots? If he uses Standard English as well, what sort of topics triggers this shift? What

does that tell you about the relationship between Scots and English at the time?

Notes

1. For whatever reason, Wright (1994 and elsewhere) associates Samuels' Type 1 exclusively with London as well, using this as a central part of her argument against acceptance of Samuels' views. What Samuels does suggest is that writers in London used Type 1. This is very different from claiming that it was an exclusively London writing system.
2. The following is to a large extent based upon the 'grand narrative' to be found in Macafee (2002) and Millar (forthcoming b). Many of the conclusions derived are my own, however.

4 Codification and ideology

4.1 Modern ideologies of language

It is commonplace among English speakers, no matter their background, to express surprise at the way that language is treated in France. It seems strange, for instance, that the French language should assume a central position in the French constitution; such a central part, in fact, that the French Republic cannot fully ratify a number of European Charters which relate to the rights of linguistic and cultural minorities (Hornsby 2010). When you are in an area where a minority may actually be in a majority, as is the case in western parts of Brittany in relation to the Celtic language Breton, it can be very striking how little open use there is of the local language. Official signs, for instance, were until very recently rarely in any other language but French. Place names, almost entirely Breton in origin in many places, were given only in a French transcription (*Quimper* rather than *Kemper*, for instance) or in such a way that no doubt was possible over which variety was preferred and official. The local language, if not exactly mute, is certainly largely invisible. Local languages in parts of Wales, Scotland and Ireland are treated rather differently (although it would have to be recognised that their status and prominence is in marked distinction to their treatment even recently).

Moreover, the ways in which the various Romance dialects of France are treated and used appears to be controlled by a heavily centralised view of Standard – Parisian – French being not just the *lingua franca* of the Republic, but also in a number of ways actually superior to 'sub-standard' varieties. Indeed there is a long (and utterly fallacious) belief, passed from generation to generation, that (Standard) French is somehow more logical than other languages (Lodge 1993). When the Romance varieties are sufficiently different from the Standard to be considered – on linguistic if not sociolinguistic grounds – as languages, as is the case with the Occitan varieties of the south, which also have a lengthy and highly respectable literary pedigree, their lack of representation in all but the most local of contexts is truly striking. Standard French could be perceived as aggressively dominant. At the same time, the perceived threat to Standard French from (American) English is given voice not just by activists, but by people in everyday discourse.

This is not a new state of affairs. At least from the 1789 Revolution on (and quite possibly for two or three hundred years before that) Standard French has been perceived by the ideologues and power brokers of France as the sole acceptable language on French territory and Parisian French – initially in its most 'aristocratic' and later in its more 'enlightened' and (upper) middle class form – as the sole entirely acceptable Romance variety within the country (and, indeed, outside it). As we have seen, other languages and varieties are rarely treated with much respect and, often, are ignored as much as possible.

Underlying these realities is a profound truth: the French language (in France and, perhaps not quite as assiduously, in the rest of the French-speaking world) and its use are controlled and used according to an ideology or ideologies constructed, at least in part, to bring together and hold together the inhabitants of France as citizens and speakers of French, in marked contrast to the considerable diversity of language, identity and loyalty of the largely feudal France of 1700.

This somewhat authoritarian treatment of language in a country which proudly celebrates its birth in *liberty* can cause considerable surprise and discomfort for outsiders; even before the Revolution, however, commentators such as Dr Samuel Johnson (1709–84), a major figure in the codification of English in the mid-eighteenth century, described the French language situation, with its Academy and intense centralisation, as representing 'despotism' when compared with the 'liberty' of language use under which writers of English prospered, as, for instance, in the preface to his *Dictionary* of 1755:

> If an academy should be established for the cultivation of our stile, which I, who can never wish to see dependance multiplied, hope the spirit of English liberty will hinder or destroy, let them, instead of compiling grammars and dictionaries, endeavour, with all their influence, to stop the licence of translatours, whose idleness and ignorance, if it be suffered to proceed, will reduce us to babble a dialect of France.

This level of self-approval – very much still present when British or American commentators make observations upon the 'absurd' French situation – has to be unpacked almost immediately. To what extent are users of English – speakers almost as much as writers – truly 'free' in their use of the language? What did Johnson and his contemporaries mean when they spoke about linguistic 'liberty'? Can this be construed as an ideology (or, indeed, ideologies) in the same way as language use and attitudes about language can immediately be analysed as ideologically driven in the French-speaking world? What results did these views create in later varieties of the language? Moreover, as Spolsky (2004) points out, what people *say* about language use in their polity and what they actually *believe* may be very different. The Irish language is the primary official language of state in the Irish Republic; yet many Irish people are less than sympathetic towards its use or promotion. Can a similar lack of concordance be found between English language ideology and reality?

4.2 The codification of English

As we saw in Chapter 3, English was essentially standardised in the fifteenth to sixteenth centuries, with one of the varieties spoken and written in London becoming the model for what evolved from being a synecdochic dialect to a fully elaborated standard. This standard was not fully codified, however, and remained essentially unfocussed into the late seventeenth century. In retrospect, it could be argued that this lack of solidity might have been potentially highly creative. But there can be little doubt that this variability in the use of the Standard upset and irritated a large number of commentators during the course of the seventeenth and eighteenth centuries.

Partly this was due to the considerable instability through which England passed in the seventeenth century (as discussed in Chapter 2). Changes in the ruling class inevitably provoked not only the insecurity of those co-opted but also disdain from those whose power base was being eroded. Moreover, the newly empowered middle classes were also both leaving their stamp on the standard language and attempting to leave behind their 'humble' origins, socially and linguistically. The social and linguistic insecurities engendered by these kinds of societal changes would again have considerable knock-on effects for the language of this and later generations.

Moreover, in a society where Classical Latin was given paramount importance by the cultural arbiters among the literate, it was inevitable that the manifest differences between that language and Standard English should have been foregrounded. These differences were, couched in a discourse which perceived them as failings on the part of English (and often of its speakers).

In either event, despite the late seventeenth and eighteenth centuries generally being a period of considerable expansion, with England (after

1707, Great Britain) becoming a major imperial power, often at the expense of France, a sense of decline from past grandeur was prevalent among thinkers on language and other cultural indices. Even Johnson, who did not fully accept or participate in the discourse of decline, stated in the prologue to his *Dictionary* that he intended to employ examples from writers from the beginning and middle of the seventeenth century rather than of his own period, since he considered the former period to be the summit of literary achievement.

At the beginning of the eighteenth century this sense of decay led to talk of an academy for English along the lines of academies already in existence for (Tuscan) Italian, (Castilian) Spanish and, in particular, French. On all of these occasions the primary role of the academy was to preserve and perfect the newly existent standard language. Since all three of these languages were descendants of Popular Latin and under perpetual influence from Classical Latin, the sense of 'unworthiness' felt by their educated native speakers in relation to the Classical variety so dominant in education and 'letters' in general was perhaps even greater, but still analogous, to that felt by English speakers. Moreover, the political and social instability felt throughout western Europe in the period encouraged a reaching after 'standards' and 'norms' which would *not* change. A number of prominent intellectuals, in particular Jonathan Swift (1667–1745), called for a similar body for English. Swift was concerned, indeed, that the language was itself in decline, commenting that

> . . . our Language is extremely imperfect; that its daily Improvements are by no means in proportion to its daily Corruptions; that the Pretenders to polish and refine it have clearly multiplied Abuses and Absurdities; and, that in many Instances, it offends every part of Grammar. (Swift 1957: 6; quoted in Crowley 1996: 55–6)

Yet the academy was not founded. Johnson's triumphant celebration of English 'liberty' a generation or so later must be interpreted as an explanation of this failure. Yet when we look deeper into the ideologies framing English 'liberty', it quickly becomes apparent that the similarities between French-language and English-language ideologies during this era are greater than their differences. The language was in the hands of a Latinate and generally leisured elite.

4.2.1 Elite culture and the language of the people

Throughout the Europe of the mid-eighteenth century, full-blown literacy was still unusual except among elite users. Most lower middle class men (and to an extent women) were literate, in the sense that they could keep accounts and run businesses – including communication with other parties beyond their immediate environs. Unlike the upper middle or upper classes, it was only those lower middle class people who had taken on an instructive or educational role – such as religious ministers or school teachers – who participated in any meaningful way with the elite literary culture of their 'betters'. Many working class people also had some literacy skills, most notably, perhaps, in countries, such as Scotland or parts of Switzerland, the Netherlands and Prussia, where radical forms of Protestantism held sway, rather than the Erastian and Lutheran traditions, as was the case in England, most of Germany and Scandinavia. These literacies were very limited, however, not only because the tools of writing, paper and books were, from the point of view of working peoples' earnings, extremely expensive, but also because many people believed at the time that introducing the 'lower orders' to literary culture would do them no good and might also break down the boundaries which maintained the elite's class privileges.

This elite culture was in many ways multinational and also multilingual – Voltaire (1694–1778), for instance, spent considerable periods of exile from France in Prussia and England; Benjamin Franklin (1706–90) was probably more revered in France than he was in either his native America or in Britain; despite the French Franklin cult, which portrayed their hero, inappropriately for a man who spent most of his life in Boston, Philadelphia or London, as a backwoodsman, Franklin's command of French (and, indeed, Latin) was considerable. Nevertheless, interest in at least some of the native languages of western Europe as 'folk' languages began to grow during this period among elite groups; in particular, perhaps, in relation to English. But despite this, the codification of English took place in a profoundly elitist environment.

While it would be wrong to say that dialects other than Standard English did not appear at any time in writing, with the exception of Scots (discussed in the preceding chapter), until the middle decades of the eighteenth century, the representation of non-standard dialects in print was relatively limited. Generally when it *was* represented, as was the case on occasion in novels and, in particular, plays, if there were any ideological assumptions underlying its use, rather than a straightforward, if on occasion hackneyed, representation of place, this was intended largely for humorous purposes. The general – although not sole – intention was to represent lack of sophistication, perhaps even lack of intelligence. In the work of an artist like Shakespeare, non-standard varieties were represented either for comic purposes or, in the case of Edmund when feigning madness in *King Lear*, to cause discomfort to the audience along with the mockery. By the mid-eighteenth century, however, novels like Fielding's *Tom Jones* (1749) demonstrate that a new cliché –dialect speakers as simple good-natured folk – was gaining ground.

With other writers, however, the speech of the unlettered was largely ignored. A late, but highly representative, example of this tendency is 'Elegy Written in a Country Churchyard' (first published in 1751), by Thomas Gray (1716–71). This poem portrays itself as the description and discussion of the lives of the inhabitants of a hamlet. Since the poem is recounted by a nameless, but undoubtedly elite, person, it is not surprising that there is little sense of the speech of the people being described (although the idea that those described only exist so that the elite may observe them *is* disconcerting). It is highly noteworthy, however, that the actual elegy, written for a man who dies in his youth, is composed in elegant Augustan English (with the admission 'for thou canst read' addressed to the reader). In reality, of course, such an inscription *would* have been represented by this form of language; the 'mute, inglorious' inhabitants of the hamlet would, however, have been unable to pay for (never mind read) such an elegy. In other words, those described act as types within a rather limited typology of people of lower rank. It is in this rather rarefied environment that the final codification of English took place.

4.2.2 Codification

During the eighteenth century, English went through its final stages of standardisation. The pre-existent dominant variety in writing, descended from the fifteenth and sixteenth centuries, became focused. All elements of the written language – orthography and morphosyntax in particular – became far less variable than in the past (although these tendencies were already at work in the preceding century). Eventually all, or almost all, variation in orthography ceased; with a few exceptions, largely related to regional norms, the same was true of morphosyntactic features.

In the course of the long eighteenth century, for instance, the use of variants such as *-or* and *-our* in words such as *honour/honor* or *-er* and *-re* in *center/centre* ceased, with decisions being made along regional lines. At the beginning of the century, while it would be inaccurate to speak in terms of free variation, certainly there was individual variation and behaviour may well have been affected by schooling, occupation and experience. Writers in British North America probably used the 'Latin' spellings – *-or* and *-er* – more often than they did the 'French' equivalents, whereas British writers favoured the opposite, but this was not carried out in a systematic way. The American Declaration of Independence (1776) in its original form varies between the two patterns, for instance. Although not discussed much, speakers appear to have been aware of, and uncomfortable about, this variation.

In his Dictionary of 1755, influential well into the nineteenth century (Beal 2004: 45, 57; Görlach 1999: 24–5; the dictionary tradition before Johnson is covered in Starnes and Noyes 1991), Johnson chose to standardise in the direction of *-re* and *-our*. Naturally, the influence and prestige of his Dictionary encouraged the spread of this absolute distinction. Interestingly, however, Johnson's patterns of *-our* use are much more consistent than those found in contemporary British English. One of the advantages of the American spelling system (as it is now perceived) is that it is entirely consistent in its spelling, including in derivatives, so that *honor* is absolutely reflected in *honorary*. In British English, this does not happen: *honour* and *honorary*. Johnson, to be fair, favoured *honourary*. In the name of consistency, indeed, he suggested spellings such as *authour* and *translatours*, as found in the quotation above, which have never caught on in Britain or elsewhere. As with so many changes (or consolidations) of this type, where usage in part must have been spread by the 'invisible hand' (Keller 1994), the general tendency is honoured, but not the finer elements of the system.

Largely because of the adversarial relationship between Britain and the newly independent United States, the American orthographic tradition, although mainly fuelled by variation on either side of the Atlantic, tended to go against the trends set by Johnson and his contemporaries. Primarily this is encapsulated in the tradition founded by the dictionaries and orthographies of Noah Webster (1758–1843), who remained consistently committed to an American language throughout his long life. As Beal (2004: 51) points out, this desire for separation from the English of England was already present in 1789:

> Customs, habits, and *language*, as well as government should be national. America should have her *own* distinct from all the world. Such is the policy of other nations, and such must be *our* policy, before the states can be either independent or respectable. To copy foreign manners implicitly, is to reverse the order of things, and begin our political existence with the corruptions and vices which have marked the declining glories of other republics. (Webster 1789: 179)

Notably, however, the fate of Webster's orthographical reforms almost exactly mirrored those of Johnson. American writers quickly assimilated the large-scale reforms; some of the more radical suggestions, however, were ignored. Webster himself eventually accepted this. Nevertheless, the Webster dictionary tradition is still a living one, unlike Johnson's, which became of historical rather than contemporary interest as the *Oxford English Dictionary* was produced.

With morphosyntax, the choices involved and the ways in which they have been enforced are less easy to plot, primarily because the variation involved is less black and white and more multi-dimensional. Nevertheless, it is likely that a correlation exists between the increasing number of prescriptive grammars published during the period (see, for instance, Beal 2004: Chapter 5) and the gradual diminution, particularly in formal written contexts, of phenomena such as 'minority' past-tense and past-participle usage and the codification of the formal distinction between adverb and adjective, as well as the complete conquest in writing of 'double negatives'. These prescriptive phenomena, while affecting in the first instance the usage of the literary elite, inevitably had more monolithic effects on the usage of the rising and expanding lower middle classes.

4.3 Towards a middle class culture

This elitist view of the English language and its use was eventually replaced (or supplemented, from another point of view) by one formed from the great social changes through which the English-speaking world passed in the period from 1750 on. Yet many of the viewpoints espoused in the earlier period continued to be present in the new era, albeit phrased and envisaged in slightly different ways.

Towards the end of the eighteenth century, the 'natural order' of society began to change significantly within the English-speaking world (and beyond, naturally, although the island of Britain was in the forefront of these changes; see Mokyr 2007 for a discussion of many of the points raised here). Primarily, the earliest large-scale moves towards industrial mass-production were made feasible through the invention of an economically viable steam engine (the theory for this type of machine was ancient, but earlier attempts at creating one had required more energy than they produced). The power which these engines made available was employed to run powered versions of machines such as looms which, along with other new technologies such as the spinning jenny, allowed cloth to be produced at speeds and costs which could not have been imaginable before. Deeper mines could also be developed, since steam engines could pump out water (and, eventually, miners and their products could be brought up from the depths without great labour on the parts of the miners, because of the use of steam hoists). By the first decades of the nineteenth century movable steam engines became possible; this meant that people and products could be carried from place to place across considerable distances at speeds which had not previously been conceivable. Everyone's mental map of his or her surroundings rapidly expanded. The railway network also meant that a rigidly adhered to synchronisation of clocks became necessary: the rhythms of the countryside in particular changed pace and uniformity spread.

At the same time, new agricultural practices were spreading in the British Isles, to begin with in prosperous regions but eventually in the poorest and most marginal regions. Essentially, the remnants of the peasant form of agriculture, where production was at the level of, or perhaps somewhat higher in good years than, subsistence, were replaced by capitalist agriculture, with property ownership continuing to be confined in few hands, but with management of the property also becoming concentrated and 'rationalised' to ensure as high a level of productivity as possible. While in the long run it is possible to see these changes as producing positive results, in the short term their effects were highly dislocating (see Overton 1996 for a discussion of these matters).

Many small tenants quickly found themselves becoming farm servants (if they were unlucky) on the new, larger farms. Since there was already a group of unlanded poor who had carried out many of these jobs under the old regime, unemployment and ensuing profound poverty became the norm for many people who previously had been able to keep their heads above water. Inevitably, many of these new poor were tempted to migrate into the newly expanding industrial areas. In doing so, their lack of skills transferrable to their new environments meant that they entered the unskilled lower working class, particularly under threat from periodic changes in economic conditions.

The presence of the new industrial poor, along with the technological developments already mentioned, meant that many formerly highly skilled artisans found their skills outmoded and undercut by the produce of the new proletariat, leading to their own proletarianisation. Inevitably, these changes in both country and town produced considerable hardship and tension between different groups. At first the urban poor and the lower middle classes (including the newly rich) made common cause against inflated prices and the restricted parliamentary franchise. The lack of agreement on much else of importance eventually made future collaboration impossible, however.

Throughout the first half of the nineteenth century elements within the newly urbanised poor became increasingly radicalised. This was echoed in the often desperate radicalism of the countryside. It is difficult to tell how close to actual revolution Britain came during this period;

certainly both reactionary and progressive observers assumed that at the very least violent upheavals would take place. The response of the authorities was often draconian – as in the 'Peterloo Massacre' of 1819, where a peaceful and unarmed crowd in Manchester were charged by cavalry. The radical hotspots – south Wales, Lancashire, central Scotland – were often kept in a state of near-martial law. And yet, when revolution flared up across Europe in 1848, Britain remained surprisingly calm. For the rest of the century (indeed, arguably, until now), the Left remained largely Parliamentary and rarely, if ever, considered seizing power. The genuine poverty of urban areas, seldom ameliorated systematically until the beginning of the twentieth century at the earliest did not appear to encourage a radical working class consensus, although Trade Union activity increased considerably.

Elements within the working classes began to move towards full literacy during the period, even before compulsory primary education was introduced in the 1870s. But it is very likely that, in the rapidly expanding industrial areas, the level of male literacy actually dipped because, as the churches quickly recognised, the connection with a particular church in those areas was not strong. Nevertheless, no matter what variety working class people spoke, their contact with spoken and written Standard English was actually considerable.

The general malaise perceived by many in the established churches throughout the British Isles meant that, in the later eighteenth century, new forms of evangelical religion, embedded within the existing churches on occasion but more often situated in new traditions, such as Methodism, developed and gained considerable popularity (Bebbington 1989). While concerned largely with saving individual souls, many of these new organisations took very seriously the idea that only literate believers would be able fully to understand the faith and develop a personal relationship with God.

It was often in the new urbanising centres that evangelical ideas were most successful, perhaps due to the *anomie* created by change and dislocation. Because the urban poor, as we have seen, were likely to have fewer chances of direct connection to literacy than many people in well populated rural areas, evangelicals quickly discovered that their desire for universal Bible literacy, made available through their reading and writing Sunday Schools, actually made their churches attractive: almost everyone recognised that literacy, up to a certain functional level, was desirable for rather more worldly reasons. The association between literacy and evangelical 'sects' was not lost on the Church of England (which retained a strong evangelical wing); Anglican Sunday Schools followed suit (Walton 1987: 186–7). By the mid-nineteenth century, therefore, a degree of literacy was widespread within many urban communities.

4.3.1 The new literacy

But what did this new literacy look like? Some evidence survives of the literacy skills of the (relatively) poor. One example of this is the corpus of letters sent to and by Thomas Holden, a hand-loom weaver from Bolton in central Lancashire, transported to New South Wales towards the end of the Napoleonic Wars for administering an illegal oath (essentially attempting to set up a Trade Union). Here is a fairly representative example:

> Sydney June [11] 30 1815
> My Dear Wife
>   I take this oppertunity of Writing to you Hoping to find to find you and My Dear Child in good health as this Leaves Me at Presant thanks Be to god for the Same and I ham very unhappy to think that you have for got me So soon for My Part I know that I ham Shut up in one Corner of the World But I hope that you wont for get to write to me hevery 3 Months as there is a Ship Sails from Portsmouth and there is nothing will Give Me More happiness than to hear from you for My Part there is never a Ship Coms to this Contry But I goes to know whether there is aney Letter for Me or no and when there is no Letter then I think you Have quite forgot Me to think that I have got ondley one Letter Since this time 3 yers So I Desire you Will Let Me know the Reason that My Brother Don't Write to Me and My Cousan James and I hope they Will find time to write if they Can and My Dear father and Mother I hear that there is Peace with all the World so I Desire you will Send the Word if it is So and Please to Let Me know how the trade is Since Peac[ ] and Whether I can get a honist Living or not and there is a Strong Report of us getting our pardon and if there is Please to Let Me Know By the first Ship and you Mentinsond Some of the Men that Came from England with Me But I will ashure you I have never Cept Company with any one Sins I Left my natife Contry for I will ashure you I find it as Much as I Can do to Mind My Self and I have Done all that Eavr Man Can Do to get my Liberty and to Come home But it is all in vain the More I strive the More I ham Behind So Dear Mother if Should Please God to Let us Meet a gain in this World I hope it will Be a happy Meetting and if it Should Please god to Call Me Before our Meeting I hope we Shal Meet in another World Where there Will Be no More Parting once I Did not think that it would Be my feat to Be So far Distant from you My Dear Mother and you My Wife and Child

Dear Mother things in this Contry is very Dear [...] and allthough the Prices is So high We are Verry glad to get at aney Price so I must inform you of my Wages I have 20 Pounds Per year in Corrency Money it will Be More than 12 Pounds in English Coin So My Dear Brother I hope you will Stay at home with your Mother and Becontented in the State you are in and I Desire you to write to Me and Send Me all the news that is going with you Both in family afairs and how trade is and the Prise of Vitling and all oather news that you Can as ther is nothing will give Me More Satisfaction then to hear from you all & when it is Dark with you it is Light with us and the natifs of this Contry they are Blaiks and they go naked Just as they Came into the world and they live on Nuts of trees as [ ] Snouts or aney oather Creeping thing [ ]n and Children goes all naked a Like So I have nothing More to add ondley Begging of you My Dear Wife that you will take Perticul[ ] Care of My Dear Child until I Return for I will ashure you I think of nothing But you and My Dear Child and My Sincere Prayr is Both Day and night that I May once More Be along with you Both and never More to Be Parted – – –

So no More at Presant from your Loving husba[ ] –

[til Death] and affectinate father and Dutifull Son

til Death Thos Holding

(Preston, Lancashire County Records Office, DDX 140/7/18; reproduced with the kind permission of the Lancashire County Records Office, Preston)

The language used in this letter is, naturally, very interesting. But it is also deeply frustrating when it comes to extracting accurate data about how Holden spoke. Examples such as *I ham very unhappy* probably tell us that Holden did not pronounce /h/ according to the same rules as do Standard English speakers, for instance. There is much that is formulaic in the letter, however; in particular in the stock greetings and farewells, something which, evidence suggests, practically all Sunday Schools would have taught, normally from a very limited number of books. Most of the evidence in the letter suggests, in fact, that Holden, although not fully versed in the standard, knew it sufficiently well to come close to it in his written performance. Those features in his writing which are dialectal or, at the very least, non-standard, are there, therefore, by accident in an attempt to represent the prestigious written variety: sins of omission, as it were, rather than sins of commission (a discussion of the linguistic nature of the corpus can be found in Millar forthcoming b).

The presence of the written standard in the lives of dialect speakers would inevitably have had considerable repercussions, linguistic and otherwise. Although represented in the (spoken) linguistic repertoire of practically every speaker of a dialect other than Standard English, it can also be seen in the late eighteenth and early nineteenth-century written use of people who we know generally spoke their native dialect. One example of this can be found in the language use of John Clare (1793–1864), from what is now eastern Northamptonshire, a man emotionally and economically tied to the soil who, for a brief period, was lionised in London literary circles. Let us consider one of his most famous poems, 'Emmonsails Heath in winter':

> I love to see the old heath's withered brake
> Mingle its crimpled leaves with furze and ling
> While the old heron from the lonely lake
> Starts slow and flaps his melancholy wing,
> And oddling crow in idle motion swing
> On the half-rotten ash tree's topmost twig,
> Besides whose trunk the gipsy makes his bed.
> Up flies the bouncing woodcock from the brig
> Where a black quagmire quakes beneath the tread,
> The fieldfare chatter in the whistling thorn
> And for the haw round fields and closen rove,
> And coy bumbarrels twenty in a drove
> Flit down the hedge rows in the frozen plain
> And hang on little twigs and start again.

This is, of course, a poem of considerable charm. A great deal of this charm derives from the use of dialect words, some, such as *brig*, being fairly transparent, while others, such as *oddling* (according to the *Oxford English Dictionary*, 'a person or thing considered odd, esp. because different from others in the same group or category', largely Northern English or North American), are guessable for any speaker of English (although *bumbarrel*, probably a type of bird, is much more opaque; the OED associates the word with a particular fashion in women's clothes for a heavily accentuated rear end in clothing).

Clare was himself a native speaker of his local Midlands dialect (Sales 2002; this is worth noting, since a number of poets have written, but not spoken, Scots). But this misses the point somewhat. 'Emmonsails Heath in winter' does not represent the at most semi-conscious use of the language of the heart so beloved of Romantic ideologues and theoreticians (as in Wordsworth's famous poetic intention to 'bring my language near to the language of men': see Rosen 2006 and Millar forthcoming a). In that sense Clare's use is not as different from that of Thomas Holden discussed above as might be thought. The use of dialect in Holden's letter is a by-product of his less than full control of the standard code; in other words, it is largely unconscious. Clare's use of dialect forms *is* conscious – indeed, highly so. Yet the standard is the central point around which both Holden's and Clare's usage orbits, a standard now under the control of the newly wealthy and powerful middle classes. The age of the 'mute, inglorious' lower orders had passed.

4.3.2 The lower middle classes as ideological and linguistic leaders

During this period, a gradual shift in ideological leadership took place under the influence of many forces discussed here. While the descendants of the eighteenth-century elite never ceased to consider themselves arbiters of language, it was the newly empowered lower middle classes who gained control of the educational along with the political apparatus. Because the nineteenth century witnessed the first attempts towards truly mass education throughout the English-speaking world, this growth in lower middle class power inevitably led to their control of the education process for almost all children. What this power represented differed from place to place, however (see Crowley 2003 for further discussion on these points).

Ideologically speaking, the lower middle classes began their rise in association, as we have seen, with radical politics. The desire for change and 'progress' was considerable and led them to ally themselves with those elements of society which looked to the remaking of that society. The difficult relationships which developed during the Industrial Revolution between the middle and 'lower' classes, along with the impact which poverty and urbanisation had upon the poorer parts of cities (and, because of the close proximity in which rich and poor lived until almost the end of the century), many members of the lower middle classes also began to move towards the political right, probably in an attempt to maintain their often somewhat shaky position in society. The fear of the mob, always present in large urban environments, led to a number of often apparently divergent linguistic viewpoints.

The first facet of this could be seen as a desire for linguistic purity. Throughout the area settled and affected by the newly highly literate western Europeans, new fears about the 'purity' of the national language were being voiced. Unlike earlier fears (as discussed above), however, where a social and educational elite were committed to maintaining 'standards' derived from their elite culture, nineteenth-century purist ideology tended to focus on maintaining a mass standard's nature and 'beauty' against at least one of the following: (1) the influence of another language or languages which was previously (or remained) highly prestigious in the territory where the language to be protected was spoken;

(2) urbanisation, with much interest being taken in the language of rural areas; and (3), the desire for 'correct' usage, following the written norm, in distinction to the perceived 'corruption' of either the 'indolent' upper classes or, inevitably and particularly, the urban working classes. The last tendency in particular is similar to the former elite views on language; but although undoubtedly a descendant of these eighteenth-century views, now carried with it was a belief that it was the 'productive' (that is, middle class) members of the speech community who were the language's guardians.

What could be described as *xenophobic* purism (Thomas 1991) was particularly common in the nineteenth century in regions of Europe where the majority language had for long been dominated by another language associated with a ruling or prestigious group. Thus significant speakers of German began to 'purify' their language of the French bor-rowings which had entered the language in the preceding two centuries. Planners for Czech, by the same token, 'cleansed' that language of the German vocabulary which had entered the language because Bohemia and Moravia had long been under the rule of the German-speaking Habsburgs, and because of the gradual Germanisation of the Czech nobility and gentry and the large number of German speakers in urban and industrial areas. Many ideologues of the time also looked away from the cities for their linguistic ideals, in marked contrast to the preceding century. Romanticism encouraged a cult of the 'genuine' which could be found only in remote country districts. In many senses this can be seen as being a variation on the first theme, but with an expressed pref-erence not for the whole language without foreign influence (or 'cor-ruption') but rather for a part of the linguistic community closer to the past and present traditions of the *Volk* (*ethnographic* purism, as Thomas defines it). The two impulses remain connected since rural dialects were often less influenced by prestige borrowings than urban ones. This feature is particularly widespread in the Norwegian designed by Ivar Aasen (1813–1896) and his contemporaries in mid-century. The Low German borrowings and Danish influence present in the middle class varieties of Christiania (Oslo) and elsewhere were far less pronounced in the language of the remote areas of the south-west of Norway, where Aasen's fieldwork was concentrated.

With English, however, it was primarily the desire for 'correctness' which was particularly favoured. Lexical purism *was* advocated by a few commentators in the nineteenth century. In the figure of William Barnes (1801–86), a talented (although largely untrained) 'philologist' and poet in the dialect of his native Dorset, we have someone who combined both xenophobic and ethnographic based purism, coining a number of new words, often from regional dialects, for which English employed Latin or, in particular, French borrowings (*folkwain* for *(omni)bus* being a representative example). Unlike elsewhere in Europe, however, language planning of this sort never connected to a larger audience – the lower middle classes, in other words, since working people's views were rarely canvassed, even when their language use was being analysed. Purists were and are considered highly eccentric figures of fun for most of this opinion-forming class.

Yet purism of a sort still affected English during the period: a purism associated with the present standard and its use. Partly this association was due to linguistic insecurity. Newly empowered and sometimes within only two (sometimes even one) generations of illiteracy (or, perhaps more often, semi-literacy), the lower middle classes appear to have been almost morbidly self-conscious in their use of language. The self-help books on pronunciation (particularly of consonants like /h/), on correcting 'errors' in grammar and morphology, along with the changes in pronunciation (as seen with *housewife, forehead* and *waistcoat,* among many others) towards a literal interpretation of the spelling, demonstrate this. But because of this group's importance as educators, whether officially or covertly, these concerns were transplanted to a far larger community (see Finegan 1998 for a discussion of many of these points).

Connected to this corrective purism was the idea that a shared language – indeed, language variety – would somehow heal the social divides which industrialisation and proletarianisation had opened. A free Englishman, no matter his social background (see Crowley 1996: Chapter 5), would consider all Englishmen his peers and his brothers if they all spoke the same. Naïve though this view is (it is not just speech which marked and marks people off socially – dress, diet and a range of other features have a similar attitudinal effect), it was widespread and, indeed, not confined either to English or to the political centre and right. Thomas Spence (1750–1814), a late eighteenth-century radical, combined trouble-making with a firm belief in the egalitarian power of elocution (Beal 1999); much later, Antonio Gramsci (1891–1937), an early twentieth-century Marxist (albeit of an unusual cast), believed that what was holding the Italian masses back in relation to Class War was their inability to understand each other, largely due to the dialectal diversity found in Italy at the time: he therefore believed that the prescriptive teaching of Standard Italian would act as a unifying factor (Crowley 1996, 2003). Nevertheless, in the England of the mid-nineteenth century, it was middle class speakers who informed and carried out what was essentially an English nationalist project.

On occasion indeed, as Crowley (1996 and 2003) has demonstrated, this passion for a common Englishness became decidedly eccentric. It was a commonplace of texts dealing with primary education, particularly of adults, that students should be taught the history of the English language in such a way as to inculcate the idea that every Englishman (and woman), no matter their circumstances, shared a common and glorious linguistic history – associated with the 'ancient liberties' of Anglo-Saxon traditions. Some authorities went further than this, encouraging the teaching of Old English for similar ideological purposes.

All of these ideologically driven educational initiatives were also carried into the expanding British Empire – in particular, but not solely, the 'white Commonwealth' of countries like Canada, Australia and New Zealand. Generations of children in these countries were taught that they were in a very real sense 'British' (or, often, 'English') and that primary allegiance was to the 'mother country'. The speed with which the dominions declared war on the British side at the beginning of the Great War in particular (although similar if less enthusiastic support was also provided in the Second World War) demonstrates the level of these commitments. A British style of English – both written and, less successfully, spoken – was enforced (in distinction to the American English style so pervasive in Canada, the Caribbean and, to a lesser extent, elsewhere). Again, the ideal of an egalitarian British Empire where everyone essentially wrote and spoke in the same way, while always unrealistic (and probably always recognised as such), lay at its centre. Ironically, it was only in the elite (largely boys') schools founded in each of the colonies and dominions in overt homage to the English Public Schools that anything like this uniformity was achieved. Even then, many schoolboys felt obliged to alter their speech when they returned to their native environments.

An issue which possibly explains the inherent ambiguity in the egalitarian single accent programme was that, as has been suggested, the accent preferred was also associated with the English ruling classes. As well as demonstrating the 'democratic' urge towards the single accent, Crowley (2003) demonstrates that, in the nineteenth and early twentieth century an informal group of academics and teachers placed 'correct' pronunciation at the heart of what was 'best' in British – and therefore Imperial – English. But this 'best' accent was always described in their writings in relation to the ruling classes (and to a degree as if possession of power and accent was something of a closed shop). In a sense this old elitism survived in alliance with populism and the linguistic insecurity of the lower middle classes.

4.4 USA: pluralism, unity, purism

While similar forces were at work on English in the British Isles and elsewhere, the development of the United States – including its varieties of English – was ideologically driven in ways different from elsewhere from its very outset (Fisher 2001). Thus while it would be difficult now to define in what ways an average American is actually more 'free' than an average English person, it is true that the former is more likely to have internalised a sense of 'liberty'. From early on, many Americans have had a sense of their country's exceptional place in the world.

Not all immigrants to what became the United States came seeking 'liberty', whether that be religious or political (or, indeed, both), of course. The Jamestown settlement in Virginia (founded in 1607) was primarily intended to have a commercial nature (although the colony itself took a considerable period to become internally sustainable, never mind profitable); most of the most powerful people in the colony had connections to the English elite and would certainly have had establishment views, politically and religiously. Even the more ideologically driven Plymouth (founded 1620) and Massachusetts Bay (founded 1628) colonies, while having Puritan or Separatist leaders, and therefore forming part of the American founding myth in ways not fully possible for the earlier colony, were populated by people from a wide range of backgrounds, not all of whom were in accord with the official view. As the colonies expanded, moreover, the cultures which developed in the Appalachian Mountains and in the Mississippi-Missouri region beyond were not generally as 'disciplined' as the eastern colonies. They were often populated by those who had been the lower classes in the more developed east. The presence of people of African origin, normally slaves, in many of the colonies (including, to begin with, in the north) must also be borne in mind.

Mobility was, of course, a central feature from the very earliest settlements. While it was possible to move from one part of England to another, as London records demonstrate, it was difficult to walk away from the authorities. This was quite possible in what became the United States until at least the late nineteenth century. Movement towards a more desirable state of living is central to the American self-construction in a way which is unlike almost anywhere else except, perhaps, and with reservations, Russia and China.

The American Revolution also added to the new country's sense of difference. Again, although Canadians enjoy essentially the same civil rights as Americans, the history of how these rights were gained differs significantly. While Canada separated itself gradually and generally peacefully from the 'mother country', the United States was born in a violent secession. Patriots came from a range of cultural backgrounds across the colonies, although almost all were middle class, with the exceptions, perhaps, of figures like George Washington (1732–99) or Thomas Jefferson (1743–1826), who were 'gentry' (although these fellow Virginians were not political allies). While too much can be made of the idea of a new country coming together ideologically at this time – the bloodiness of the Civil War almost a century later must always be borne in mind – there is little point in denying that a common set of values, already much talked about in European circles, was crystallised both in the independence struggle and also in setting up an ideologically driven system of government based upon individual rights.

In often contradictory ways, therefore, the United States constructed itself as a 'city on a hill', an exceptional place where liberty was central to every citizen's self-construction. No matter the reality of the American Dream, there can be no doubt of its importance as a belief and an ideology. How to make idealism of this type work is, of course, a rather more difficult matter. As French people, citizens of another country engendered through the ideals of the European Enlightenment, also regularly find, it is easier to use words like *liberty* and *equality* than to know exactly what they mean in a particular context – whether to you or to other people – and how they combine. When you say *e pluribus unum* 'from many one' (one of the United States' mottoes), do the egalitarian sentiments inherent in it imply that people should act in essentially the same way? If it does, how does this relate to liberty? All these points are, of course, open to interpretation.

4.4.1 Language use in the United States[1]

To what extent have these ideological issues affected language use – and its perception – in the United States? In the first instance, we need to look at how the varieties spoken in the colonies were perceived.

A striking feature of eighteenth-century writing on what is now the United States is that observers regularly say that local people do not have many non-standard features in their speech, some commentators going so far as to suggest that the people with whom they spoke sounded 'English' (of course this point is not without its own issues). This is in marked contrast to other commentary – particularly in nineteenth-century discussions – which comment on how divergent (often, how 'ugly') various forms of American English can be. Indeed in July 2011 a light-hearted article on 'Americanisms' on the BBC website (http://www.bbc.co.uk/news/magazine-14201796) sparked considerable numbers of often spiteful comments on how 'ugly' Americanisms are; inevitably, hardly any of the words and phrases mentioned originated in the United States. That such views still appear demonstrates how deep the conflicts between British and American ideologies of correctness must be.

In Chapter 6 we will discuss some of the developmental stages through which colonial varieties pass in their formative stages. Anticipating somewhat, it appears to be the case that, in the language of the second and third native generations, considerable uniformity prevails, before social roles again dictate divergence. Homogeneity can last a considerable amount of time. While social differences can be found between the speech of working class and middle class Australians across that country, regional differences are notoriously difficult to spot, with few phonological differences expressed between even distant cities such as Sydney and Perth and often small-scale lexical variation taking its place. It should be noted that large-scale English-speaking colonisation has been ongoing in Australia for more than two centuries. Is it possible, therefore, that the initial apparent homogeneity observed for eighteenth-century American English was due to relatively recent Anglophone settlement and that later diversity was due to 'normal' regional and social factors being brought to bear on language use as the colonies matured?

There may be something in this. A couple of points need to be made, however. In the first instance, there is a long-standing view that the differences in language along the Eastern Seaboard and inland are due to different settlement patterns in different regions, important in relation to the 'old country' origins of new settlers. Thus, according to this view, features in the speech of New England, for instance, such as the merger of /ju/ in *tune* and /uː/ in *moon* can be traced back to the East Anglian and southern Lincolnshire origins of many early settlers; equally, many features of the tidewater south, such as lack of full rhoticity and monophthongisation of a number of diphthongs, as in *ride*, might be related to the dialects of the south-east of England; Appalachian English, by this argument, is primarily the language brought from Ulster by Scots speakers in the seventeenth and eighteenth centuries.

But while at some levels this argument makes sense, there are good grounds for suspicion. In the first instance, it is difficult to demonstrate that particular regions *did* have overwhelming immigration from the regions in the British Isles suggested (although equally while people from a wide range of backgrounds moved to New England in its first few generations, the ruling elite was often of the eastern English background proposed as central to the make-up of New England speech, thus suggesting something like the *founder principle* discussed in Chapter 6). Secondly, the primary means by which British Isles origins are suggested is through comparison between modern dialects on both sides of the Atlantic, although time depth is built into the analysis by some scholars. The ancestor of the dialects of modern East Anglia may well have had the merger discussed above, but we cannot assume this merely from the modern evidence. Nor can we assume that because there is a correspondence between dialects now that there is a 'genetic' relationship between one and the other. On the other hand, just because dialects are not alike now does not mean that there was no connection in the past. In the contemporary southern states, *y'all* is often used as the second person plural pronoun. Nothing like this is now found in the British Isles. But Middle Scots did use *ye/you all* in such plural contexts. Given how many Ulster Scots speakers migrated into the southern mountains and piedmont, it seems likely that this Scots feature must have been carried over into the mainstream varieties of the region. Yet even here there is no evidence for the transfer from immigrant Scots speakers to immigrant English speakers (see Montgomery 2001 for a discussion of these points; Millar 2005: 162–71 provides a broader context).

Nevertheless, these dialect differences are likely to have been affected by the mix of immigrants in each region. This would particularly have been the case since, unlike Australia almost 200 years later, the English colonies along the Eastern Seaboard were not well connected to each other. Indeed, up until the time of the Revolution (and, in fact, for some time afterwards), it was often easier and quicker to go from, say, Charleston to Boston via Bristol or London than directly along the North-American coast. Roads barely existed and when they did they tended to be colony-internal. The colonies were different from each other politically – some having a proprietor, while other colonies were run by a self-perpetuating oligarchy or by some form of representative government. They were also different religiously, with Virginians regularly being Anglicans, while their neighbours in Maryland were often Catholic and many Pennsylvanians were Quakers or representatives of other radical Christian sects. In the mountains to their west, radical dissent of other sorts was to be found, with Presbyterianism and Congregationalism being strong, later overlaid by Baptist and Methodist evangelicisation. There was no love lost between inhabitants of different colonies, to the extent that the idea that they all formed one unit was risible to many; it is likely that most colonists had not met many people from other colonies, unless they lived in Boston, Philadelphia, New York City or a small number of similar, if smaller, centres. Even without turning to the British Isles-origin theory for dialectal diversity, we can see that diversity would quickly have become the norm in the colonies both through geographical isolation and also early identity construction based not upon the idea of being a 'British American', but rather a Virginian, from Connecticut, or elsewhere.

But if that is the case, the homogeneity observed by early visitors still needs to be explained. Is it possible that what is involved is largely a result of the *observer's paradox*, the fact that, when we observe humans, we are therefore ensuring that we will not see normal behaviour? Might the presence of a prestigious outsider in a community have encouraged all members of a community to speak in a more standardised manner? Alternatively, did these prestigious strangers only meet prestigious members of the communities they visited, whether those were members of the rural 'gentry', urban merchants or even, particularly in the back country, religious ministers and schoolteachers? While something can be said for both explanations, it has to be recognised that neither can be true *all* the time. They also ignore a central point of American life from an early period: along with geographical mobility stood social mobility. While a 'lower class' did exist from an early period (even if we ignore the slaves), many people both aspired to, and were able to achieve, middle class status or equivalent, even if they came from a relatively humble background. A good example of this, although somewhat later than others, can be seen in the family of Abraham Lincoln (1809–65), the sixteenth President of the United States, who grew up in considerable poverty (although his family had been somewhat more affluent before he was born) and was descended from indentured servants. Even if your present prospects were less than wonderful, hope for improvement existed; indeed it might even have been seen as your right.

A further feature of early American life also needs to be recognised: literacy. Although there were many non-literate people in the colonies, literacy was probably rather more widespread than it would have been in similar situations in western Europe at the time. At the heart of this is the adherence many Americans had to non-hierarchical forms of Christianity, whether from before arrival in the colonies, as for many New Englanders, or through the religious revivals of the eighteenth century which laid people open to evangelical traditions such as Methodism or the various Baptist confessions. The ability to read the Bible went hand in hand with the Lutheran tenet of 'the priesthood of all believers'. This meant that, even in upcountry districts, you were likely to find people who had regular contact with written Standard English and were therefore likely to reproduce fairly convincingly this code in speech.

Moreover, in a highly geographically mobile environment where literacy was prized, figures associated with education, such as school-teachers and religious ministers, would have represented a considerable element in the social glue which held society outside the main cities together. This may explain why American English, with its highly pre-scriptive stress on, for instance, the use of subject pronouns in subject complement contexts, as in *this is she* (rather than *this is her*), sounds slightly pompous to speakers of British English, where prescriptivism, while certainly present, rarely reaches this level. Literacy of this type may also explain why American English speakers can be intolerant towards those whose speech is sharply divergent from the standard and which is associated (often unfairly) with low levels of literacy. In par-ticular, these views may be aimed at the speech of Southern whites, both from the low-lying parts of the region and the hill country and, before everything else, the dialects of black Americans, often termed African American Vernacular English, which we will discuss in more detail in Chapter 6.

4.4.2 American English and rhetoric

Nevertheless, the generally egalitarian background to the spread of American English can be said to have affected its public expression. Let's compare speeches given by three presidents of the United States: Thomas Jefferson (President 1801–9), Abraham Lincoln (President 1861–5) and Harry S. Truman (President 1945–53). It is not surprising, of course, that levels of formality would decline between the late eight-eenth and mid-twentieth centuries – this would be true for practically every language of western European origin. What is more interesting, however, is the style and language used by these men, each of them Head of State and Commander in Chief of the Armed Forces, and how this has altered over time.

The first passage is an excerpt from the beginning of the State of the Union Address given by Jefferson on 8 December 1801:

Fellow Citizens of the Senate and House of Representatives:

It is a circumstance of sincere gratification to me that on meeting the great council of our nation I am able to announce to them on grounds of reasonable certainty that the wars and troubles which have for so many years afflicted our sister nations have at length come to an end, and that the communications of peace and commerce are once more opening among them. Whilst we devoutly return thanks to the beneficent Being who has been pleased to breathe into them the spirit of conciliation and forgiveness, we are bound with peculiar gratitude to be thankful to Him that our own peace has been preserved through so perilous a season, and ourselves permitted quietly to cultivate the earth and to practice and improve those arts which tend to increase our comforts. The assurances, indeed, of friendly disposition received from all the powers with whom we have principled relations had inspired a confidence that our peace with them would not have been disturbed. But a cessation of irregularities which had affected the commerce of neutral nations and of the irritations and injuries produced by them can not but add to this confidence, and strengthens at the same time the hope that wrongs committed on unoffending friends under a pressure of circumstances will now be reviewed with candor, and will be considered as founding just claims of retribution for the past and new assurance for the future.

Among our Indian neighbors also a spirit of peace and friendship generally prevails, and I am happy to inform you that the continued efforts to introduce among them the implements and the practice of husbandry and the household arts have not been without success; that they are becoming more and more sensible of the superiority of this dependence for clothing and subsistence over the precarious resources of hunting and fishing, and already we are able to announce that instead of that constant diminution of their numbers produced by their wars and their wants, some of them begin to experience an increase of population.

(Downloaded from http://www.infoplease.com/t/hist/state-of-the-union/13.html, 26 August 2011)

This is an elegant piece of writing (and speaking) and very much a product of the Enlightenment. Rhetorical turns of phrase, such as the *litotes* of 'a cessation of irregularities' in reference to the winding down of the first stage of the Revolutionary-Napoleonic Wars, demonstrate a form of reference which is strikingly different to how American politicians have spoken for most of the period following. There is little overt emotion expressed – this would not be in keeping with the elevated viewpoint assumed by the President from his office. References to divinity tend not to be particularly Christian (not surprising given the level of deist, theist and Unitarian beliefs current among Jefferson's peers in Europe and America). Jefferson was only the third President of the United States, after all; the only other non-monarchical head of state who could exercise this level of authority at the time was Napoleon Bonaparte, First Consul of the French Republic. There are no real attempts to engage the audience, particularly not in a 'folksy' manner. This is an enlightened gentlemen speaking to his educational and intellectual equals. Although in many ways a political radical, Jefferson was also a landed gentleman, well educated and comfortable among the social and intellectual elite of the Eastern Seaboard and, indeed, Europe.

This stance is quite different from that found in Abraham Lincoln's Gettysburg Address, given on 19 November 1863 at the dedication of a memorial on the Gettysburg battlefield, at the height of the American Civil War. This speech has for long been considered one of the most important given in the United States, regularly learned by schoolchildren and often quoted by politicians and others at times of national stress and distress. At the time, however, it was given largely damning reviews. It was very short for the period, for instance. The 'warm-up' speaker had orated for over an hour and had indulged in a great many rhetorical flourishes and classical allusions which were practically obligatory at the time.

But although this speech is not rhetorical in the classical sense, it is as finely crafted, although tapping into a different tradition:

> Four score and seven years ago, our fathers brought forth upon this continent a new nation: conceived in liberty, and dedicated to the proposition that all men are created equal.
>
> Now we are engaged in a great civil war . . . testing whether that nation, or any nation so conceived and so dedicated . . . can long endure. We are met on a great battlefield of that war.
>
> We have come to dedicate a portion of that field as a final resting place for those who here gave their lives that this nation might live. It is altogether fitting and proper that we should do this.
>
> But, in a larger sense, we cannot dedicate . . . we cannot consecrate . . . we cannot hallow this ground. The brave men, living and dead, who struggled here have consecrated it, far above our poor power to add or detract. The world will little note, nor long remember, what we say here, but it can never forget what they did here.
>
> It is for us the living, rather, to be dedicated here to the unfinished work which they who fought here have thus far so nobly advanced. It is rather for us to be here dedicated to the great task remaining before us . . . that from these honored dead we take increased devotion to that cause for which they gave the last full measure of devotion . . . that we here highly resolve that these dead shall not have died in vain . . . that this nation, under God, shall have a new birth of freedom . . . and that government of the people . . . by the people . . . for the people . . . shall not perish from this earth.
>
> (Downloaded from http://showcase.netins.net/web/creative/lincoln/ speeches/gettysburg.htm, 26 August 2011)

Although very well read across a wide range of subjects, Lincoln was not a product of the eastern elite as Jefferson was. He was born in Kentucky when that was genuinely on the frontier, before moving into the rapidly developing Midwest. Sharp-witted and rapid in his dealings, he was in many ways the prototypical farmboy made good (although behind the image lay a much more complex individual). He knew his constituency well: literate, but with the Bible at the centre of that experience. Classical analogies were of no interest, or use, to them.

There is a long-standing debate over what Lincoln's religious beliefs were. There is a good possibility that he was not at least a conventional Christian; he may indeed have been agnostic or even atheist (see, for instance, Gienapp 2002: 37). But he knew what people from his background (who were by this time the heart of the expanding United States) were used to hearing and found emotionally stirring.

Because the Gettysburg Address is so well known, it is sometimes easy to forget how heightened its lexical choice is. The vocabulary is centred in the 1611 Authorised Version of the Bible and the literature – hymns, poetry and prose – influenced and inspired by it. The first phrase, *Four score and seven years ago* is highly marked to speakers much more used to *eighty-seven years ago*. Lincoln is taking upon himself the mantle of prophet or patriarch, a role which non-elite Americans understood. A literate American audience knew why he was doing so and what it meant. Indeed, although most of the rhetoric of the founding fathers was based on an ostensibly disinterested Enlightenment blueprint, there was a counter-tradition, embodied in the writing of the radical Thomas Paine, which tapped into the same tradition Lincoln did (Wood 2003: 54).

The final example of presidential speech is an excerpt from an address Harry S. Truman broadcast to the United States Armed Forces on 17 April 1945. The War in Europe was in its very final stages when President Franklin D. Roosevelt died. It should be noted that Roosevelt had been president for a long time – over twelve years. Many of the younger people to whom Truman was speaking may have had only hazy memories of life before Roosevelt. Moreover, Truman was an unknown property, having only become Vice-President that January. Unlike the 'aristocratic' Roosevelt, Truman came from a lower middle class midwestern background. He had been a successful grocery store owner.

To the Armed Forces of the United States throughout the world:

After the tragic news of the death of our late Commander in Chief, it was my duty to speak promptly to the Congress, and the Armed Forces of the United States.

Yesterday, I addressed the Congress. Now I speak to you.

I am especially anxious to talk to you, for I know that all of you felt a tremendous shock, as we did at home, when our Commander in Chief fell.

All of us have lost a great leader, a far-sighted statesman and a real friend of democracy. We have lost a hard-hitting chief and an old friend of the services.

Our hearts are heavy. However, the cause which claimed Roosevelt, also claims us. He never faltered—nor will we!

I have done, as you would do in the field when the Commander falls. My duties and responsibilities are clear. I have assumed them. These duties will be carried on in keeping with our American tradition.

As a veteran of the first World War, I have seen death on the battlefield. When I fought in France with the 35th Division, I saw good officers and men fall, and be replaced.

I know that this is also true of the officers and men of the other services, the Navy, the Marine Corps, the Coast Guard, and the Merchant Marine.

I know the strain, the mud, the misery, the utter weariness of the soldier in the field. And I know too his courage, his stamina, his faith in his comrades, his country, and himself.

We are depending upon each and every one of you.

At first glance, this appears to be rhetoric-free. But on reflection it is a cleverly constructed composition intended to appear artless while still using heightened styles, as the use of partial repetition in *All of us have lost a great leader, a far-sighted statesman and a real friend of democracy. We have lost a hard-hitting chief and an old friend of the services* demonstrates. An avuncular tone is attempted – the President is no longer the disinterested enlightenment sage or the engaged prophet, but rather a man of standing within the community, as a shopkeeper often was in the Midwest, his store an (unofficial) debating chamber.

These examples both show the ways in which political rhetoric developed in the United States, in a culture where rhetoric and learning rhetoric has continued in ways which would seem somewhat unlikely in other parts of the English-speaking world, where little reference is made to rhetoric in central aspects of study at school or university level (for a discussion, see Miller 1997). We can explain this in relation to a perceptual ideology of the country and its speakers – religiously inspired and perceived as a single, egalitarian, community. Jefferson's founding hierarchical rhetoric could not survive in that kind of environment.

Whether the egalitarian, religiously exceptional heart of this United States ideology framed through rhetoric might be the expression being taken for the achievement or not is beyond the remit of this book. But the importance of the written word (and its spoken equivalent), inevitably related to the use of a Standard English, has a particular power in the United States. Those who use divergent codes – such as African American Vernacular English, although these attitudes reach far beyond this variety – may make other Americans uncomfortable, particularly when perceived as being anti-egalitarian in its claim for a 'special case'. We saw in Chapter 2 how lack of full rhoticity in the speech of New York City was considered by some Americans – including many New Yorkers – as being in some senses un-American. Democracy of a populist bent encourages both familiarity and uniformity, while at the same time rendering diversity dubious for a particularly powerful lower middle class elite.

4.5 Lower middle class language ideologies in modern Britain and beyond

Practically since literacy began, a tradition of criticising others' language use has been strong, often analysed as criticism of a decline in 'standards'. It is not surprising that this complaint tradition has grown and often become associated with conservative politics. There cannot be a week goes by where a British newspaper does not carry a linguistic complaint letter. At times they may be more common, particularly during periods of uncertainty. Most linguists are deeply suspicious of the tradition, since linguists view description, not prescription, as their primary purpose. Those who publicly espouse prescriptivism are often perceived as reactionary cranks, people to avoid if possible. But Cameron (1995) makes the persuasive point that the difference between description and prescription may not be as great as linguists think: after all, a description by its nature encourages a sense of what is 'normal' within a system. More importantly, she suggests that it is a good idea for linguists to listen to what people interested in language have to say about it, primarily so that we can understand *why* they hold views which, from an insiders' viewpoint, appear ill-conceived or even meaningless.

In recent years, it has become apparent that it is possible to make a living from being a 'language pundit'. The success of Lynne Truss's *Eats*,

Shoots & Leaves: The Zero Tolerance Approach to Punctuation (Truss 2003) and of many works which followed in its wake, including Humphrys (2004), demonstrate that linguistic complaint literature has continued into modern times and, most interestingly, sells well. Naturally, the perceived 'ills' of modern language use may be different from writer to writer. Truss, for instance, is primarily interested in punctuation, which is, arguably, non-linguistic (although many people felt that she was on a 'grammar crusade', primarily, perhaps, because of her interest in the possessive apostrophe), while Humphrys concentrates on the 'dumbing down' of language and the misuse of words and phrases. Nonetheless a sense of a common core of worries exists among those interested in language as an institution.

A number of linguists have attempted to engage in this debate, either as an interested outsider, as with Cameron (1995), or as in some ways a 'corrective' to some of the assumptions about linguistic decline around, as with Milroy and Milroy (1999), coupled with an attempt to understand what Standard English actually is and whether it truly has a unique position in relation to other varieties of English. Crystal (2006) attempted to grapple with the arguments of self-appointed language pundits. While essentially moderate in his treatment of the issue (too moderate, perhaps, for some linguists), his work was shouted down by a number of pundits.

Most of these debates and furores are essentially good clean fun, cooked up by journalists and 'personalities' to further their careers and strike a populist chord with a sizeable constituency. But there are less amusing tendencies afoot in this populist 'backlash' against 1960s liberalism in relation to language teaching. I probably speak for many linguists when I say I regret how few students come up to university with anything more than a limited sense of how to analyse their native languages. This is, it should be noted, a very different regret from one passed on students' not knowing 'proper' grammar. The two are regularly equated, of course, but the ideological bridge is extremely rickety. In the late 1980s, however, the rather authoritarian Thatcher government in Britain, running out of steam in a variety of ways, began to use teaching standards as being a way to develop a new populism aimed at 'loony lefties' and other bogeymen and women in various local council offices and schools. The move was extremely popular with Thatcherism's natural constituency, the lower middle classes. In the end, however, as Cameron (1995) eloquently demonstrates, the results of this policy were unimpressive, since it was recognised that the fetishised rote learning of 'grammar' was both unworkable and self-defeating in terms of developing a sense of language and structure. The process did lead, however, to a bureaucratisation of education throughout England and Wales, discouraging individual initiative by teachers, which may have been the intention all along.

Of the same time and ideological background, although not necessarily connected directly to Thatcherite educational initiatives, is the work of Professor John Honey, whose primary viewpoint, related in a range of publications, including Honey (1991), is that *not* using Standard English (by which he normally means RP) will affect someone's life chances. This is not necessarily incorrect. There is no doubt that in a country such as England, where a significant part of those holding power have gone to a limited number of schools and universities (as have, often, their parents) and where most of this elite use Standard English as a native dialect in ways that most people do not, having a regional accent, even when speaking Standard English, is a drawback if you have considerable ambitions. But Honey takes this a stage further by saying that 'liberal' educationalists and linguists who encourage the retention of local accents and the perpetuation of dialects – particularly urban dialects – are actually doing those taught a disservice. There are a number of issues with this argument, of course, not least the equation of Standard English and RP. The ideology involved is dangerous, however, since, as Crowley (1999) points out, he is essentially blaming those who do not have the 'correct' speech forms for not acquiring them, rather than enquiring why a small minority who speak in a particular way should be able to assume power over the masses who do not. Insidious and popular, this type of argument has a long history, as we have seen. Indeed in using examples from the recent past, I have merely opted for materials which are readily available. Similar arguments and examples could be found at any time in the last 200 years. This ideology of the connection between middle class morality and adherence to 'correct' linguistic norms is very powerful indeed.

4.6 Discussion

While the English-speaking world does not have the overt linguistic ideologies which the French-speaking world has, ideology has played and plays a significant part in the ways the English language is perceived by native speakers. These perceptions have changed over the years, due to social changes, but a centralised, non-dialectal, variety lies at its heart. Although ideological differences exist between those countries following the American model and those essentially following the British (or 'Commonwealth'), equivalent at the heart of both lies the social and linguistic power of the lower middle classes, expressed through the maintenance of 'uniformity'. Again, the difference between these views and those found in France is not great.

Further reading

Beal (2004) and Görlach (1999 and 2001) are all excellent treatments of language change in the late modern era. Crowley (1996 and 2003) are readable, thought-provoking and act as a means of bringing macrosociolinguistics and literary theory together. Milroy and Milroy (1999) and Cameron (1995) provide fascinating (and complementary) insights into the ideas underlying 'language standards'.

Some issues to consider

1. Visit the website of an organisation such as *US English* (http://www.us-english.org/, accessed 12 January 2012) or the *Queen's English Society* (http://queens-english-society.com/, accessed 12 January 2012). What ideologies underlie their views? How are these represented?
2. What subjects are dealt with in dialect poetry found in ONE of the following varieties: English 'West Country'; Appalachian Mountains; Cockney; Lancashire; Northumberland? What does this tell you about attitudes towards that variety?
3. Find out what you can about the decisions made on what was to be used, what to be excluded, in the *Oxford English Dictionary*. With what you know, can it really be said that it represents *all* of English?

Note

1. Many of the points made here are discussed by the contributors to Algeo 2001.

5 Contact and shift as agents of change

5.1 Typological change from Old English to Middle English

There can be little doubt that, in the period 850–1250, English passed through a series of changes which profoundly affected the nature of the language. An essentially synthetic language, where most important functional information was carried by inflectional morphology, quickly became one where most functional information was carried by the position of phrases within a clause. In short, grammatical gender and, more vitally, grammatical case were expunged from the English morphosyntactic system, as the following discussion will demonstrate.

The following brief excerpts of Old English and Modern English give a fair idea of what changes have taken place (although we have to recognise that the text involved is a translation, originally from Greek but via Latin in the case of Old English and that its sanctity makes its wording more resistant to change):

Old English (late tenth or early eleventh century)

Fæder ure þu þe eart on heofonum si þin nama gehalgod tobecume þin rice gewurþe þin willa on eorðan swa swa on heofonum urne gedæghwamlican hlaf syle us to dæg and forgyf us ure gyltas swa swa we forgyfað urum gyltendum and ne gelæd þu us on costnunge ac alys us of yfele

Present-day English (New Revised Standard Version)

Our Father in heaven, hallowed be your name. Your kingdom come. Your will be done, on earth as it is in heaven. Give us this day our daily bread. And forgive us our debts, as we also have forgiven our debtors. And do not bring us to the time of trial, but rescue us from the evil one

Although Old English and Present-Day English are obviously closely related, anyone approaching the former without German or a background in medieval English would have serious difficulties parsing the structures found. We cannot present here an exhaustive analysis, but a few phrases can suffice. In Modern English, for instance, the noun phrase *our daily bread* gives us no information about its function (it is the direct object of *give*, but without context this would be impossible to predict). In Old English, on the other hand, the equivalent phrase *urne gedæghwamlican hlaf* tells us that the case employed is accusative (the *-ne* ending can only mean this), which generally means direct object function (grammatical case is rather more subtle and complex than association with particular functional roles, but that need not concern us here), The *-ne* ending also tells us that *hlaf* 'bread' is a member of the masculine gender class. Indeed *all* the endings (or sometimes lack of endings) on the words in the passage are meaningful (unlike in Modern English, where they are normally unpronounced detritus from an earlier stage in the language's history). Thus the *-um* on *heofonum* tells us that the noun is dative plural. With the preposition *on*, dative case implies stasis while accusative case means movement, so we know that the phrase means 'inside the heavens' rather than 'into the heavens'. In Modern English, we can of course imply the same difference; but we need two (or even more) different prepositions to carry this out.

This is, as I have said, a profound change; that does not mean that it is unnatural, however. If we consider all the Germanic languages we can see that similar changes are ongoing in all varieties. To take the noun phrase in the first instance, we can see that English and Afrikaans are the only Germanic languages to have lost grammatical gender entirely. But a number of other languages – most dialects of Swedish, Danish and Dutch, for instance – have 'simplified' the system somewhat, with only two genders (common – originally masculine – and neuter gender) rather than the original three (masculine, feminine and neuter). Grammatical case has been lost, with the exception of a few fossilised or near-fossilised usages, in English, Afrikaans, most Scandinavian varieties and Dutch. It should be noted that those languages not mentioned here – German, Faeroese and Icelandic – while maintaining something like the original case and gender system of the Germanic noun phrase, do so in a less morphologically 'rich' way than was previously the case. This can be seen readily if we conduct a similar comparison of versions of The Lord's Prayer in Old High German and Modern High German:

Old High German (ninth century)

fater unser thu thar bist in himile, si giheilagot thin namo. queme thin rihhi, si thin uuillo, so her in himile ist, so si her in erdu. unsar brot tagalihhaz gib uns hiutu. inti furlaz uns unsara sculdi, so uuir furlazemes unsaren sculdigon. inti ni gileitest unsih in costunga, uzouh arlosi unsih fon ubile.

Modern High German

Vater Unser im Himmel, Geheiligt werde Dein Name, Dein Reich komme. Dein Wille geschehe, Wie im Himmel, so auf Erden. Unser tägliches Brot gib uns heute, Und vergib uns unsere Schuld, Wie auch wir vergeben unseren Schuldigern. Und führe uns nicht in Versuchung, Sondern erlöse uns von dem Bösen.

Modern High German has both grammatical gender and case (*im Himmel* 'in heaven', for instance, contains the clitic *-m*, a form of *dem*, the definite article form for dative case with nouns of the masculine and neuter gender classes in the singular; as with Old English, the sense of 'inside' is carried by the dative use). But the modern version of the language is far less morphologically rich than the earlier, implying that much of the original morphological diversity was unnecessary and that simplification does not have to mean breakdown.

5.1.1 Drift

This set of changes could be connected to a process proposed by Sapir (1921; in particular pp. 144 ff): *drift*. Sapir's starting point is a startling truth: language change can often appear to be a matter of similar processes being applied to different parts of a language, at the same time or often in succession. Using English as a laboratory, Sapir demonstrated that functional marking in the noun phrase, originally found on nouns, adjectives and determiners, is now only recorded with the relative/interrogative pronouns (*The man whom I saw yesterday* or *Who am I?*) and most of the personal pronouns (*I gave her the book*). Within the relative/interrogative pronouns, however, there is, Sapir demonstrates, a general tendency towards the loss of function-marking in colloquial speech and, increasingly, in writing. Thus most native English speakers would now say *The man who I saw yesterday* (or, often, variants like *The man I saw yesterday* or *The man that I saw yesterday*). The functionally marked forms have remained, but are now generally available only as features learned later in life. Their artificiality is demonstrated by the fact that most native speakers occasionally use them 'wrongly', as with **Whom am I?* From Sapir's point of view, the next in line for the forces of *drift* would be the personal pronouns. As a number of English-based pidgins and creoles demonstrate (as well as, to a degree, the traditional dialects of south-western England), it is not actually necessary to use function-marked forms there. All native speakers would understand the information carried in *I gave it to he* as readily as *I gave it to him*, even if only a few would recognise the former as 'normal'. It is quite likely that the unmarked forms would be rather more widespread than is the case if literacy, a naturally conservative force, had not been at work on most English speakers over the last few hundred years.

A number of scholars (see Malkiel 1981) take Sapir's ideas further, suggesting that *drift* can be employed to explain why related languages continue to act in a similar manner *after* they have ceased to be part of a dialect continuum. Thus it is striking, as noted in Chapter 2, that a very similar series of sound changes – the Great Vowel Shift – took place in almost all West Germanic varieties in the late medieval and early modern periods. While some of the details of these changes differ from language to language, the general tendency for lower vowels to rise and high vowels to diphthongise is found in a range of languages – English, Dutch and German – where immediate influence along a geographical continuum is unlikely. Some linguists would suggest that there was a 'weakness' in these languages which was inherited from the ancestral variety and which, at the right point, was triggered by societal forces – in this case, the rise of a lower middle class as a major economic and eventually political force in urbanising societies.

Returning to the noun-phrase systems of the Germanic languages, *drift* could have been at work in the typological changes involved. Thus Afrikaans and English are at the analytic end of a continuum of change at the other end of which are Icelandic, High German and Faeroese:

As we have already noted, however, even these structurally con-servative varieties exhibit the same set of changes, albeit in a lesser, incipient form, as do languages which have participated more fully in the same set of changes. Therefore *drift* lies at the heart of the changes. But this analysis ignores a number of difficult questions. Why have some varieties gone through this set of changes in a more thorough manner than have others? Why is it that Afrikaans and English, geo-graphically peripheral to the West Germanic languages as a whole, have been affected more thoroughly than have more central languages like Dutch? Moreover, as we will see, although English as a whole took around 350–400 years to complete these changes, in each dialect the change appears to have taken only a few generations. Why is this the case? What forces brought it about? A good way to display the changes and their rapid transfer can be achieved through the analysis of three brief excerpts from representative, essentially non-literary, texts.

Languages in *italics* = earliest recorded form of language; Languages in **bold** = modern varieties, descended from italicised variety to their right.

Figure 5.1 *Drift* in the Germanic languages

5.1.2 Rapid Diffusion

5.1.2.1 Textual analysis 1: the Anglo-Saxon Chronicle

We begin with a brief excerpt from the *Anglo-Saxon Chronicle*, concerned with a series of events which took place in the middle of the eighth century, but actually composed in the late ninth or early tenth centuries. The dialect employed is the West Saxon form of English used at the royal court in Winchester and, self-consciously or not, as we saw in Chapter 3, broadcast as 'English' to the 'provinces'. Possibly because the West Saxon kingdom was something of a backwater until the Viking invasions, its language, as represented in a considerable written corpus, was both idiosyncratic – particularly in phonological terms – when compared to the other written dialects and also conservative in terms of its retention of the inherited inflectional morphology.

Text 1

Her Cynewulf benam Sigebryht his rices ond Westseaxna wiotan for unryhtum dædum, buton Hamtunscire. Ond he hæfde þa oþ he ofslog þone aldormon þe him longest wunode, ond hiene þa Cynewulf on Andred adræfde ond he þær wunade oþ þæt hiene an swan ofstang æt Pryfetes flodan; ond he wræc þone aldormon Cumbran.

Translation:

In this year [755] Cynewulf and the councillors of the West Saxons deprived Sigeberht of his kingdom for unlawful actions, with the exception of Hampshire; and he kept that until he slew the ealdorman who remained faithful to him for the longest period. And Cynewulf then

drove him [Sigeberht] away into the [Kentish] Weald, and he lived
there until a herdsman stabbed him at the stream at Privett; and he [the
herdsman] avenged the ealdorman Cumbra.

Although this text is relatively easy to follow, even if we have not
studied Old English for any time, it is immediately obvious that the
language is, to a considerable extent, based upon different precepts from
Modern English. In the noun phrase, for instance, grammatical gender
– the morphological marking of nouns in large-scale noun classes which
may, but need not, bear some relationship to natural sex – and case – the
morphological marking of nouns, adjectives and determiners according
to function – are very much still in operation and work in tandem. For
instance, in the excerpt:

> Her Cynewulf benam Sigebryht his rices ond Westseaxna wiotan for
> unryhtum dædum, buton **Hamtunscire**. Ond he hæfde **þa** oþ he ofslog
> þone aldormon þe him longest wunode
>
> In this year Cynewulf and the councillors of the West Saxons deprived
> Sigeberht of his kingdom for unlawful actions, with the exception of
> **Hampshire**; and he kept **that** until he slew the ealdorman who remained
> faithful to him for the longest period.

There is a potential danger in Modern English that we would not know
who or what *that* referred to in the second sentence. An attempt to
demonstrate this relationship in the translation could be carried out by
subverting the natural (and normally quite rigid) element order rules
of Modern English ('and **that** he held'). In the Old English, however,
the fact that *scire* is a member of the feminine gender class and that *þa* is
(among other things) the demonstrative pronoun used in place of feminine gender nouns in the accusative case (largely associated with direct
object contexts) must have made the connection between *Hamtunscire*
and *þa* obvious to native speakers.

The element order rules for Old English are also much more lenient
– or, perhaps more accurately, more various; this allows emphasis
within clauses to be realised far more subtly than is possible today. For
instance, in:

> ond **hiene** þa Cynewulf on Andred adræfde ond he þær wunade oþ þæt
> **hiene** an swan ofstang æt Pryfetes flodan
>
> And Cynewulf then drove him [Sigeberht] away into the Weald, and he
> lived there until a herdsman stabbed him at the stream at Privett.

hiene, the accusative case form of *he* 'he' is used not in a SVO (Subject
Verb Object) construction, now practically demanded, then the default

element order pattern, but rather an OSV (Object Subject Verb) one, now practically unknown, but possible in Old English, albeit marked. Why would someone choose to use the marked form? The answer we think is that by placing the direct object in what would be the unmarked position for the subject, the listeners' (or readers') attention is drawn to this element as the feature the speaker (or writer) wishes us to concentrate upon. Of course, as Mitchell (1994) points out, Old English is normally not that syntactically different from Modern English. *Pragmatic word order*, as we have just discussed, is nowhere near as common or straightforward to employ as it is in, say, Russian. But nevertheless there is still a lot going on morphosyntactically here in this low register prose which Modern English *cannot* do, and noun-phrase concord is at its heart. In the next two passages we will see how this system broke down.

5.1.2.2 Texts 2 and 3: the Peterborough Chronicle

In the aftermath of the Norman Conquest of 1066–7, it was practically inevitable that much of the West Saxon vernacular project was jettisoned by the new French-speaking monarchy and its bureaucracy (see, for instance, Loyn 1991). The *Anglo-Saxon Chronicle* tradition continued, as far as we can tell, in a number of places in England for ten to fifteen years after the Conquest before the annual description of events ceased to be issued at the centre. In Peterborough, in the south-east midlands of England, however, the *Anglo-Saxon Chronicle* manuscript continued to be added to until the middle of the twelfth century. The material recorded becomes more idiosyncratic and personalised; it is very likely that its continuation was essentially a hobby.

Most of the twelfth-century material in the *Chronicle* is the work of two hands (and authors), the First and Second Continuations. As we will see shortly, although relatively close chronologically (we have no reason to assume, for instance, that much hindsight is involved in the construction of the annals), the two Continuations demonstrate a considerable linguistic leap in relation both to each other and the Old English, which they obviously revered, in the preceding pages of the manuscript. Rapid and consuming language change is also taking place between the two continuations. If we recognise how conservative the written form is in comparison with the spoken, in fact, the change involved becomes very profound.

Text 2: the First Continuation

MILLESIMO cᵒxxvᵒ. On þis gær sende se king Henri toforen Cristesmesse of Normandi to Englalande ⁊ bebead þet man scolde

biniman ealla þa minetere þe wæron on Englelande heora liman – þet
wæs here elces riht hand ⁊ heora stamen beneðan: þet wæs for se man ðe
hafde an pund, he ne mihte cysten ænne peni at anne market. ⁊ Se biscop
Roger of Særesbyrig sende ofer eall Englalande ⁊ bebead hi ealle þet hi
scolden cumen to Winceastre to Cristemesse. Þa hi ðider coman, ða nam
man an ⁊ an ⁊ benam ælc ðone riht hand ⁊ þa stanes beneðan. Eall þis wæs
gedon wiðinnon þa twelf niht, ⁊ þet wæs eall mid micel rihte, forði þet
hi hafden fordon eall þet land mid here micele fals þet hi ealle abohton.

Translation

1125 In this year [1124] before Christmas King Henry sent from
Normandy to England and gave instructions that all the moneyers
who were in England should be deprived of their members, namely the
right hand of each and their testicles below: the reason for this was that
anyone who had a pound found it would not buy goods worth a penny
in a market. Bishop Roger of Salisbury sent over all England, and com-
manded them all to assemble at Winchester by Christmas. When they
came there they were then taken one by one, and each deprived of the
right hand and the testicles below. All this was done in the twelve days
between Christmas and Epiphany, and was entirely justified because they
had ruined the whole country by the magnitude of their fraud which they
had paid for to the full.

Note: ⁊ is an abbreviation used for 'and' before the advent of the
ampersand.

At a casual glance this passage appears to be 'standard' late West Saxon
Old English. A closer examination of the text demonstrates, however,
that while the passage is certainly indebted to Anglo-Saxon models,
in fact there has been considerable change. While many phrases have
retained their historical morphology, for instance in *sende se king Henri*,
'[the] king Henry sent', where *se* is used correctly with a member of the
historical masculine gender class in the correct nominative subject contexts, this is also regularly confused, particularly perhaps in final syllables, for instance, in the example *he ne mihte cysten ænne peni at anne market*,
cysten would have had <-an>, and *anne* would have been <anum>.
This ambiguity reaches epidemic proportions with *⁊ bebead þet man scolde
biniman ealla þa minetere þe wæron on Englelande heora lima*, where *ealla þa
minetere þe wæron on Englelande* morphologically looks like the direct
object, particularly since it has *þa*, historically associated with the accusative case in the plural. Moreover, it is in the position immediately following the verb where the direct object would be regular. Yet it is in fact
the indirect object. In Old English this distinction could be marked by

endings and dedicated dative case forms. Here this is no longer possible, yet the scribe still proceeds with the formation: this is grave ambiguity.

Grammatical gender also appears to be breaking down, as the example *ðone riht hand* demonstrates. In 'classical' Old English *hand* was a member of the historical feminine gender-class. Here it is found with *ðone*, which historically was triggered only by masculine nouns in the accusative case. This is an example of right case, wrong gender.

Finally, element order has changed a great deal since Old English. In Old English, generally where a verb was represented by both an auxiliary and an infinitive or participle, the latter would be found at the end of the clause. In this passage, the two parts of the verb are generally found together or in close proximity; in other words, as in Modern English. The element order system here is largely incapable of the subtleties of meaning Old English was; this must be due largely to the breakdown in the function-morphology relationship already discussed.

Text 3: the Second Continuation

Millesimo cliiii. On þis gær wærd þe king Stephne ded ₇ bebyried þer his wif ₇ his sune wæron bebyried æt Fauresfeld; þæt minstre hi makeden. Þa þe king was ded, þa was þe eorl beionde sæ; ₇ ne durste nan man don oþer bute god for þe micel eie of him. Þa he to Engleland com, þa was he underfangen mid micel wurtscipe, ₇ to king bletcæd in Lundene on þe Sunnendæi beforen Midwintre Dæi, ₇ held þærc micel curt.

Translation

1154 In this year King Stephen died, and was buried with his wife and son at Faversham; they had founded that monastery. The earl [i.e., Henry, count of Anjou, heir to the throne] was overseas when the king died, and yet no man dared do other than good for their great fear of him. When he came to England, he was received with great ceremony, and was consecrated king in London on the Sunday before Midwinter's day and held there a great court.

Much of what was said for the First Continuation is also true here, with the proviso that what were ongoing developments in the first passage have been largely completed. Grammatical case has all but disappeared. Grammatical gender is also gone (on the sole occasion when it might have survived, *þæt minstre hi makeden*, *þæt* is more likely to stand for the new 'pure demonstrative' than be the marker of neuter gender in the nominative and accusative cases). The original formal complexity of the simple demonstrative paradigm has been replaced with a split between *that* for distal demonstrative meaning and *the* for definite article meaning, no matter the historical case or gender.

It is obvious, therefore, that the inherited Old English system is practically moribund and that, while the Second Continuation scribe can read and basically understand his models, he is incapable of replicating what is now an essentially foreign system.

5.1.3 Nature, dating and direction of change

These changes were not confined to the *Peterborough Chronicle*, of course. The loss of gender and case marking, along with marking of definiteness and plurality in the noun phrase, was thoroughgoing eventually in all dialects. But what is interesting about the process is that it happened much earlier in some dialects than in others. Essentially, the further north your origin, the more likely it was that your language would be affected early; the further south and east you lived, the more likely your variety was to go through the changes late. Thus texts like the English gloss to the *Lindisfarne Gospels*, produced in the tenth century by a monk named Aldred in Chester-le-Street, County Durham, is already showing a partial breakdown of grammatical gender marking. One example of this is the use of demonstrative pronoun in *þiu wide geat* 'the/that wide gate'. In 'classical' West Saxon Old English the 'simple demonstrative paradigm was:

	Masculine	Neuter	Feminine	Plural
Nominative	se	þæt	seo	þa
Accusative	þone	þæt	þa	þa
Genitive	þæs	þæs	þære	þara
Dative	þæm	þæm	þære	þæm

In late Northumbrian Old English the <s> forms were replaced by <þ>, by analogy with the vast majority of forms in the paradigm. *þiu* is therefore equivalent to West Saxon *seo* and thus should represent nouns with feminine gender class in nominative contexts (i.e., largely in subject contexts). In the phrase cited, *geat* is indeed the subject of the phrase. The problem is that the noun is historically a member of the neuter gender class, and should have *þæt* as its determiner.

The final examples of gender-class marking in English can be found in the *Ayenbite of Inwit*, written by Dan Michel around 1350 in Kent; in other words between 400 and 450 years after the change appears to have begun. This seems in many ways a reasonable amount of time for such a change to take place. This is missing the point, however. In those dialect areas where we have sufficient evidence, there is seldom more than three generations between using a system largely indistinguishable from the Old English and one where little survives of the inherited system, as we have seen with the *Peterborough Chronicle* continuations.

We can also map out how the change passed through English and, indeed, England. Originating in northern dialects in the ninth to tenth centuries, it spread to the east midlands in the eleventh and twelfth centuries, the (south-)west midlands in the twelfth century, the south-west of England in the thirteenth century and Kentish in the thirteenth and fourteenth centuries.[1] From an historical linguistic point of view, the primary issue with this change is why and how it happened by this somewhat circuitous route, since there is an undisclosed issue: northern dialects of English were not, we think, particularly prestigious in the Middle Ages, as has remained the case since.[2] Most linguistic change, moreover, appears to have radiated out from the populous south-east (the raising and rounding of Old English /ɑː/ to /ɔː/ in words like *stone* being a particularly striking example, eventually reaching all dialects spoken to the south of the Rivers Ribble and Humber).

Samuels (1989a) observes a counter tendency, however. Features – lexical and morphological in particular – of northern dialect usage gradually spread through the midland and southern dialects in the course of the Middle English period. On occasion these borrowings from the north may represent means for getting around systemic ambiguities. For instance, in Old English 'he' was *he* /heː/, 'she' was *heo* /heːɔ/ (with the accusative form *hie* /hiɔ/) and 'they' was *hie* /hiɔ/. In West Saxon at least the stressed forms would have been readily distinguished (something which cannot probably be said for the unstressed variants likely to have been common in speech, thereby representing the first potential stirrings of ambiguity). In the early Middle English dialects of the east midlands, however, all of these forms fell together at /heː/.

Since the ambiguity between 'he' and 'she' was particularly marked because the pronouns were of the same number, it is natural that attempts would be made to rectify the situation.[3] In northern England new forms – 'unusual' phonological developments from the old forms – began to make their presence known. Employing only a slight systematisation, it can be said that <h> variants begin to be replaced with variants on <ȝh>. A generation or so after this these variants are replaced with ones spelled with <sh> or <sch>, or other variants, suggesting /ʃ/. Samuels (1989a) demonstrated that this set of changes in spelling (and, it can be assumed, pronunciation) gradually moved southward in the Middle English period, in a manner somewhat reminiscent of capillary action. In each dialect the change would take two to three generations, but the cumulative effect for the language as a whole would have taken considerably longer.[4]

The issue with ambiguity between the third person singular and plural forms was also sorted through the borrowing of Northern usage, although on this occasion through what had been an actual Norse borrowing (although it would be very unlikely that southern speakers would have been aware of the new form's provenance – if they cared): *they*. Interestingly, the subject form came south earlier than the oblique *them* and possessive *their*. Chaucer, for instance, uses the first but not the other two, where he retains native <h> forms. This type of usage represents what I have termed *conservative radicalism* (Millar 2000; in particular pp. 63–4). Northern forms are employed to sort out issues in more prestigious dialects, but only in 'small homeopathic doses'. The problem (if that is the right word) is that the injection of linguistically radical material into a more conservative framework tends to encourage more radical importations. Thus *them* and *their(s)* entered written London dialect (and therefore Standard English) in the generation after Chaucer's death, possibly because *hem* was too close to *him* and *hare* to *her*. If the 'northern' forms had not been available, everyone would probably have 'soldiered on', however.

Moreover, the borrowing of *they* meant that the descendant of Old English *þeah* 'although' was often its homophone. Since both of these are function words, native speakers must have felt uncomfortable with using both, meaning that the northern (in origin Norse) conjunction *though* was brought into southern systems. This borrowing led to a further ambiguity, since the plural of *that* in southern England was *tho*, which was now often homophonous with *though*. A new plural – *those* – was therefore created. Samuels (1989a) demonstrates that these problems can be traced back to northern England and were spread by 'capillary motion' to more southern areas. These changes are part of a much larger set, all of which suggest that northern influence, particularly at a subconscious or covert level, was always present on the edges of more southerly dialects and may have assumed a role as a 'fix' to sort out ambiguity created by change.

English therefore lost all trace of the inherited grammatical gender system and almost all of the grammatical case system, with the change beginning in northern England, and gradually spreading to more conservative dialects to the south. As with the smaller-scale changes discussed above, 'capillary action' was also at work under these circumstances, leading to a gradual movement of the new system to the south. Probably because both case and in particular gender marking systems were already compromised to the south (an example of Sapir's *drift*, no doubt), these changes were more thoroughgoing than others (including other grammatical features, such as the radical simplification of verb number).

In relation to the collapse of grammatical gender (and with it grammatical case) similar patterns are analysed in Jones (for instance 1967ab and 1988). There appears to have been a period immediately before the complete loss of case where gender marking was jettisoned in favour of the marking of function, something we have seen in the examples from the gloss to the *Lindisfarne Gospels* and the *Peterborough Chronicle* First Continuation discussed above. This attempt at systemic reform could not stand up to the forces placed upon it by more radical change, however (Millar 2002).

The question then is: was *drift* the only catalyst for these changes? Given the speed of the change within dialects and the directionality from north to south, it is worth asking whether other features might have contributed to the processes involved. Language contact, as a catalyst of change, is one which should be examined.

5.2 Language contact as catalyst

English has, of course, gone through numerous language contacts of different types in its history. Two stand out during the late Old English and early Middle English periods, however: contacts with speakers of Old Norse and of Old French.

5.2.1 Contact with speakers of North Germanic dialects

During this period, for whatever reason, speakers of North Germanic dialects moved out of their heartlands and into the more developed parts of north-west Europe and beyond (a brief and approachable discussion can be found in Sawyer 1982; Richards 2010 is a good recent treatment of Viking England). Some came as short-term raiders, others took part in attempts to gain political power in specific territories (sometimes succeeding) and many settled, more or less peacefully, to exploit better soils and climates. In some places, such as what became Normandy (of which more shortly), the new Scandinavian rulers and settlers lost their native language relatively quickly – perhaps in the second to third generations. In other places, however, Scandinavian settlers appear to have maintained their native dialects for considerably longer, particularly in parts of the north of England. It should be remembered, perhaps, that Old English and Old Norse were quite close relatives, so mutual intelligibility might, again, not have been utterly problematical, based minimally on an awareness of common words and structures (we will return to this point in the following sections). This might have allowed speakers to maintain their native languages somewhat longer than might otherwise have been the case.

The tenth and early eleventh centuries were the most intense period of Scandinavian involvement in the politics, economics and social structure of England. Resurgence by the West Saxon kingdom (the only English-ruled polity left standing) under Alfred and his descendants led in the first instance to a line being drawn across England, from the Irish Sea to the Thames at London. North and east of the line was the Danelaw, the area where Danish rather than English legal traditions functioned. In its original establishment it was probably envisaged that the Danelaw would have been administered by Scandinavians, although whether this implied that the region was perpetually removed from England is impossible to answer: it appears not to have been the West Saxon kings' interpretation. In the course of the tenth century the land south of the Humber was fully reincorporated under English rule. Nevertheless, the dialects of the southern Danelaw – Leicestershire, Nottinghamshire, Derbyshire, Lincolnshire, and so on – retain a considerable amount of lexical influence from Scandinavian. Indeed, aspects of Norse legal practice, such as the smallest basic unit of military and civil administration was, until the 1970s, not known as *hundred*, as in the south, but instead as *wapentake*, suggesting a central weapons cache.

North of the Rivers Humber and Ribble, however, West Saxon hegemony was less complete (although kings whose times and characters lent themselves to expansion, such as Athelstan, who reigned from 924 or 925 to 939, were able to exercise supremacy over the north). Nevertheless, the English kingdom of Northumbria – in particular the southern sub-kingdom of Deira – was essentially replaced by a Norse Kingdom of York, with connections throughout the Scandinavian world, from Russia to Greenland and beyond. The present county of York, with its three-way division into *ridings* (Old Norse *þriðungar* 'three parts') can be seen as its political, cultural and, to a degree, linguistic continuation. Many features of Norse – particularly lexis – can be found in its dialects, many of them not found in other varieties, with the exception of northern Lancashire and Cumbria to its west and north, also heavily settled and occasionally ruled by Norse speakers. The level to which Norse replaced English can be seen in place-names. A number of Yorkshire towns, such as Whitby (previously known as *Streonshal*), assumed a completely new name. On other occasions, however, names were remade to suit the rather different phonology of Norse, *York* being a good example, as an opaque descendant of Old English *Eoforwic*.

Although the West Saxon expansion began to lose speed in the late tenth century, due both to the general unfitness of some of its rulers, and a reversion to highly organised raiding and settlement under the Danish Kings Sweyn Forkbeard (king of England 1013–14) and his son, Cnut (king of England 1016–35), these changes were at times largely confined to who ruled, rather than who settled. Cnut in particular ruled England largely as an English monarch, using the same governmental apparatus and traditions of consultation employed by his English predecessors. Nevertheless, truly 'Viking' involvement with England did not cease until after the battle of Stamford Bridge, near York, in September 1066, where an English army under the leadership of Harold Godwinsson defeated an army led by Harald Hardrada, King of Norway. In the most influenced parts of England, Norse quite possibly lasted as a spoken language for another century and more, an argument made much of by Samuels (1989b). Whether the people who spoke these dialects considered themselves anything other than English is another matter, however. In relation to the ongoing Viking threat, Christian identity was probably analysed as being of greater importance than linguistic, although this point would be difficult to prove.

5.2.2 Contact with speakers of Norman French

As we have seen, the Duchy of Normandy essentially came into being through the Scandinavian expansion. A major force of Scandinavian raiders was employed in the early tenth century to keep off their kinsmen from the area around the mouth of the Seine, in an example, perhaps, of 'poacher turned gamekeeper'. This land – which was quickly extended to the west and north – was given by the king of the western Frankish lands as an hereditary fiefdom to their leader, Rollo (or Hrolf). Normandy quickly became a major power in north-west Europe, although, as we have already noted, the Scandinavian settlers rapidly assimilated linguistically (and to a lesser extent, perhaps, culturally) to the local norms. The Normans were inherently outward-looking; England was not their only colony (although the only one ruled by the ducal family). Within a few centuries Normans gained power (via England) in Wales and Ireland, while the King of Scots invited English Normans into Scotland to carry out political and economic change. Sicily, southern Italy and Malta were 'liberated' from their Moslem overlords by Norman adventurers. Parts of Greece were also occasionally ruled by Norman knights (Chibnall 2000 presents an impressively even-handed treatment of the subject).

Contacts between England and Normandy began before 1066. Edward the Confessor (reigned 1042–66) had spent a large part of his life as a refugee from the rule of the Danish kings in England, probably largely in Normandy. Moreover, his mother, Emma, was the daughter of Duke Richard of Normandy (Emma went on to marry Cnut, ensuring that the ruling houses of a considerable part of northern Europe were intimately connected). This meant that a distant relationship existed between Edward and Duke William of Normandy. Given the length of his stay and his family relationship with Normandy, it is likely that Edward spoke Norman French fluently. He may even have considered it his first language. Certainly he was something of a Normanophile. Significantly, the earliest French borrowings into English, such as the ancestor of *pride*, actually predate the Norman Conquest. It is very likely that Norman – and beyond that French – culture (and language) would have had a considerable effect upon England even without 1066, as was the case in German (and other languages) during the same period.

The events of 1066–7, however, gave a particular flavour to the Norman influence. The Normans came as conquerors. While it would be inaccurate to say that all English landholders lost their lands during this period, land *was* regularly seized in the two generations after conquest. French-speaking colonists did include artisans and lower ranking soldiers, of course, but the vast majority of immigrants during this period were at least gentry and often noble. In a sense, therefore, language use became a socially stratified matter in Norman England. Those English landowners who remained after the great change were likely to move over to French in order to show class solidarity.

Despite its considerable status, however, French eventually declined in England. Leaving aside the royal house – first Norman, then Plantagenet – whose language use was likely to be different from that of the nobility, it is highly probable that the second or third generation after the conquest would have had considerable command of English. Given that very few English people, we think, ever learned French, knowledge of English would have been necessary for the ruling class to interact with servants, tenants, most merchants and the soldiery. This might well have been 'kitchen English', but that does not mean that native-speaker levels of competence were not present. Lack of much contact with other French speakers, particularly if you were a member of the minor gentry living somewhere quite remote, must have made this shift even more inevitable.

Moreover, as we saw in Chapter 3, the loss of Normandy in 1204 meant that Norman immigrants to England had to make the choice of losing their French or English lands. Many chose the latter. It might have taken some time to sink in, but essentially after that they became Englishmen of Norman descent. Their native dialect was no longer connected to that of Normandy (with the exception of the Channel Islands), was increasingly divergent from any form of French and, no matter its prestige, became useless on a day-to-day basis. By around the middle of the fourteenth century, it was probably dead as a first language.

5.2.3 An initial analysis of the contacts

Given the amount of contact between speakers of different languages in England during the late Old English and early Middle English periods, it is unsurprising that English was affected by both Norse and French. In most mainstream histories of the English language these considerable influences are considered largely in relation to the level of lexical influence – evidence which is assimilated easily by students with little or no background in historical linguistics as well as relatively straightforward to date through the employment of resources like the *Oxford English Dictionary*. This masks, regrettably, a number of issues which are central to our understanding of the sociolinguistic and linguistic path of the English language during the Middle Ages, however.

That is not to downplay the effect that French in particular has had on the vocabulary of English, of course. But we must bear in mind that, impressive though the level of borrowing was – perhaps more than 50% of present English vocabulary is not English in origin, most of this from French – it is fairly straightforward under most circumstances to learn and borrow foreign lexical items. Incorporating structures from other languages is less than straightforward; plotting how two systems interact is difficult.

Leaving this aside for the moment, we also need to note that, smaller though Scandinavian lexical influence is on English, its distribution is considerable and quite different from that of French. With the exception of Scots, where a different history made Central French influence strong in the later Middle Ages, practically the same set of French borrowings can be found in all dialects of English. You cannot say the same for Norse. While all varieties of English have some Norse vocabulary, its influence is far greater in northern England than elsewhere (with Scotland and the north-east midlands being similar, but not so greatly affected). In other words, these are the areas where primary contact between English and Norse took place ('the Great Scandinavian Belt') and where, as was suggested above, Scandinavian dialects possibly continued to be spoken for a considerable period. Finally, the kinds of lexis borrowed from Norse – largely homely words – are different from those borrowed from French, where many of the words are connected to the concerns of the ruling class – words associated with warfare, rule, law and fashion.

5.2.3.1 Non-lexical influence

If we go beyond lexical influence, however, Norse is more influential upon English than its lexical input would suggest. By the same token, French is less well represented than we might expect.

In terms of phonology, most scholars believe that the separation of voiced and unvoiced fricatives into separate phonemes (something not apparent in Old English) was due to the importation of French words which demonstrated this phonemic split. Thus [f] and [v] were distributed in Old English according to position in the word, the former being found in initial position, the latter in medial and final position. Then French words came into the language which had [v] in initial position – *virtue* and *voice* are good examples. If only one or two words had entered, it would have been possible for the English /f/ phoneme to maintain its original distribution. But because of the weight of initial <v> words and, quite possibly, the prestige involved in pronouncing French words 'correctly' in post 1066–7 England, phonemic split became a reality.

Beyond this, the other French influence of considerable importance was prosodic. Old English, like all early Germanic varieties, had a rigid stress pattern, with stress falling only on the first central (not prefix) syllable. French, like all Romance languages, had variable stress, with each word possessing its own stress pattern. Words derived from the same root might be stressed on different syllables. Given the number of French words brought into English in the high Middle Ages, fundamental change in English prosodic patterns is not surprising.

What is noteworthy about these large-scale French-induced changes is that they are dependent upon the massive lexical borrowing. Other structural changes not connected to this are limited (and also contested), such as the origin of the Modern English impersonal pronoun *one* in the ancestor of Modern French *on*. Norse influence upon English is of a different type.

Phonological influence from Norse upon English is rather muted. Unlike English and French, English and Norse were close relatives with much in common. Some features, however, such as the presence of /g/ before front vowels in Modern English words like *give* and *get*, where previously only /j/ would have been possible, cannot represent anything other than evidence of Norse upon all varieties of English. In structural terms we again have to accept that similar systems do not necessarily illustrate transfer well. A number of possibilities nonetheless present themselves, including the replacement of native –*th* by –*s* as marker of the third person singular present tense verb, the ability to form a relative clause without a relativiser, such as *the man I saw yesterday*, possible in the North Germanic languages but not in English's West Germanic sisters. Like Modern High German, in a construction *ich habe das getan* 'I have done that', Old English had a tendency to construct periphrastic verb structures along the lines of:

S v dO V

(where the auxiliary, inflection-carrying part of the verb is separated by the direct object from the lexical verbal element). From the early Middle English period, however, this word order was no longer prevalent, with:

S vV dO

(where auxiliary and lexical are never separated by the direct object) constructions along the lines of *I have done that* becoming the sole acceptable constructions, a construction which appears to have been the norm from an early period in Old Norse (language internal explanations are also possible for this change; both processes probably worked in tandem). The absolute distinction between *the* and *that* which Modern English has – in comparison with Modern High German, where *das* can have both article and demonstrative functions – could also be due to the influence of Norse patterns (Millar 2000a).

The question is, therefore: to what extent can the typological transitions through which English passed in the late Old English and early Middle English periods be associated with these long-term contacts? The problem with what we have set out in the preceding text is that little or no theoretical understanding of contact informs it. In order to weigh up influence, it is necessary to consider these matters more rigorously.

5.3 Language contact from a theoretical viewpoint

Linguistic contact is an ongoing feature in almost everyone's experience. Sometimes this can be at a very banal level: my knowledge of a few Hindi or Urdu words and phrases, largely related to food and music, being a good example. But many contacts between languages have brought about changes which have altered the very nature of one or both varieties, or even produced a new variety derived from, but unlike, either input.

For instance, the earliest recorded Armenian (from the first Christian millennium) realises the inflectional morphology of a typical Indo-European language. Modern Armenian, conversely, has a largely agglutinative morphology (where each piece of functional morphology is placed sequentially in an ending; a plural like English *men* would be impossible). During the period from around 900 to the present, speakers of Armenian have been in perpetual contact with speakers of Turkic languages (in particular Turkish and Azeri) (Millar 2007b: 159). Although these relationships were (and are) complex, multilingualism has normally been common and often necessary. The new agglutinative noun-phrase structure of Armenian is not directly derived from Turkic; rather it is based upon native 'building blocks'. Nevertheless, its conceptual framework is Turkic in origin.

Such an absolute rejection of ancestral word formation patterns for constructions analogous to patterns found in neighbouring languages can only really be explained by contact, however; contact at a profound level. In Latvia, a number of Baltic dialects spoken in the north of the country have ceased to employ grammatical gender in the noun class system – a central feature of Indo-European languages. It is very unlikely that the presence of speakers of Estonian and other Finnic languages (which do not have grammatical gender either) to the north of these Latvian dialects (and, historically, among them) is coincidental (Thomason and Kaufman 1988: 238–51). Like many examples of intense language contact, these changes are also intrinsically connected to language shift, a point to which we will return on a number of occasions in the following.

Most impressive of all, however, is Michif, a language spoken by a few thousand people along the western prairie border between the USA and Canada. It has, simplifying somewhat, French noun-phrase morphology but the verb phrase morphology of Cree, an Algonquin language. Since, in Cree, the grammatical gender of the noun is marked on the verb, each noun has two grammatical gender associations: French and Cree. What is interesting about Michif is that few, if any, of its speakers can speak both French and Cree; only a few more have command of either. It is very likely that in the first decades of the nineteenth century a group created by contact between Cree-speaking locals and French-speaking trappers actually *chose* to develop a new language (which probably partly existed because of contact already) as a group identity marker, taught this variety exclusively to their children and abandoned previous linguistic connections (Bakker 1997). While this example is unusual, it nonetheless establishes the extent to which linguistic contact can affect the development of a language and its speakers, both in a sociolinguistic and linguistic way.

In some senses, all language contacts are similar; in other ways each is unique. Despite this, it is nevertheless possible to produce typologies of contact either according to the social relationships between speakers of different languages or the extent and depth of contact (the two states cannot, of course, act independently of each other). It is to these points that we will now turn.

5.3.1 Social patterns of contact

Contact between two (or more) populations speaking different languages is rarely socially equal (although we will be considering relationships of this type later in this chapter). It is much more common for one population to dominate the other(s) politically, economically and socially. That does not necessarily mean that the language of the dominant community actually displaces the dominated, although this was certainly true for all the extant languages of continental western Europe some 2000 years ago (except Basque), replaced by Latin under Roman rule. But there are also occasions where the language of the dominated overwhelms that of the dominant, such as the linguistic 'conquest' of the Turkic-speaking Bulgars by their Slavonic-speaking subjects in the early medieval Balkans or the gradual loss of their Manchu language for Chinese by the Qin conquerors of early modern China, even though their disdain for their Han 'slaves' was considerable. There are also occasions where both languages survive in an evolving relationship for a considerable period, as illustrated by Finnish and Swedish in Finland. Contact effects upon all varieties involved are practically inevitable, however.

Perhaps most common (although it is difficult to quantify these phenomena) is where a dominant language affects a dominated. Most Indo-Aryan dialects of the Indus and Ganges valleys have been influenced by various Persian dialects, the chancery language of the Moslem overlords of the area from the ninth century on (although the rulers often spoke Turkic dialects). This influence is particularly marked in Urdu, the primary language of the Mogul court at Delhi and vehicle of a considerable literature in the nineteenth and twentieth centuries. Even decades of linguistic nationalism – particularly notable for Hindi – have not erased entirely the Persian influence on other north Indian, non-Moslem, varieties, however. Although the contact mainly encouraged lexical borrowing, structures in particular were often excised from the language of prestige by those who wished to share in its prestige while employing a native language.

Similarly, as we already have seen, Turkish before the twentieth

century was filled with Arabic and Persian vocabulary, phonological and structural features, although it must be noted that the written
Ottoman variety possessed rather more of these features than did
the spoken varieties of the unlettered. The various language reforms
initiated by Kemalist Turkey since its establishment in the 1920s
have meant that few of these features survive in writing. It is worth
noting, nonetheless, that the word for 'republic' used in the title of the
Republic of Turkey – *cumhuriyeti* – is a representation, in Turkish spelling, of Arabic *jamhūrīyah*. The prestige of Moslem concepts of good
government obviously trumps the prestige of westernising modernity.

Relationships of these types are called *superstratal*, with the dominant
language being the *superstrate* or *superstratum*. Rather less visible are
substratum influences. It must be pointed out, moreover, that because the
political and economic power associated with the superstrate ensures
that it is the dominant parts of the population which receives most
attention, it is not always obvious when substratal influence is taking
place.

It does exist, however. In the vernacular English of Ireland, a phrase
such as *I'm just after having a cup of tea* meaning 'I have only very recently
had a cup of tea' is very common. With the partial exception of some
speakers of the Highland English of Scotland, this construction is peculiar to Ireland. Interestingly, Irish has a separate tense – termed *anterior*
or 'hot news' – which describes essentially the same state of very recent
completion associated with the Irish English phrase (see Filppula,
Klemola and Paulasto 2008: 186–8 for a discussion). While it would be
almost impossible to prove this connection, the proximity of the speakers, the fact that we know that Irish used to be spoken across a far wider
area in Ireland, that many Irish speakers switched to local varieties of
English and that the construction is hardly known among a large part of
the English language's native speakers, would make the construction's
origin in native speakers of Irish carrying across linguistic material from
their first language to English practically impossible to gainsay.

Much less common than either substratal or superstratal contact-
induced change is *adstratal* influence. In an adstratum environment,
speakers of two or more different languages live essentially in an equal
relationship. One group of speakers may possibly have more access
to the political and economic power of a given place. But the ways in
which power and prestige are shared out means that the difference
between one group and another is not great.

A good example of this is the linguistic contact which existed between
Germanic-speaking Franks and the Latin-speaking population in post-
imperial Gaul. The Franks were, of course, militarily and, to a degree,

politically powerful. But the indigenous Gallo-Roman populace had considerable cultural capital (their Roman culture being portrayed as infinitely superior to the 'Barbarian' culture of their conquerors, a viewpoint many Franks shared); many of the old landed families of Gaul preserved their property under the Franks; their children often married into the Frankish aristocracy, regularly ensuring the development of a new hybrid culture.

Frankish has had a considerable effect on French. This is particularly true with lexis, where a definite concentration on the language of warfare, such as *maréchal*, historically 'leader of the horse', and weaponry illustrates where the Franks were particularly dominant. Interestingly, a number of French colour terms are also Germanic – *bleu* 'blue' and *brun* 'brown' being the most well-known – itself a more advanced state of a distribution also found in Italian and Spanish. Other borrowings are generally reflections of everyday life and everyday interchange. We know little about the influence Latin had on Frankish, primarily because the dialects which we assume to have been the most affected were those which were the first to succumb to language shift to what was becoming French. There is evidence in dialects spoken on the margins between Germanic and Romance varieties that certain Romance features were borrowed. In Luxembourgish and some other Germanic varieties spoken within the *limes* of the former Roman Empire, for instance, the equivalent of English *what* is used as a relative pronoun. In other varieties of 'German', this would be unthinkable; it is normal in the Romance varieties, however.[5]

The nature of language contact makes it important to recognise that it is not only the social relationships between speakers, however, but also the levels of inter-penetration between varieties, which affect the outcome(s) of contact.

5.3.2 Levels of contact

In an attempt to make sense of the many examples of linguistic contact analysed by scholars (about many of which we know less than we should), Thomason (2001) provides a four-point typology of language. Too much detail would be involved in a complete representation of this scale (interested readers should consult Thomason's work directly or via Millar 2007b: 387–96). It should be borne in mind that these stages are little more than arbitrary points upon a continuum, not states.

Thomason proposes a general tendency that borrowing alone is an example of relatively limited contact, while considerable impact on structure demonstrates a contact of considerable strength. Within lexical borrowing, she suggests, the borrowing of open class words – nouns, verbs, adjectives, and so on – demonstrates a much less potent contact than does the borrowing of closed class words – prepositions, pronouns, conjunctions, and so on. Structural borrowing is also graded. The borrowing of a phoneme, for instance, demonstrates a less profound contact than the borrowing of morphosyntactic structural concepts, as discussed for Armenian above.

An illustration of a particularly weak contact is the influence Dutch has had upon English. Although Dutch words are found throughout the English lexicon, they are particularly common in relation to sailing and art (*skipper, landscape, easel*, and so on). Many of these borrowings date from the sixteenth and seventeenth centuries, when Dutch speakers were at the forefront of technological innovation in both fields. Other Dutch borrowings, such as *coleslaw* and *boss*, represent later contacts, often where English language colonists came into contact with Dutch speakers, in places like the Cape of Good Hope or what is now New York State and New Jersey.

At times, quite a few English speakers have known Dutch, particularly perhaps through seafaring, but most of the words borrowed are used by people with no Dutch. Except to a small extent with the more Afrikaans-influenced of South African English varieties, no structural influence has been felt by English from any Dutch variety, except in the ephemeral features the generation who switch languages display (indeed there is greater English influence upon the Dutch of bilingual communities in Iowa in the United States, as Smits 1996 demonstrates).

At the other end of Thomason's scale is the contact felt between different Indo-Aryan and Dravidian languages in Kupwar, a village in central India, as discussed, among many others, by Gumperz and Wilson (1971) and Thomason and Kaufman (1988: 86–8). Here is a brief example of how much contact has taken place:

In Kupwar and the villages around it, multilingualism is the norm and this appears to have been the case for centuries. The three primary languages originally represented discrete groups, but although this is still the case to some extent, practically all locals have at least passive knowledge of the languages which are not their mother tongue. Of the three main languages, two – Marathi and Urdu – are not particularly close relatives (in other words there would be little chance of mutual intelligibility as there would be, say, between the languages spoken in the Punjab and the Ganges valley). Urdu was introduced by Moslem settlers in the last millennium, while Marathi is the local Indo-Aryan language. Kannada is the local Dravidian language and is therefore entirely separate from the other two languages at all levels of language.

Ur.	pālā	dʒarā	kāṭ	kē lē kē	ā - jā
Ma.	pālā	dʒarā	kāp	un ghē un	ā - lō
Ka.	tāplā	dʒarā	khōd - i	tagōnd - i	ba - yn
	greens some	cut	Abs. take	Abs. come	TA

'Having cut some greens, having taken (them), I came'
= 'I cut some greens and brought them'

Abs. = absolutive construction marker; TA = tense and agreement marker
Ur = Urdu; **Ma** = Marathi; **Ka** = Kannada

Figure 5.2 Structural convergence in the languages of Kupwar

Yet this is not what is portrayed in the example given. There are normally lexical differences between the three (although we must note the quantifier *dʒara*, common to all), but structurally they are practically indistinguishable. It should be noted that all three languages are highly structurally distinct where this multilingualism does not prevail. In a sense, if this kind of concordance were replicated across a much larger cross-linguistic corpus, which to a degree it is, it would be tempting to see the apparently separate languages as merely three surface realisations of the same structure.

From the point of view of this typology, French exerts a superstratal influence over English; the high levels of lexical borrowing but limited structural influence suggests a relatively weak contact. The Norse influence, on the other hand, is adstratal. Although lexical borrowing is limited in comparison with the French influence, structural influence is far greater (although nowhere near the level reached in the Kupwar example mentioned above). But is this all that we can say about contacts of this type?

5.3.3 Intimate contact

Thomason's typology seems to describe well the levels by which language contact can affect the development of a language or languages. There is, however, one point which is left out of her model (although it can be placed quite readily within its framework).

On a number of occasions, language contact does not necessarily show itself entirely through the transfer of material from one language to another. Instead, compromise features may be prevalent, as I have already suggested. This may be particularly the case when the contact varieties are quite closely related to each other, although it is certainly common elsewhere as well. The contact between the West Germanic Low German dialects and the North Germanic varieties of Scandinavia in that peninsula in the late Middle Ages and early modern era is a useful example.

At the time, Low German was dominant across large parts of northern Europe, primarily due to the Hanseatic League, a trading confederation of cities including Bremen, Hamburg, Lübeck, Danzig (modern Gdańsk), Königsberg (modern Kaliningrad) and Riga. So powerful was the League that it acted in many ways like a sovereign state, sending embassies to and making treaties with, other powers. Its influence upon Scandinavia and its environs was particularly profound, and can still be felt in the architecture of cities as far apart as Aberdeen and Tallinn. For a number of centuries practically all trade to, from and within Scandinavia was carried out by speakers of Low German. Many towns – most notably Bergen and Stockholm – had German quarters; it was quite possible to be born in Sweden, for instance, and have Low German as your mother tongue.

Although this dominance was far from popular with some local people, the contact between the West and North Germanic varieties which resulted affected everyone's speech eventually. There was some transfer from Low German directly to Scandinavian – many vocabulary items and some structures, such as a passive construction based upon the verb 'become', so that Norwegian *det gjøres* and *det blir gjørt*, both meaning 'it will be done', the latter based on a Low German construction and using the borrowed verb *bli(ve)(n)* 'to become', the former exhibiting the native 'medio-passive'. But there are features which cannot be attributed to either source but seem to have been, at the very least, encouraged by the contact.

Old Norse had, for instance, a complex paradigm both for the noun phrase – expressing case function and gender as well as number – and verb phrase – including the marking of number and person. The modern Scandinavian languages have barely preserved any of these features. Practically all varieties realise no number or person information for the verb. While a few marginal dialects of Norwegian preserve case to some degree, most varieties do not, beyond a vestigial –*s* to mark possession (which itself is considerably less popular than other constructions representing possession). The noun phrase itself is strikingly lacking in many of the inflectional features it had 600 years ago. The majority of these changes passed through the languages when Low German was dominant.

As is often the case in these circumstances, there is no 'smoking gun'.

No one is likely to write that he or she is being profoundly influenced by language contact: it really does not – and should not – matter to anyone as they go about their daily business. It is also true that the first indications of these changes began to show themselves *before* the language contact was intense. But the speed with which the changes passed through the grammatical systems of the Scandinavian languages (and not, at least in a systematic sense, their near relatives spoken in the North Atlantic islands, which retain a much more archaic inflectional morphology) is at the very least indicative of different linguistic histories and ecologies.

Underlying the most extreme forms of contact are features which most linguists would consider to be part of a set: pidginisation and creolisation. These, like the example above, do not generally demonstrate their presence through the transfer of linguistic material (particularly in terms of inflectional morphology). Essentially, pidgins appear to be varieties which are limited in their use to relatively straightforward relationships and transactions. No one has a pidgin as a first language. Generally they come into being when people who need to interact have no language in common. Pidgins are therefore highly unlikely to have complex phonological, morphological or syntactic structural patterns, since this deters and impedes learning. The vocabulary regularly comes from one primary source, the *lexifier language*, which may be a language of considerable prestige – a language associated with power, more often than not. But the words borrowed and the ways they are used may be idiosyncratic and may include the use of morphemes and words in ways which are not normal in the lexifier. While speakers of the latter variety may be able to recognise words and phrases from their own language, they will be unlikely to understand the pidgin with any ease. It has become, at least in linguistic terms, a new variety.

The actual means and routes of development in the construction of pidgins are much debated among creolists; this debate, while most interesting, need not concern us here. But the results of the contact(s) involved are not confined to transfer from one language to another; instead many of the features are *not* regularly found in any of the source languages, thus making the contact's primary contribution *interference*. Indeed the similarity of pidgins and creoles around the world (much vaunted in the 1980s, although later downplayed) may have some basis in the ways in which they came into being).

Although quite extreme, these results help produce insight on a rather less powerful contact phenomenon: *koineisation*. Again, we will be considering this process in detail later in this chapter and the following one. What can be said, however, is that, when two or more language varieties which are either dialects of the same language or, on occasion, closely related languages come into contact, the result will not be primarily a matter of transfers between varieties (although this certainly happens), but rather elements of interference, particularly when a feature is highly marked as associated with one variety or makes comprehension difficult between varieties.

There is, as we might expect, a continuum of level of effect inherent in these processes. In work on the variety developing in Milton Keynes, a 'New City' established in the south midlands of England in the 1960s and 1970s, Kerswill and Williams (2000) demonstrated that, while London features in the phonological system predominated, reasonable since the majority of settlers were from the London area, features from elsewhere, including the south midlands, were found along with features which could be said to be of no provenance prior to the city's foundation. Unlike pidginisation, therefore, concordance between varieties is much more possible (given the close relationships involved); indeed, it appears to be welcomed. Kerswill (1994) demonstrated similar phenomena for the Norwegian varieties spoken in Bergen, Britain (1997) for the English Fenland and Scholtmeijer (1999) for the Dutch polders.

This is also the case with much more powerful examples of koineisation. For instance, on the islands of Fiji a large part of the population is of South Asian origin, with particularly strong inputs from the middle Ganges and the Punjab (although descendants of speakers of other Indo-Aryan languages, such as Gujerati and Marathi, are also present). The varieties involved in their original nineteenth-century input were to some degree mutually intelligible or at least close enough to each other that it was possible to 'feel' resemblances. The leaps that had to be made were obviously much greater than with Milton Keynes English, and may well have been facilitated by relatively low levels of literacy. Some of these compromises and new developments are illustrated in Table 5.1.

Here we can see that, unlike the considerable variation in suffix formation in the 'mainland' Indian varieties, Fiji Hindi is uniform in its usage; this usage is not always (although it is sometimes) derived from one source. Perhaps most interestingly, however, is the fact that, in comparison with the relative morphological complexity of the source dialects, where number and person is always represented and gender is represented in some varieties for the second person, the Fiji variety has apparently simplified, with only a distinction between third person (both singular and plural) and the other two numbers being maintained.

Table 5.1 Indian Hindi dialects and Fiji Hindi definite future suffixes (from Siegel 1987: 115)

	Bhojpuri	Avadhi	Braj	Fiji Hindi
1 singular	bō, ab	bū	ihaū, ūgau	egā
1 plural	ab, bī, iha	ab	ihaī, aīgai	egā
2 singular (masculine)	bē, ba	bē, ihai	(a)ihai, (a)igau	egā
(feminine)	bī, bis			
2 plural (masculine)	bâ(h)	bō, bau	(a)ihai, (a)igau	egā
(feminine)	bū			
3 singular	ī	ī, ihai, ē	(a)ihau, agau	ī
3 plural	ih, ē, ihen	ihaī, aī	(a)ihaī, aīgai	ī

It would be very easy to construct an argument based on the idea that relative simplicity made the new variety easy to learn, easier to learn than any of the 'home' varieties.

Thus contact-induced linguistic compromises and what might seem to be simplifications of the system can have as profound an effect as structural transfer. Whether this insight can be applied to English will be dealt with shortly. Before that, however, we need to consider a common side effect of contact – language shift – and its potential results.

5.3.4 Language shift as an agent of linguistic and sociolinguistic change

In cases of profound contact the 'death' of a language may produce quite powerful results in the surviving languages. Since recorded history began, there has always been evidence that some language varieties, previously spoken by a considerable population, had lost most, if not all, speakers and were, essentially, dead. Indeed evidence for language shift can be found in the place names of most areas of the world where there has been long-term habitation. Many place names in Greece – *Corinth* for instance – are not native to Greek (indeed impenetrable since they were first recorded). The same is true for common Greek words like *hyakinthos* 'bluebell, hyacinth' and *thalassos* 'sea'. The language posited for these remains – called Eteo-Cretan or Pelasgian by linguists (van Windekens 1952; see also Finkelberg 2005: Chapter 3 for an alternative interpretation) – would otherwise be unknown.

Reasons for abandoning your own language in favour of that of your neighbours' are manifold, although certain tendencies are appreciable in most circumstances. Sometimes shift takes place due to traumatic changes in the environment. When a language only has a few thousand speakers – the experience of a large part of the world's population – it does not take much (in global terms) before speakers – who are often bilingual or even multilingual in any event – switch. A tribal grouping in Amazonia, tropical Africa or south-east Asia, numbering two to three thousand, can easily disintegrate through disease, famine or the workings of large-scale economic processes (for example, the felling of rainforest to develop sugar plantations, common in Borneo). With the exception of rare instances of conscious genocide, many members of these groups survive the trauma. But they will often find themselves in very different ecological niches where the use of other languages will benefit them more. Their children are unlikely to use the ancestral language.

Related to this set of circumstances are the linguistic experiences of border communities. Gal (1979) demonstrates how a Calvinist Magyar-speaking community on the Austrian side of the Hungarian frontier moved towards the language (and occupations) of their Catholic or Lutheran German-speaking neighbours during a period of industrialisation, prayer and the black market being among the few occasions when only Magyar was used.

If you are a member of an immigrant community, it is also likely that your heritage language will eventually come under threat. For instance, in 1685 Louis XIV of France revoked the Edict of Nantes of 1598, a guarantee of tolerance and protection to the minority Protestant population, often termed the Huguenots. The revocation led to large-scale migration from France to Protestant polities in Europe and beyond, particularly among the most skilled and wealthiest members of the Huguenot population. Inevitably, many came to England. Their names carry on in that country, in situations as diverse as Courtauld, a prestigious carpet producer, Laurence Olivier (1907–89), the actor-director, and *Roget's Thesaurus*, initially designed by the polymath Peter Mark Roget (1779–1869). Yet the Gallo-Romance dialects they brought with them were gone within three generations. In the end, the difference between two Protestant groups (with the immigrant one no doubt being bilingual from an early period) was not great enough.

More successful survivals take place when language is only *one* of the distinctions between the host community and the newcomers. Most Jewish people who emigrated to the United States in the late nineteenth and twentieth centuries were Yiddish speakers (although many also spoke other languages, including Polish, Russian, Hungarian and German). Yiddish is only really healthy in the USA today when used by ultra-Orthodox groups such as the various Hassidic sects, however. Unlike most American Jews, who have assimilated to a lesser or greater extent to the mainstream, the ultra-Orthodox, although normally fluent in English, generally prefer to keep the mainstream at arm's length, maintaining communities where Yiddish remains not only the everyday language and which partakes of the general sense of *yiddishkayt*, 'Jewishness', which, in their view at least, subsists among them. A further factor may be that some members of the community, especially if they are members of a particular rabbinical bloodline, may be expected to marry equivalent men and women who live in Israel, France, Switzerland and many other parts of the world; on these occasions, Yiddish may be the only language in common and for that reason may be conserved, its use encouraged. This type of survival, however, although impressive, must be considered unusual. Indeed even under these auspices contact-based linguistic change can flourish, with the Yiddish of American ultra-orthodox Jews often lacking grammatical gender marking on the nouns, adjective and definers, probably under the influence of English (Katz 2004: 389–90).

While the experience of language shift is commonplace, what actually happens during it is less well-known. In pioneering work from the 1970s and 1980s, however, Dorian (in particular, 1981) developed a model for what happened when native speakers of a particular language did not speak that variety for decades or who had considerable passive knowledge of the native language of their ancestors but had rarely if ever spoken it. Dorian termed these individuals *semi-speakers*. Some people, although they might only occasionally speak their ethnic language, nevertheless did so without many 'mistakes'; there were others, however, who had no problem understanding their ancestral language, but could not reproduce its structure consistently. Thus a semi-speaker of Dorian's Gaelic-speaking population in east Sutherland in Scotland might have problems reproducing the VSO default element order for Gaelic because the SVO structure of English was dominant. The use of initial consonant mutation to describe function was disfavoured by many semi-speakers both because it is not a phonological feature of any Germanic language and because modern English makes only limited use of any feature remotely like grammatical case.

Sasse's (1992) analysis, based primarily on Dorian's theoretical conclusions and his own work on Arvanitika, the Albanian varieties spoken in Greece, presents a more in-depth theoretical model of what actually happens during language shift. From a sociolinguistic viewpoint, what happens in the last generations of the use of a language, Sasse suggests, is a gradual move away from the ancestral language by significant elements of the Abandoned language (A) community. These might be people who have social aspirations for themselves or their children. In a period when the target language is considered prestigious, and certain linguistic domains practically require its use, A may be considered incapable of carrying abstract or prestigious ideas. It may also become a social handicap to use an 'accented' variety of the Target language (T) or to have features which are carried over from the grammar of one language to that of the other. All of these factors and more will encourage some elements of the community to move away from A. This means that, in the last few generations, some children will not learn the local variety through the normal means of contact with their family and neighbours, which many sociologists of language (for instance, Fishman 1991) believe ensures a 'normal' acquisition of all registers and structural properties of a language. Instead, they will learn it from other children and older people who are outside their immediate circle. This means that they will be able to understand A well, but may make basic errors producing it. Many speakers of A will consider these varieties to be 'corrupt' and may even cease using A, preferring to use T when speaking to younger people. This type of behaviour, naturally, has touches of self-perpetuating prophecy about it. Denison (1977), among others, suggested that some language deaths are actually 'language suicides'.

From a linguistic point of view, therefore, reduction in speaker numbers, a breakdown in normal transmission and a 'shaky' command of the language's structure by some inhabitants of the semi-speaker continuum provide evidence for what happens as a speaker base collapses. At its end, Sasse concludes, is a situation where only a few words and phrases remain in use in the A community, normally kept going because they have some group-internal resonance, whether that be for cultural, religious or other reasons. Many Jewish people of Ashkenazi origin who no longer speak (or may never have spoken) Yiddish maintain a few phrases, such as *shabbos goy* 'gentile (normally a young man) who is paid to light fires and carry out other prohibited activities in a Jewish household on the Sabbath' or many words about ethnic specific food, even if they are not actively religious. These holdovers represent something like a marker of identity, no matter how playfully used.

Yet the influence of A goes beyond this, because these final generations, in switching to T, tend to carry material from A into T. In the period just preceding that with which this chapter is concerned, a considerable language shift took place which has not always been considered by scholars as a source of contact phenomena in English: the Brittonic languages.

5.3.4.1 The 'death' of the Brittonic languages of Lowland Britain

The south-east of Britain was not, of course, always English-speaking. The traditional view has been that Germanic speakers entered the former Roman province of *Britannia* in some numbers in the early- to mid-fifth century, probably originally as mercenaries to the Celto-Roman polities which had inherited, in a piecemeal manner, Roman authority, used against both similar polities and the 'Barbarian' forces from outside the Roman *limes* which were threatening parts of the former territories (for a discussion of these and similar issues, see Millar 2010c: Chapter 5). According to the mainstream interpretation that flows from this account, Germanic speakers quickly overwhelmed their employers, seizing land along the coasts and up the river valleys. The original inhabitants were dispossessed, and a considerable number were driven west, in the wake of total defeat and behaviour which might – anachronistically – be described as 'ethnic cleansing'. To nineteenth-century (and, indeed, many twentieth-century) scholars, this narrative explained two striking truths of the early history of English: why there are so few (early) p-Celtic borrowings (the grouping of dialects which later included Welsh, Cornish and Breton) into any variety of English, as well as why no Celtic varieties are reported in eastern English territory, even in the very earliest records.

More recent historical, archaeological and linguistic scholarship has gradually questioned many elements of this account, eventually leading to scholars doubting the veracity of the 'truths' discussed in the preceding paragraph.

The first of these 'corrections' is based upon advances in our understanding of the historical and archaeological record for late Imperial and post-Roman *Britannia* and similar regions on the Continent.

By the third century CE, the *Lowland Zone* of Britannia – its fertile southern and eastern regions – had become almost as culturally Romanised as Gaul. In London in particular a cosmopolitan social and ethnic mix developed, 'Roman' in the sense that such a mix would only have been possible due to the size and diversity of, and freedom of movement possible in, the Empire, but probably not dominated by people from the original Italian heartland of Rome. No matter what other languages citizens, visitors and slaves spoke, Latin must have been the default lingua franca, as well as being a prestigious language associated with government, justice and education. It is likely, of course, that different varieties of Latin – native and non-native, literate and non-literate, and so on – existed side by side and that many speakers had control of more than one variety.

Outside the cities, considerable economic (and doubtless political) power was in the hands of a propertied elite – again, anachronistically, something like a 'gentry', with some of the richer and more powerful members of this society behaving rather more like an aristocracy. Many – perhaps most – considered themselves Roman, although evidence from contemporary Gaul suggests that, not far underneath Roman social and political structures, native tribal leadership structures and conditions continued and were, to a degree, perpetuated. The rural poor would, most scholars assume, have retained their British language, although it is likely that most would have had some competence in Latin, perhaps of a limited and occasionally 'broken' type (for a discussion of this and similar features, see Millar 2010c: 117–23).

It is also likely that most people in country districts, and also probably many in urbanised environments, could speak the local language, whether at native-speaker or at a rather more 'broken' level. Use of this language may even – although this is not actually reported for Britannia – have involved something like local identity expression, particularly at times in the third and fourth centuries when Britannia – along with Gaul – was essentially part of a breakaway Imperial structure. In Gaul, Gaulish expressions and titles were used during these periods even if, we assume, very few people by this time used that language in everyday communication (Van Dam 1985: 31, 46).

How can the survival of British in Britannia be squared with the death of the originally far more numerous Gaulish? One argument is that, with the important but still marginal exceptions of London and York, Britannia was something of a backwater to the Romans in comparison with Gaul. Because of Britannia's marginality, along with its physical separation from the Continent, it might be assumed that fewer native speakers of Latin lived on the island than in Gaul, less off-putting to the inhabitants of what was, essentially, a Mediterranean empire. If you lived in the more rural parts of the Romanised provinces of Britannia, you would have had to have spoken some British.

In addition to this, British remained dominant, we believe, in the *Highland Zone* of Britannia, the higher, less fertile, but militarily important, northern and western parts of the Roman provinces. Here, there were only limited attempts at Romanisation, probably confined largely to centres such as Carlisle, Chester and Caerleon. In the main, we believe, similar social structures, based upon tribal units with chieftains of some sort or other, survived, even if the actual units and their cultural apparatus were inevitably altered by the change in governmental structures. Something like the vernacular culture of pre-Roman times probably survived the conquest. Chieftains still patronised vernacular poets, for instance. In post-Roman Britain, it is tribes from the northernmost part of the Romanised zone, in what is now southern Scotland, whose deeds were celebrated in early Welsh poems like 'The Ride of the Gododdin'. This meant that a reservoir of Celtic speakers remained nearby to the Romanised Britons, in a way impossible for the people of Gaul. No matter how much the 'tribals' made Roman citizens of British descent cringe, their presence also made it necessary to continue the use of British, due to trade and, eventually, the protection which the inhabitants of the Highland Zone might be able to offer to the rather more pacific inhabitants of the Lowland Zone.

There was also, of course, a strong Roman military presence in parts of the Highland Zone. Latin may well have been the lingua franca for relations between locals and the soldiers, so necessary to the survival of Roman units. Although Roman soldiers were not officially allowed to marry, relationships inevitably developed and children of mixed parentage were born. More importantly, many individual soldiers must have begun to be 'tribalised' in their relationships with the locals. This would inevitably have involved some knowledge of the local language(s).

As the aftermath of Roman disengagement proceeded, our knowledge of what was actually happening in Britain becomes fractured. There are occasional 'brighter' moments, such as the reports by a range of historians, both Continental and based in Britain, of the visits of St Germanus to (southern) Britain in the late 420s and (possibly) the 430s in an attempt to root out heresy. These reports appear to demonstrate that in the first decades of the fifth century there were still sufficient Latin speakers among the gentry and the merchants of towns who were able to understand debates, homilies and sermons in that language. By the end of the next century, no evidence appears to remain for the knowledge of Latin among any of the 'Welsh', with the small exception of priests and monks (and even here levels of competence in the language varied). Moreover, the fact that there are very few references to Welsh speakers living in the new English kingdoms needs to be explained. Where did the British speakers go?

To some extent this set of facts (or lack of facts) appears to support the old view that something like genocide (or at least forced migration) affected the Lowland Britons. But only to some extent. While it cannot be said that the relationship between incoming English and the natives was ever cordial, there is evidence, both historical and archaeological, for continuity of residence and culture in many sites across the Lowlands from post-Roman to Anglo-Saxon. This even includes the continuity of Christianity, albeit probably as the faith of a circumscribed minority, speaking a minority language. We also have evidence of the legal recognition of Britons' rights within the Anglo-Saxon kingdoms in later literate times, although the fines paid for killing or maiming a British noble were rather lower than for his Anglo-Saxon equivalent. Of course it could be argued that memory of British status might have been perpetuated even without the knowledge of the ancestral tongue – analogues, such as the language use of post-exilic Jews and their perpetual association with their religion and its sacred language, are not difficult to find. Some scholars, most notably Tristram (2007 and elsewhere), have suggested – although in her case with the assumption of the continuation of use of the ancestral languages – that a form of *apartheid* existed, with British speakers, no matter their status, being considered less important than English speakers, with unequal economic conditions providing the means by which even better-off Britons were, slowly but surely, pauperised (Woolf 2007).

Prejudice against Britons must have been common – perhaps even societally embedded: the dismissive name *Welsh* – foreigners – suggests this. I doubt very much, however, that such prejudice was officially reinforced beyond the legal distinctions mentioned above or that a barely literate society could institutionally 'remember' former status. Moreover, even though a British noble was worth less than an English one, his life was still given a value. This does not suggest a savage and repressive regime. Finally, we cannot ignore facts: moving from one status to another was probably relatively straightforward. For instance, the semi-legendary founder of the West-Saxon royal house – later to become the most 'English' of the English houses in their resistance to the Scandinavian invasions of the ninth to eleventh centuries – was called *Cerdic*, which is a British rather than an English name.

To what extent, therefore, has this apparently long-term survival of at least British traditional cultural attributes and most likely actual British language within an essentially English cultural framework affected the English language? How is this affected by the supposition that, as far as we can tell, most English speakers were descended from British speakers? We will return to these questions after we have given further thought to the French and Norse influences discussed earlier in the chapter.

5.4 Weighing up the evidence: contact and linguistic change

As we have seen, traditional accounts of the history of the English language, focused largely on lexical borrowing, tend to consider French the primary actor in the changes through which English passed in the late Old English and early Middle English periods. This is probably due to French influence being highly visible. But to what extent is such an attribution tenable?

Despite claims made by, among others, Dominigue (1977), where the Norman Conquest is analysed as producing a pidgin or creole-like set of changes in English, it has to be said that French cannot have been the primary cause of the changes involved, essentially because, as we have seen, the changes began in a period where little or no French influence was felt by any English variety. That does not mean, however, that the influence French had socially as the changes spread across English did not have at least some effect.

Norse influence upon English appears a rather more hopeful source for the great transition. For a start, we have compelling evidence that the morphosyntactic changes through which the language passed originated in exactly the same places where the Norse influence was strongest. Furthermore, the less Norse influence there was on a dialect, the more likely it was to be later in its application of the changes involved and for those changes to be entirely implemented. Of course, this argument, while attractive, does not actually mean that this influence was the primary source for the whole change. Scholars, have, however, developed the idea considerably, adding theoretical lessons learned from other contact situations.

Middle English is, of course, *not* a creole. But the morphosyntactic changes through which English passed have creole-like features. This led Trudgill (1986) to coin the term *creoloid*, referring in particular to the changes felt in the Continental Norse languages in the late Middle Ages, under the influence of Low German (as discussed earlier in this chapter), English in relation to Norse and Afrikaans, the Dutch contact variety developed at the Cape of Good Hope from the seventeenth century on. These three Germanic varieties are, of course, the ones which have drifted furthest from the original synthetic-based typology of their ancestor variety. A *creoloid*, Trudgill would argue, is a variety which shares many structural features with creoles, but which has not gone through pidginisation and is therefore still treated by linguists as being part of the history of one language, rather than the development of a new variety which shares only some features with its lexifier language.

As I have suggested elsewhere (Millar 2000a: Chapter 2), Afrikaans represents a rather different set of contacts than do the other situations Trudgill considers. Primarily this distinction is due to relationship between varieties. Both English and Continental Norse came into contact with relatively close relatives.[6] Afrikaans came into contact with languages which were not related to it, such as Khoisan varieties (the languages of the 'Hottentot' herders and the San gatherer-hunters), east Asian and Indonesian varieties and, later, Bantu languages, or were relatively distantly related, such as the Gallo-Romance dialects brought to the Cape by Huguenot refugees in the later seventeenth century.[7] Indeed evidence suggests that there was a creole Dutch used at the Cape and that some Afrikaans varieties – particularly those spoken by 'coloureds' or deeply rural people – possess a far more creole-like status than does standard Afrikaans, heavily influenced until the twentieth century by the standard Dutch of Church and State and, indeed, mutually intelligible to a considerable degree, with the Dutch of the Netherlands. Given this sociolinguistically triggered diversity, it might be argued that the term *creoloid* is best suited to Afrikaans alone. With the other two contexts, it might be argued that terms connected to *koine* might be sought (it should also be noted that, as we will see, Trudgill has now abandoned the Norse influence on English scenario).

Thomason and Kaufman (1988) are at pains to downplay the amount of influence Norse had on Old English, while not denying that contact between the two varieties caused or encouraged a number of developments. To register this lower level of contact and also, I believe, to distance their views from some of the more extreme creole-based analyses which preceded them, they use the term *Norsified English*; Fennell (2001), after reflection, supports their analysis. In Millar (2000a: Chapter 2), I discuss their views, demonstrating – I believe – that the series of changes which English passed through can still be analysed as more exceptional than such a term suggests; that does not mean that, small points of detail aside, I fundamentally disagree with their desire not to associate the developments involved with anything as extreme as creolisation.

Millar (2000a) brings together these and other views to attempt an explanation both of how the initial contact affected English and how the changes involved spread out into English. I envisaged a situation in areas of considerable Scandinavian settlement in the 'Great Scandinavian Belt' of northern England where it was quite normal for cross-cultural relationships to be formed and for children to grow up where their parents were speakers of different 'languages'. These children would be very likely to speak a variety which played up the similarities between English and Norse – found in particular in the lexicon – while downplaying dissimilarities – largely morphological – between the two languages, a practice which we know nonliterate people across a relatively wide language continuum were able to do, for instance, in nineteenth-century central Asia. Expand this apparently unique scenario to a wider society; let it be played out over a few generations;

then it is possible to envisage both how radical and rapid change could be, particularly when hardly anyone could read, meaning that they had little sense of what a particular variety should be like and in a situation where many people might not even have known whether the variety they were speaking was *English* or not.

Naturally, change of this type would take some time to become apparent in writing, even in the northern English focal area. There is a degree of conservatism inherent in writing and in the preservation of written forms, particularly, perhaps, when literacy was limited and society itself was under considerable stress, as was the case in northern England in the eighth to eleventh centuries. Yet even with these provisos, it is worth noting that the English glosses to the *Lindisfarne Gospels* demonstrate occasional 'slips' towards more vernacular norms, as we have already seen.

We have already charted how this change moved from north to south within England. Millar (2000a) suggested that this should be seen as a series of spreads, with the more conservative midlands and then southern dialects incorporating only so much of the 'new' English to prop up the system in place there, itself under considerable (although lesser) pressure from the drift phenomena already described. As we saw, however, incorporating the new material almost inevitably led to bringing in more features of the northern innovations to cope with these new issues. This explains why change took a short time in individual dialects, but took considerably longer in the language as a whole: a mixture of distrust for the lower prestige northern varieties was essentially at odds with the solutions which at least some of the innovations presented for the problems faced by the more conservative dialects.

In essence, the contacts and changes involved in the original English–Norse contact in the north of England could be framed as the creation of a koine, a situation where unmarked features are preferred above highly marked ones. The extent to which speakers of one variety could understand speakers of the other is highly debateable (and also unlikely to produce a ready solution). The possibility that people could form a use variety from close relatives does not seem much more unlikely than the coming together of divergent varieties in one place bringing about a compromise variety, as we will see in the next chapter. The later, more small-scale, contacts and accommodations between English varieties across England I termed *koineoids* in Millar (2000a); I am now convinced that the term *koine* would work as well for them.

But although we seem to understand the direction which these changes took through the language, we have to recognise that we have no absolute proof that it was contact with Norse which caused the original typological shift (as we have already seen, the very situations which brought about the contact also meant that documentary evidence is rare and contradictory). This has led a number of people to suggest that contact with Celtic languages might have acted as the catalyst.

The traditional view (see, for instance, Baugh and Cable 1993: 72–4) is that very little Celtic influence can be felt on English. The number of British lexical items which have been borrowed into mainstream varieties of English – with the exception of the English dialects of Devon and Cornwall and southern Wales, where contact with p-Celtic varieties continued for much longer – is in many ways pitiful. Most are topographical – *coomb* for a valley, *tor* for a peak, for instance; at least one refers to wildlife: *brock* 'badger'; one refers to baked goods: *bannock*, a name given to various types of unleavened bread. It has to be recognised that few of these words are common. The topographical terms mentioned above are little used outside south-western England; *bannock* is only common in Scotland and parts of Ireland. According to Thomason's typology, this would represent a *very* limited type of contact-based influence.

But a number of scholars – most notably Jackson (1953) – have built up a large-scale hypothesis based on this (lack of) information. Instead of agreeing with the nineteenth-century scholars who employed this paucity of p-Celtic borrowing to support their view that there had been little or no contact between the English and the 'natives', this new viewpoint argued the opposite: long-term and deep bilingualism on the part of the British-speaking inhabitants of the English-dominated parts of Britain. In a situation where all British speakers in this situation were essentially native (or near-native) speakers of English as well, it is quite possible that bilingual speakers kept their two languages separate, particularly when one of them is associated with a less powerful unit in the polity.

The argument for this type of relationship between the languages is difficult to dispute: it sounds likely. More recent scholars have, however, argued for direct Celtic influence upon the phonology of Old English (for instance, Schrijver 2009) and possibly its syntax (for instance, Poppe 2009). A direct discussion of all the points made and their implications for our understanding of the history of the English language is beyond the scope of this book. What can be said, however, is that it is likely that some of the ideas are correct and that the Celtic influence upon all varieties of English was so pervasive as to be at least one of the reasons why English appears structurally distinct from its continental West Germanic sisters. Indeed Trudgill (2010: Chapter 1) makes contact between the Celtic languages and English the primary spur for the structural changes which affected English in the late Old English and early Middle English periods. There are problems with a full acceptance of this viewpoint, however, as we will see.

It is perhaps significant that many, if not most, of the verifiable Celtic influences upon English actually appear to have taken place at a somewhat later date. Although recounted in a range of publications, their spirit is best presented in McWhorter (2009). While this essay makes a strong case for the Celtic influence upon English as a whole, the features which are most solid either appear to date from rather later in the history of the language – such as the spread of the *do-periphrasis* or the expression of progressive aspect through the *be* + *ing* construction – or are associated with a particular contact zone from which it has never spread – such as the Irish English 'hot news' past tense mentioned above. That this is the case is not, of course, surprising: the further back in time we reach, the less certain any explanation for linguistic change – particularly, perhaps, those based on language contact – can be. It does not in any way disprove the hypothesis (or hypotheses) of Celtic influence upon the early development of English, but it does provide a frustrating hindrance to the gathering of direct evidence for it. As we will see, this hindrance is also associated with a different influence which some who support the Celtic influence model rightly or wrongly consider to be a competitor: the influence of Norse upon English in the north of England in the late Old English period.

This frustration has led to some worrying argumentation. Most notably, Tristram (2007) essentially claims that all (or practically all) of the structural changes through which English apparently passed relatively rapidly in the late Old English and early Middle English periods were retarded in writing due to the essential conservatism of the language of the fully Anglicised 'theocratic' elite, who had control over literacy, in comparison with the rather less 'Germanic' English of the Celticised general populus, basing this viewpoint upon the somewhat less traditional writing of some glosses and of the writings of the 'transition period' itself. In other words, for four centuries a conservative variety was maintained in the face of large-scale change from below by means of what some scholars term 'apartheid'. While not impossible, this is rather unlikely, particularly in a situation where the level of literacy and the possibility of centralised governmental policy on education was very low indeed. That these discrepancies did exist towards the end of the Old English period should not blind us to the comparative lack of evidence in earlier times.[8] Particularly worrying from this point of view is the fact that early Northumbrian Old English is actually deeply conservative in morphological terms, yet late Old Northumbrian is highly radical and, as we have seen, the apparent source for the typological changes through which English moved.

Trudgill (2010) supports the Celtic influence hypothesis, although without the idea that the 'new' features of English were the result of transfer, instead seeing the changes as being the result of second language (L2) interference. In supporting the Celtic interference model, Trudgill cites the authority of Thomason and Kaufman (1988) in suggesting that adstratal relations between close relatives actually causes *complexification*, while the substratal relationship between British and English was, due to the nature of A influence on T, likely to encourage the *simplification* we find in English during the 'transition period'.

While, again, elements of this argument are noteworthy, it uncovers what appears to be a central flaw in Thomason and Kaufman's views. Thomason and Kaufman generally concentrate on the transfer of linguistic material from one language to another (although they do also consider L2 influence and its contribution to *interference*, to be fair). Closely related varieties, like English and Norse, do not necessarily emphasise transfer features when they come into contact, although this certainly also happens. The considerable similarities between close relatives accentuate when they do not agree, as we have seen, and encourage remedial action. Koine-like creations of this type do not encourage complexity, as Trudgill's work on new varieties of English, discussed in the next chapter, demonstrates.

5.5 Discussion

What we can say, therefore, is that substratal influence from Brittonic, while its speakers went through language shift, is likely to have been the catalyst for effective and longer lasting change eventually in English as a whole. But the fact that the location for change appears to have been solely in the 'Great Scandinavian Belt' suggests the agency of Norse-English contact also. The fact that its radical effects are felt first (at least in writing) in the first century after the latter contact became central is also significant (especially when comparison is made with the conservative morphosyntactic nature of early Old Northumbrian), both sociolinguistically – the social order attenuated, perhaps broken down – and linguistically. By the same token, the loss of a conservative literate elite after 1066–7 may well have encouraged the development of new written forms of English closer to everyday speech. But in distinction to Tristram's views, as we have seen, the influence for change came from one geographical source and was spread through English in an appreciable way. Speakers of French, it could be argued, provided this gap through their prestigious position in English society. The arrival of a large number of words from French not categorised according to the native gender pattern might also have further destabilised the already shaky grammatical gender system.

This discussion demonstrates how, with some difficulty, sociolinguistic views on language contact and language shift can be employed in a discussion of linguistic developments in the relatively distant past. In the next chapter many of the same insights will be brought to bear on more recent and far better documented contacts.

Further reading

The seminal book on a sociolinguistic overview of contact-induced change is Thomason and Kaufman (1988), which includes a discussion of the Norse influence on English. Fennell (2001) largely follows their argument, while developing it. A critique of Thomason and Kaufman's analysis can be found in the second chapter of Millar (2000a); this does not in any way lessen the book's importance.

Some issues to consider

1. Why has the Celtic influence on English been downplayed by scholars?
2. What made the north of England so productive in terms of linguistic change in the period covered?
3. Research the scholarly treatment of the effects of contact between English and one of the following: Latin, Low German, the languages of South Asia. How do these differ from the contacts described in this chapter?

Notes

1. Roberts (1970) presents convincing evidence for these changes taking place in an otherwise mainstream late West Saxon text. This could be taken to imply an early assumption of the new paradigm in the south-western dialects. It is possible that this is the only evidence found for a different system of noun-phrase marking which under-lays the 'official' one, a point to which we will return later in the chapter. But such a small amount of evidence is more likely to represent the usage of a scribe born elsewhere in England who has fully

assimilated to the prestigious West Saxon system orthographically, but not morphosyntactically.

2. Wales (2006: 83–4, and elsewhere) criticises my argument in Millar (2000a) on this as an example of an 'anachronistic fallacy': because northern dialects are non-prestigious now, they must always have been so in the past. This would indeed be a fallacious argument; it is not the one I made, however. Instead I argued that the numerical superiority of Southumbrians over Northumbrians, the economic advantages that much of the south had over the north following the Scandinavian settlements and the destruction caused by William of Normandy's punitive northern campaigns along with the language attitudes of southerners to northern varieties recorded in the Middle Ages (and given considerable space by Wales in her book) suggest that medieval speakers from the south generally did not assign prestige to northern dialects. That the latter gained more prestige in the early modern period does not negate this argument. As I have said, the body of evidence of phonological change radiating from south-eastern England acts as further evidence for the place from which prestige was considered to be situated at the time.

3. There *are* a number of languages – Finnish being a particularly striking example – where no distinction is made between male and female in the third person singular pronoun. Even in those Indo-European languages which have lost grammatical gender, however, the distinction is recognised as being central to the pronoun paradigm, possibly for cultural reasons, or even, perhaps, inertia.

4. The origin of the new form has been suggested to be a Norse pronunciation of the falling Old English diphthong as a rising (a good example being the change from Old English *Eoforwic* to *York*). /hj/ would quite naturally become a voiceless palatal fricative [ç]; this is likely to be what <ʒh> stands for. This sound, while common enough during that period in other parts of the English syllable, was not found at the start of words; instead the similar /ʃ/ sound, common in initial position, was employed.

5. It is worth noting that working class dialects in south-eastern England also produce this construction. It is far more difficult to accept primary Romance influence as the essential basis for this construction; it must be assumed, therefore, that constructions of this type are potentially native to the Germanic languages, appearing through *drift*.

6. Given the period in which English was influenced, the length of

time from its split from Norse was considerably shorter than was the case with the Scandinavian varieties and Low German, although essentially the same phenomena were inherent.

7. Afrikaans *did* come into contact with its close relative Standard English. But this language only assumed prominence at the Cape in the late eighteenth century, by which time Cape Dutch had already moved considerably away from Netherlandic structural patterns.

8. Latin *did* have this kind of relationship with the Romance dialects. But the status – and unchangeability – of Latin was infinitely higher than that of (written) English, which also had a 'stepdaughterly' relationship to Latin.

6 Linguistic contact and new dialect formation

In the previous chapter we considered the nature of long-standing contacts between English and other languages and how this affected the development of English as a whole; inherent to much of the discussion was language shift. In this chapter we will again be considering the nature of contact, but generally in situations where the primary contact was between different varieties of English, although of course this was touched upon in the last chapter and contacts between languages will be considered on a number of occasions in this chapter. The primary point of interest here, however, is what happens when migration causes a new settlement to come into being where, eventually, a new variety of the colonising group is created.

6.1 Colonial dialects: an introduction

In recent years considerable scholarly interest has been focused on the development of varieties of a language outside its traditional geographical confines. Essentially the primary concern has been: what happens when speakers of a language move to a new place where previously that language was not spoken, but where – unlike most languages of immigration – these speakers are dominant in the new territory, demographically, politically or economically (or all three of these)?

While groups have always moved around and created new communities where a new variety of the 'home' language is spoken, the last 500 years have proved a test bed for such movements. Western European languages – including Spanish, French and English – have been spread around the world by sea, as have Chinese and some South Asian languages. Russian, during the same period, has spread across a vast swathe of northern Asia. Very rarely, if ever, are all of the linguistic colonists from exactly the same place. Inevitably this means that some degree of dialect contact and dialect change takes place.

A good example of this can be found in New Zealand English. As

Gordon et al. (2004) and Trudgill (2004) point out, albeit with different associated interpretations, the majority of people who came to New Zealand in the first few generations of *Pakeha*, 'European', settlement were from non-rhotic parts of the English-speaking world; it is therefore not surprising that New Zealand English is non-rhotic (with the exception of some Southland varieties where the settlement was almost entirely Scottish and the area involved was until recently quite cut off from the rest of the country). But Scottish settlement (and settlement from parts of Ireland which have been heavily influenced by Scotland) was considerable. There are a number of lexical items found in all forms of New Zealand English – *pinkie* 'little finger', *wee* 'small' or *byre* 'cow house' – which appear to derive from this source.

Although there are occasions in which the new variety develops in a *tabula rasa* environment – including two of the varieties on which we will concentrate in this chapter, St Helenian and Tristan da Cunha English – where no, or practically no, indigenous people were settled before European arrival, most of the time colonists have arrived to find people already settled. Although relationships between settlers and natives have often been disastrous, it is most unusual for there to have been no influence from the indigenous languages on those of the settlers. Despite the fact that natives and settlers were regularly at loggerheads from early on in colonisation, American English has borrowed from a wide range of local languages, deriving, as we might expect, words concerned with flora and fauna which were new to Europeans, such as *chipmunk, raccoon* and many others, but also examples of political terminology, such as *caucus* 'decision-making body within a political grouping', which have an aboriginal source. Even phrases like *this neck of the woods* may represent a calque upon a native idiom. If technological advantage lay with the settlers, as was increasingly the case for those of European origin after about 1600, then shift away from the native language was inevitable, but not without linguistic effect, on both native and settler languages.

Perhaps the most systematic treatment of how this set of developments interacts is presented in Schneider (2007), where both plantation colonies (where slave or coolie labour were exploited by a relatively small group of English speakers) and settlement colonies (where English speakers immigrated in considerable numbers and generally worked the land – or, on occasion, waters – themselves or became merchants selling other people's produce and labour) are treated. Essentially, Schneider suggests that there are five phases associated with the colonisation and nativisation process: *foundation, exonormative stabilization* [norms formed on the outside], *nativization, endonormative stabilization* [norms formed on the inside] and *differentiation*. Essentially, he suggests, all colonies follow this pattern of nativisation and homogenisation, with class-based dialects only being differentiated at the end of the process. Throughout, both sociolinguistic and linguistic issues are considered, both separately and as interlocking units. Moreover, interest is taken in both the settler community (and their language use) and the indigenous community (and their language use).

Following Schneider's model, it becomes apparent that, as time passes, the settler community gradually sever connections – political, certainly, but also cultural – with the 'mother country', beginning instead to consider themselves native to the new settlement. There is, of course, no set time period for this to happen, nor is there one way for this separation to take place. The United States of America, for instance, separated itself by violence from Britain, while practically all other 'Old Commonwealth' countries – including, it should be noted, countries like Australia with strongly developed and articulated nativist traditions – have become fully formed countries through incremental reform (South Africa is a somewhat different matter, which will not be dealt with here in depth, largely because it involves a second, and often dominant, European influence). Moreover, it should be noted that, despite Australia and New Zealand's relative similarity in age and geographical position, settlers of British descent in New Zealand tended, at least until recently, to look towards Britain as a cultural and political model far more than natives of Australia have done for generations. Partly these differences are due to the nature of identity construction. New Zealand and Canada, for instance, have relatively small populations and are sited either beside or close by countries with much larger populations – the USA and Australia – whose inhabitants have a strong sense of their identity and have long since broken emotional (although not necessarily full political) ties with the colonising power. In Canada, in particular, the connection with the royal family is emphasised, with photographs of the queen regularly exhibited in public buildings, in a way which seems quite exaggerated to British people. Average Anglophone Canadians are probably no more emotionally tied to the monarchy than are, say, average Scots. But this is a useful way to demonstrate difference from the hegemonic American influence so central to their experience. Some Canadian linguistic features – such as at least the knowledge of those occasions where British and American English differ significantly in terms of lexis – appear to support this identity-based connection.

Throughout the model, Schneider emphasises the different ways in which linguistic contact affects the development of a colonial variety. In the early parts of colonisation, Schneider suggests, the primary linguistic accommodation lies between different varieties of the 'home' variety. A good example of this, although one dating further back in time than most colonial varieties discussed in the literature, is the dominant form for 'each' used in English writings from Ireland in the Middle Ages, *euche*. McIntosh and Samuels (1968) demonstrate that this form, found only in a small region in central England, is the product of accommodation in Ireland between different varieties of Midlands English (from where most settlers came), most notably *uche* and *eche*. If any influence from the indigenous language is found in the settlers' English, it tends to be related to either toponyms or the names of flora and fauna largely previously unknown to the settlers.

As the settler population begins to consider itself native to the territory it occupies – normally in the second to third generations – the debate over what the local variety of English should be like becomes intense, with disputes beginning to appear between innovative speakers, who play up the local features of the local dialect and those who continue to attempt to maintain close linguistic ties with prestigious varieties at 'home'. Elements of the latter viewpoint still exist in New Zealand in particular. It used to be highly visible in Australian television drama, with older actors generally coming quite close to RP in their speech, unless they were comic characters, in which case 'Strine', the stereotypical working class/outback dialect, was the norm. Younger actors generally spoke Middle Class Australian exclusively (unless, again, there was a reason for their speaking with a less prestigious accent). Eventually the local variety wins out, even if a 'complaint literature' on the inappropriateness (often 'ugliness') of the local dialect continues for some time, as do Education Department documents (Trudgill 2004) attempting to construct policy to reverse 'declining standards' in speech. The truth of the matter is that many of those complaining about, or developing policy against, the local variety use it themselves (although code switching may well have been particularly marked with some individuals).

Part of the linguistic nationalism which becomes prevalent during the increasing divorce between colonising country and colony may include the use of indigenous innovations in relation to English. Prior to this rapprochement, it is likely that any indigenous English features would have been severely criticised by the settler authorities and generally avoided by the settler population as a whole. There are some colonial varieties where there is generally little if any indigenous influence upon settler English, Australian English being a particularly striking example of this. On such occasions, it is likely that ethnic relationships have been particularly fraught, and that racism towards the indigenous population may, until quite recently, have been the societal norm, thus making contact less likely. In South Asian English, however, not only does a considerable degree of borrowing from indigenous languages take place, largely for cultural reasons (as can also be seen in Māori borrowings into New Zealand English). The form of English developed by non-native speakers has essentially become standard across South Asia (perhaps because most speakers of these varieties are themselves non-native speakers). These can include phonological and structural features, such as the use of retroflex consonants in words such as *bottle*, it is most marked in lexis, however. The Scots dialects of Shetland, discussed later in this chapter, also exhibit these tendencies quite strongly. Finally, Schneider claims that originally relatively homogenous varieties – homogenous perhaps in part because of the new identity being produced – will eventually develop considerable social variation as inequalities in wealth and access to the levers of power increase.

Useful though this model is, however, we have to recognise that it does not fully explain what is happening during this process of nativisation. Recent research on this matter by Trudgill (2004) will now be focused upon, since his work appears to present a means of visualising the stages involved in new dialect formation.

6.2 Theoretical models

6.2.1 The 'inevitability of colonial Englishes' (Trudgill 2004)

In work from the mid 1980s on (such as Trudgill 1986), Trudgill has added to his considerable standing as a microsociolinguist by investigating what happens when relatively closely related varieties come into contact in a new place. This culminated in his 2004 book, concerned primarily (but not solely) with the development of New Zealand English. His findings, although undoubtedly attractive and argued with Trudgill's considerable ability as a writer, have not been fully accepted by many within the scholarly community (as can be seen in the discussion of Trudgill's views by a range of eminent scholars in *Language in Society* 37 in 2008). The background to his views needs therefore to be discussed briefly before we turn to Trudgill's analysis of how new varieties come into being, before moving to a discussion of his model as a whole.

For almost as long as there have been extraterritorial varieties of English (and, indeed, other languages), scholars have been attempting to explain what the – geographical and social – origins of these varieties are. In the case of Southern Hemisphere Englishes, all of which, no matter how populous, such as Australian or South African English, or relatively low in number of speakers, such as Falkland Islands English (Sudbury 2001), share much with each other at all levels of language, it has long been posited that the primary source for all the varieties was working class dialects, rural and particularly urban, from the south-east of England, possibly primarily London and Portsmouth, both cities with a maritime tradition and, in the case of London, a large population associated with great inequalities in education and wealth. This influence, it was argued, can be seen both in the lack of rhoticity and the rounded nature of the diphthong in *ride* (in comparison with Received Pronunciation) in all of these varieties.

There are, however, some issues with accepting this single source explanation. There are features in all the Southern Hemisphere Englishes which are not present in the working class varieties of the English south-east. For instance, in most Southern Hemisphere varieties, /h/ is realised exactly where it is in Received Pronunciation and most other varieties of English. This would most certainly not be the case with non-standard South-East English varieties (with the exception, at least until recently, of some East Anglian varieties). On these occasions, commentators have regularly looked at who else entered the colony, particularly in its early days. Australia, for instance, had a Scottish population as well as a rather more sizeable Irish group in its original 'mix' (if this metaphor is apposite for a largely penal settlement). New Zealand has had a sizeable Scottish minority (in places a majority) practically since Pakeha immigration began. Scholars could therefore turn to this type of evidence to explain why retention of this sort was allowed (on this occasion, practically no varieties of Scottish or Irish English have 'lost' /h/). Although this type of argumentation was rather *ad hoc* (and sometimes assumed that, as in the case of Scottish and New Zealand centralised pronunciations of /ɪ/, just because there are similarities, these must derive from a common predecessor rather than being merely independent innovations), it nonetheless carried with it the seeds of later understanding.

The origins of New Zealand English have long fascinated scholars (and, indeed, laypeople). As a variety which has a fair-sized (but not massive) speaker population and is situated on a set of islands which are some distance even from its nearest large-scale English-speaking population (Australia), it can be seen as – at the very least to an extent – an excellent laboratory for more scientific views on dialect origin. New Zealand English is also blessed by having considerable amounts of evidence for the way people spoke in the first few generations of settlement.

In the period immediately after the Second World War, the New Zealand Broadcasting Corporation instigated a project to record the memories of those who survived from these generations, using mobile recording units which covered a fair part of the country. Although not intended for linguistic analysis, the recordings' rediscovery in the last twenty years has sparked considerable activity in assessing what the actual sources for modern New Zealand English were.

What was immediately striking about most of the recordings of the first New Zealand-born generation was that their accents bore very little similarity to the recognisably local and relatively homogenised varieties used by the second and third generations. On the other hand, while many of the people recorded did bear some resemblance in their speech to 'old country' dialects – particularly, perhaps, in those areas where Scottish settlement was highly prevalent – this was often not the case. Indeed, the accents recorded appeared to mix a number of varieties; this was not always due to a combination based on parents' different origins. Some of the varieties recorded are even – from a systemic point of view – essentially impossible. For instance, there is typological continuum in English which dictates that, if you do not have /h/ in words like *hot*, you will not have /ʍ/ in *what* (for a discussion of the patterning of the /ʍ/ versus /w/ variables, see Schreier 2005: 82–112). In the Black Isle dialect of Northern Scots, for instance, unique in Scotland in not having /h/, *what* is /at/. In more mainstream varieties of 'English', such as Cockney, *what* has, of course, /w/, but the principle remains the same. Yet one of the first native generation recorded in New Zealand, Mr Ritchie of Arrowtown (Trudgill 2010: 171) had no /h/, but used /ʍ/ practically universally in its historical position. This type of pattern (on this occasion of a particularly marked type but by no means unrepresentative of the distribution patterns of the speakers as a whole) begs an important question: how could this level of variation lead to relative homogeneity in the next generation?

In order to explain this, Trudgill builds up a typology based both on the New Zealand evidence and on previous analyses (by him and by others) on what actually happens when strangers from different linguistic backgrounds meet for the first time in a new environment, by considering the processes involved to be fivefold.

In the first instance there is *mixing*, 'the coming together in a particular location of speakers of different dialects of the same language, or of readily mutually intelligible languages' (Trudgill 2004: 84). If we find ourselves in a new environment, most of us, largely semi-consciously at most, tend to adjust towards the other speakers, particularly if your usage is unusual in relation to most of the other people's varieties. When

I lived in Canada, for instance, I ceased pronouncing *tomato* /tə'mato/, preferring instead /tə'meto/ (see Trudgill 1986: 110 for further discussion of this type of accommodation). My primary reasoning behind this was that, in Toronto, many people are not native speakers of English (in particular, perhaps, in the catering and grocery trades) and that using my Scottish Standard English pronunciation would only have created an unnecessary problem for people not used to it. It is worth noting, however, that my 'North American' pronunciation was no such thing. The diphthongisation of stressed vowels so common in Canadian English is not shown in mine; the medial /t/ remains voiceless and not retroflex. I had produced a mixed form, more comprehensible than my native pronunciation but still grounded in the phonotactic constraints of my native variety.

These mixing phenomena tend to be *ad hoc* and generally ephemeral. They certainly encourage the perpetuation of large-scale searches for major systemic correspondences. Nevertheless, over time, these compromises may become regular or, at the very least, a major factor in the general variation patterns found in any new community.

Following on from this is *levelling*, which Trudgill defines as 'the loss of demographically minority variants' (2004: 84). In some ways this is similar to Schneider's *nativization*. In almost all Southern Hemisphere Englishes, for instance, full rhoticity is not found. As we have seen, many commentators have suggested that this lack is due to the influence on all these varieties from the (non-standard) dialects of south-east England. This does seem a sensible conclusion. But we have to explain exactly how this transfer of features took place.[1]

Trudgill suggests that the spread of non-rhotic pronunciations in New Zealand English is a matter of numbers, in the end. Non-rhotic speakers made up more than 50% of the speakers and therefore their usage became the norm. Similar points could be made for the New Zealand pronunciation of the diphthong in words like *ride*, which is more open than the Received Pronunciation equivalent, something it has in common with Cockney and some other non-standard south-east England dialects. But the population from the south-east which had this pronunciation who came to New Zealand was probably not in the majority. On this occasion, a majority can be put together by bringing in immigrants from the south-west of England and from midland and southern parts of Ireland.

While this argument is very attractive and does, at least on these occasions, appear to make sense, some scholars feel that the forces which designate the feature considered the victor in the 'contest' are somewhat mechanistic, almost 'just add water' in their denial of human agency. We will return to a discussion of this point very shortly. Nevertheless, the extreme variability associated with first-generation speech seems to be in line with the improvisation and experimentation inherent in these first two stages; this certainly appears to be highly speaker-centred.

The third stage is associated with *unmarking*, 'the tendency for unmarked forms to survive even if they are not majority forms' (Trudgill 2004: 85). On this occasion, if a feature is too closely associated with a particular pronunciation or usage, particularly when that has negative connotations, then a minority form may be preferred. Thus the /h/-full nature of modern New Zealand English may be due to there being a majority of settlers – from Scotland, Ireland, East Anglia and elsewhere – having this phoneme in its standard distribution. But even if that is not the case, 'h-dropping' was heavily associated with a particular part of England, with strongly negative associations for many and was moreover from at least the early nineteenth century on, subject to an onslaught by schoolteachers and other language pundits towards which the first and second generations of New Zealanders cannot have been immune. This disapproval – or at least *marking* – of 'h-dropping' could well have given the final push to the use of the phoneme.[2]

The next stage lies at the heart of our understanding of the process: *interdialect development*, which Trudgill defines as the emergence 'of forms which were not actually present in any of the dialects contributing to the mixture, but which arise out of interactions between them' (2004: 86). We have already seen a similar, although not identical, development in the spread of the medieval Irish English form *euche* for 'each'.

Other examples might include Canadian English *riding* 'parliamentary constituency'. In British English the Old Norse borrowing *hustings* is occasionally used (now normally in the expression of journalists when referring to events taking place during an election as a whole: 'Here is a round-up from the hustings tonight'). The word *riding*, also, as we have seen, an Old Norse borrowing, can only refer in England either to the three ridings of Yorkshire or of Lindsey (itself a third part of Lincolnshire). These were to some extent administrative divisions; but there was never an exact correspondence between their use and parliamentary elections. It is probably the case that either someone in Canada associated their less than fully autonomous parliament (which in its early days was overseen by the Westminster parliament) with the local divisions in Yorkshire or, more likely, some confusion between *husting* and *riding* took place. No matter what, however, the term has stuck and has become a full-blown marker of Canadian identity.

The final stage in Trudgill's model is what he terms *reallocations* and *focusing*, 'the process by means of which the new variety acquires norms and stability' (Trudgill 2004: 109). All elements which produced the stable New Zealand English of today were present in the first generation recordings (along with, as we have seen, many features which are not). There was no perceptible framework, even in the usage patterns of individuals, which immediately leads to the present system. Nevertheless, Trudgill would claim, the seeds of the modern regularity can be found in the past irregularity. The present centralised pronunciation of /ɪ/ in New Zealand speech came out of a range of pronunciations of the KIT vowel (as defined in the Wells classification of vowels in English), from front and high to something approaching /ʌ/. It would be tempting to suppose that the presence of large numbers of Scottish people in the original settlement encouraged this use (although the Scottish vowel is rarely as back as the New Zealand). More likely, however, the predisposition towards centrality was caused by a set of system internal sound changes rather than original inputs (Trudgill 2010). It may also be worth noting that the pronunciation of KIT is a central *shibboleth* (a linguistic feature held to be peculiar to and representative of a particular group) in the relationship between Australian and New Zealand English, with the former having a high front pronunciation (almost at [i]).

This final point raises an issue with Trudgill's model: *determinism*. His model is subtle and, I believe, gives a fair schematisation of what must happen in the development of colonial varieties. But a considerable number of scholars (see, for instance, Hickey 2004a) have baulked at the apparently mechanistic nature of the model. There appears to be no agency in the development of a new variety; instead its development seems largely to be a matter of majority usages winning out over minority, with the exception already noted about unmarked forms being preferred over marked, even if the latter is the majority usage. This view appears to undermine one of the central tenets of sociolinguistics: individual language choice is constructed partly by individual and group identity.

Trudgill has made the telling point on a number of occasions that conscious views on language use rarely affect real language use. To return to our earlier discussion of /r/ in late eighteenth- and early nineteenth-century south-east England English, the spread of this innovation was, as far as we can tell, frowned upon by middle class opinion makers. Nevertheless, its spread was rapid. The same can be said for the spread of /ɑː/ in words such as *bath* in the same area. What is now seen as a mark of privilege was then analysed as a sign of, at the very least, lower middle class origin. Moreover, it is quite possible to explain the shibboleth status of KIT discussed above as being produced *after* rather than *before* the sound changes had taken place. This could be taken as meaning that the variation and change is entirely unconscious, but is then reinterpreted consciously. This begs the question, however: to what extent is socially conditioned linguistic variation truly the product of social relationships between speakers? There are a number of theories which attempt to interject the speaker in what is coming worryingly close to the neogrammarian viewpoint that linguistic change is in a sense mechanistic, constructed within the system without human agency. The most important of these counter-proposals is Mufwene's *founder principle* (Mufwene 2001 and elsewhere).

6.2.2 *The* founder principle

Mufwene's primary focus in this matter is not, as is the case with Trudgill's work, on the emerging dialects of voluntary colonists; instead it is concerned with the development of varieties, such as African American Vernacular English, formed largely in the context of slavery and its aftermath. This is an important point, because there are serious problems involved in the analysis of the development of African American Vernacular English, particularly in relation to varieties which can certainly be described as creoles. The question of whether African American Vernacular English (AAVE) has a creole basis is much disputed. What lies behind this dispute is worth considering.

It is not the purpose of this chapter to present a complete treatment of the debate over the origin of African American Vernacular English. We need to understand the central points, however. Essentially, the field is split into those who believe that African American Vernacular English is a *decreolised* creole (see Rickford 1999: Chapter 10 for a discussion) and those who believe that it is essentially a mainstream English variety which has taken on some features from varieties much closer to the canonical idea of *creole* (see, for instance, the papers in Poplack 2000).

For those who argue for a creole origin, the necessity is quickly apparent for evidence demonstrating how, when and for what reason the decreolisation took place. Let us consider the historical evidence. Most notably this includes the recordings made in the 1930s of the recollections of former slaves along with the witness of language use in African American colonies planted outside the United States in the period running up to and during the American Civil War, in places as disparate as Nova Scotia, the Dominican Republic and Liberia. But this evidence does not illustrate varieties which are more creole than modern African American Vernacular English (Poplack and Tagliamonte 2001). It could be argued that, given that house slaves, those most likely to come into contact with Standard English, generally lived longer than field hands, due to the nature of their work, the 1930s recordings may have been biased towards the language of the former rather than latter group. Higher levels of literacy – and, indeed, liberty – were likely to be found among the descendants of those who took part in voluntary 'repatriation' and colonisation than among the African American population as a whole. But inviting though many of these arguments might be, they still leave us with absolutely no evidence for the straightforward descent of African American Vernacular English from a creole.

The dialectal viewpoint suggests that African American Vernacular English is essentially a variety of Southern States English, highly similar to, but not exactly the same as, the local dialects of the white population. Given the obvious similarities between white and black dialects in these areas, it is difficult to argue against such a viewpoint. It has to be accepted, however, that, in its simplest sense, this explanation fails to explain the apparently creole features of African American Vernacular English which do not occur in the local white dialects. It is at this stage that Mufwene's arguments begin to assume importance.

Like many other historical linguists, Mufwene turned to evolutionary biology to provide metaphors for the processes he saw in new variety development. Unlike Trudgill, he does not see the first few generations after first settlement as representing only the 'settling' of a new variety based, at heart, upon the victory of majority features over minority ones. Mufwene would not deny that this type of development is central to colonial language formation. He does, however, believe that in this competition some varieties have greater strength because they represent the language of the *founder* population.

The founders are not, Mufwene claims, necessarily the first people to settle in a place. Instead, they may well represent the first *significant* population, a group connected intrinsically to the new community, possibly as leaders and opinion makers but also possibly as those with whom other groups regularly interact. This influence is likely to continue, even when the founder population is no longer in the majority. In relation to the United States, for instance, the first European settlers on the Eastern Seaboard were English speakers (with the exception of small Spanish settlements in Florida). Their linguistic influence has, of course, continued and, indeed, grown over the last 400 years. Yet fewer English speakers moved to the region than did German speakers over the period. Nevertheless, while German was a major language in the USA in the nineteenth and early twentieth centuries, there has

never been a time when its speakers dominated the country linguistically or even appeared to want to do so. The fact that they had entered
an English-speaking environment where that language was dominant
seems to have been challenged by very few German speakers.

Returning to African American Vernacular English, Mufwene essentially suggests that the plantation environments so crucial to the development of English creoles in the Caribbean were a relatively late feature
in the history of African settlement in North America. On plantations,
speakers of mainstream Englishes rarely interacted regularly with the
slave population, meaning that new varieties of a creole type could
develop unchecked. But for a large part of the seventeenth century (and
into the eighteenth century in many places), African slaves in North
America did not live on large plantations, growing cotton, tobacco or
rice, depending on where the plantation was situated. Instead, most
lived in much closer proximity to their owners and, crucially, indentured servants, essentially temporary slaves of European – normally
English-speaking – origin, on a much smaller farm. While there might
be a number of slaves on the larger farms, the numerical preponderance
of Africans associated with later plantations was nowhere in evidence.
Mufwene terms this period the *homestead stage*.

    This close proximity did not necessarily make the slaves' lives easier
than they were later, but it did make it possible for Africans to learn the
dominant language directly and continuously from native speakers in a
way which fundamentally differs from the situation in which Africans
found themselves in the large Caribbean plantations, where mainstream
varieties of English were normally in short supply. It is likely, of course,
that the primary influence on the evolving English of Africans during
this period was not the language of the prosperous but rather of those
with whom they had most contact; in particular, perhaps, the English
of the indentured servants. This probably explains some of the features
of African American Vernacular English which seem to have much in
common with a range of dialects of the British Isles. Most of what has
been said here could be applied to the non-standard dialects spoken by
southern whites, of course, since the sources for black and white speech
were very similar.

    Naturally, other features in African American Vernacular English
cannot be explained in the same way. Mufwene therefore proposes a situation where creole and other 'foreign' features were incorporated into
the ancestor of African American Vernacular English through contact
both with new slaves coming directly from Africa (and also indentured
servants who spoke languages other than English, including German,

Welsh and Irish and Scottish Gaelic) and with slaves who, whether in Africa or in the West Indies, had already learned an English pidgin or creole. These features would tend to be perpetuated – they may even have been assumed as something like an identity feature – but were never used by a large enough (or prestigious enough) population to make them omnipresent as they are in varieties more closely associated with the concept of creole.

The Africans who were brought as slaves to what is now the United States during the eighteenth century came in far greater numbers than those of the homestead phase. Moreover, the plantations they primarily inhabited and worked upon exhibited, as we have already seen, a far greater separation between blacks and whites than had been possible earlier. In addition, many of the slaves who had come directly from Africa learned English only in these rather limited contexts, rather than from native speakers in everyday interaction. These would appear to be perfect environments for pidgins and creoles to develop. Yet the only true North American English-based creole is Gullah, spoken largely on islands off the Atlantic coasts of South Carolina and Georgia, in areas with long-standing connections to the Caribbean and where large-scale plantations, cultivating rice in particular, led to an overwhelming majority of inhabitants being of African descent (the cultural and linguistic result of which are analysed in the essays in Twining and Baird 1991). Why did African American Vernacular English not develop in this way?

Mufwene argues convincingly that the founder principle governs here. The original slave population and their descendants, grounded in the homestead stage, passed on their knowledge of English into the new plantation era. Because of the concept of perpetual bondage which developed in North America during this period which assumed that, unlike earlier forms of slavery, it was almost impossible for slaves to gain their freedom either by buying themselves out or by manumission through particular services to their owners or on an owner's death, those who had been schooled in the old ways inevitably had an influence on how later populations behaved linguistically. As Africans were trained in English during the homestead stage by native speakers from a variety of geographical and social backgrounds, plantation slaves largely learned English from native speakers of English from an African background.

It is likely of course that features carried over from native languages to English would have had some effect on the development of African American Vernacular English during this period. But the variety remained essentially the same, primarily because of the founder effect. Even though it is likely that the speakers of homestead African American Vernacular English were always in a minority during the plantation stage, their considerable prestige within the slave community – as seasoned slaves with local knowledge and obvious dexterity in the new language – would have encouraged its acquisition. Thus, unlike Trudgill, Mufwene claims a degree of human agency – of a largely collective type – in the preference of one variable (and, indeed, variant) over another. How these two theoretical strands interact will be related to two lesser-known new English varieties representing two inter-related but actually rather different new dialect formations: St Helena English and Tristan da Cunha English, respectively the earliest and most recent formations of this type in the southern hemisphere. From the outset it should be noted that this discussion is based primarily on the work of Schreier (2003 and 2008), although some of the conclusions are mine.

6.3 Case studies

6.3.1 St Helenian English

St Helenian English is one of the least known Southern Hemisphere varieties of English, largely because the island itself has, for most of its occupation by Britain, been off the main trade routes. Moreover, the relatively small population (at present a little over 4,200) means that the chances of anyone meeting a St Helenian (the locals' preferred adjective construction) are actually quite low. Often, on first contact, the hearer might analyse the speaker's accent as being New Zealand or South African (or sometimes a combination of the two, confusingly). In time, however, other features begin to make these identifications less secure. In the following, therefore, I will sketch out some of the most distinctive features of the dialect, with the proviso that no attempt at full coverage is intended.

In terms of phonology, the vowel patterns of the St Helenian dialect (StHE) tend to bear considerable similarities with (non-standard) Southern British varieties (and also with Australian, New Zealand and, to an extent, South African varieties). Diphthongs such as that represented in Wells' work by PRICE tend to be low and rounded. There are, however, features in StHE which are very unusual elsewhere, such as: THOUGHT/ FORCE/ NORTH/ POOR merger at the tense diphthong /oə/ as well as with the *choice* diphthong (which, from personal experience, can make a St Helena resident briefly sound like a Western Scots speaker).

Consonants deviate somewhat from the mainstream (including, to a large extent, the other Southern Hemisphere Englishes). /w/ and /v/ are merged, often at [β]. Although almost all St Helenians can pronounce dental fricatives in the mainstream way, particularly in formal contexts, most use /f/ and /v/ in TH contexts in informal speech. Merger of /w/ and /v/ *was* present in some South-East English varieties in the nineteenth century, and can be found in some lesser-used English varieties, sometimes at the creole end of the new variety continuum (Trudgill 2010: 61–75). TH-fronting, as it is sometimes called, is common in many varieties of urban British non-standard English, although the spread from the London area is quite recent. In London it is not regularly commented upon until the twentieth century. Authors like Dickens, who had a particularly good ear for the London street speech of his era, never have working class characters realising this variant. It is also found in a number of creole and post-creole environments. This duality of non-standard South-East English and the effects of creolisation as points of origin is something of a leitmotif in St Helenian English.

All the following examples derive from Schreier's fieldwork. Morphosyntactic features of the dialect include 'double comparison', as in, *people were **more genuiner** than what they are today*, a feature found regularly in non-standard varieties. There are also differences between local use and the standard in relation to article use. These can include occasions where *a* would normally be expected, such as, *she had to get **operation*** and *he had generator to run the 'lectricity. The* is, on the other hand, used when it would not be in the standard (although some of these features are certainly found in other dialects), such as *she was infected in the leg, all from **the diabetes**.*

Very striking is the use of pronouns. On occasion object pronouns are used in subject position, as with ***us** come up Peak Hill way see*. Subject pronouns are also regularly used in possessive contexts, as with *that's **they** occupation*. The former usage is reminiscent of the dialects of south-west England, but both it and the latter are regularly found in creoles, the latter being regular in African American Vernacular English. Another pronominal feature, a discrete second person plural pronoun along the lines of *So **y'all** be goin back soon?* is unusual in the British English sphere, but is, of course, common in the southern states of the USA (and was found in Middle Scots, among other varieties).

There are also a number of noteworthy features with the verbs. Aspect, for instance, is often represented in ways rather different from those found in Standard English. These include an habitual *be* construction: *it don't **be** pain like fore days it don't **be** real pain*; a similar habitual *do* construction: *that's what all of us **do** query*, and a completive *done* construction: *I **done** beat him now*. While examples of the final construction can regularly be found in Southern and South-Western colloquial American English, the first two features can be associated with many creoles (and also African American Vernacular English). In the same vein are examples of non-standard verb-subject concord, as with *it **don't** be pain like fore days it **don't** be real pain* discussed above, as well as the use of invariant *is*, as shown with *I's quite happy* and *I think they's divorce*. A further feature, rather more unusual in terms of World English, is the reduction of a construction along the lines of *must have to* to ***mussy***, as with *they **mussy** take that down and buil' the house*.

Perhaps the most striking feature of St Helenian verbs, however, is the ways in which non-finite verbs, in particular infinitives, can take (past) tense markers, as shown with *my daddy used to **got** the flax* 'my daddy used to get [i.e., collect, harvest] the flax' and *I didn't **went** out nowhere* 'I didn't go out anywhere'. With the exception of a variety which we will deal with shortly, this kind of construction is practically unknown in any other variety of English.

How then can we explain St Helenian English's divergence from the Southern Hemisphere English norm? In the first instance we need to understand something of the history of the island and its inhabitants.

It is worth noting in the first instance that St Helena, unlike all other British Southern Hemisphere colonies (with the partial exception of South Africa, where a peculiar blend of slavery and peonage survived at the Cape from Dutch times), was a settlement where slavery was common, albeit without its becoming absolutely central to the island's economy in the way it did in the Caribbean. Although St Helena is relatively close to Africa and connections both with West Africa and Portugal's Angola colony were at times strong, many, perhaps most, of the slave population were originally from Madagascar. Such a large and occupationally and socially discrete population is likely to have maintained its native language for some time. Indeed Larson (2009) has recently demonstrated how Malagasy speakers have attempted (and often succeeded) in maintaining their language and strengthening contacts with other Malagasy exiles in other parts of the French and British empires since the beginning of European slave hunting and imperialism on Madagascar in the sixteenth century. This (enforced) immigration is very unlikely *not* to have had some effect on the developing English dialect, although there seems to be little evidence of direct borrowing from Malagasy. In relation to this immigration it should be noted that, while there was considerable evidence of racism, particularly 'colour' prejudice, in nineteenth-century St Helena, this appears, very unusually, to have utterly dissipated. Almost everyone on the island is now of 'mixed race'.

A number of other ethnolinguistic groups have been present in the island from time to time – French speakers, both during the exile of Bonaparte following the collapse of his empire and earlier, when a number of French protestant exiles settled (albeit often temporarily) on the island, as well as speakers of major imperial languages, such as Portuguese (no doubt often in its pidgin and creole forms, vehicular languages of the oceans and the slave trade), south-east Asian and Indian languages spoken by coolie labourers, including Cantonese speakers, and Afrikaans, the language both of a number of prisoners-of-war on the island during and after the South African War of the early twentieth century and of traders practically since the foundation of the colony. But the only linguistic input which can be considered greater than Malagasy is the non-standard varieties of southern British English brought by settlers in the first few generations of the colony. Standard British English has always had an administrative presence on the island, stronger at certain times, such as when Bonaparte's exile dictated a large military presence, although always as a minority and largely external variety. Educational opportunities, growing from the late nineteenth century, led to an increasing exposure to (and use of) that variety, however.

If we look at the linguistic evidence already discussed, a good case could be made for there being features which appear creole-like; in particular, similar to features found in the Caribbean creoles. But the actual dialect itself, while exhibiting features which are unusual for Southern Hemisphere Englishes, is much more mainstream than the basilectal Caribbean creoles are. This need not mean that no actual creole was ever spoken on St Helena. Occasional comments on the 'broken speech' of slaves are present from relatively early on. The fact that no ethnic varieties as such occur on the island is both a testament to the enlightened ethnic politics of the last 150 years and also explains what probably happened. In general, the variety of the 'white' settlers from southern England was the basis of the new dialect. The many speakers of the post-creole were able to incorporate elements of their own speech into the new variety, some of which may have acted (and act) as local identity markers.

Schreier (2008: 119) provides a diagrammatic illustration of this complexity (see Figure 6.1).

What can our theoretical models do to explain what happened on St Helena? In the first instance, as far as we can tell, since historical forms

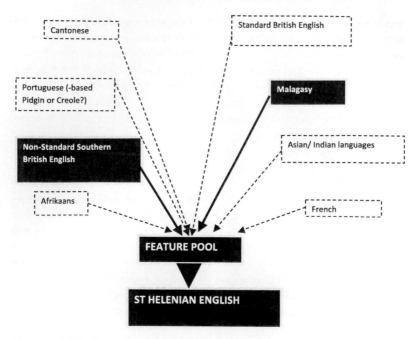

Figure 6.1 The feature pool of St Helenian English

of St Helenian English are not as well documented as New Zealand English, while its time depth is greater, Trudgill's model, moving from often extreme variability in the first generation to considerable homogeneity in later generations (most early recordings of St Helenian English are strikingly similar to what we have today, even if standard influence, undoubtedly largely through education, may have helped decrease the frequency of non-standard features), largely holds true. Indeed, although we cannot really illustrate it, his views on how koineisation takes place in the earliest period appears highly likely. From this model's point of view, a serious issue is present, however. If, as has been suggested, a relatively large minority of St Helenian English speakers spoke a creole, their language should have had little or no influence upon the majority usage.

In theory, the same problem exists for the founder principle explanation favoured by Mufwene. If the free white settler population was the founder population, then, again, we would not expect much creole influence. But here is a central subtlety in Mufwene's project. It is not only the dominant variety which derives support from the founder principle. Instead, each discrete variety would have a founder principle as support. Moreover, in the racial homogenisation of the last two hundred years on St Helena, it must regularly have been the case that households would consist of speakers of both 'white' St Helenian English and its creole counterpart. In each household's children, therefore, creole features would have had the same weight as non-creole, encouraging their adoption in the new variety. While this experience could probably not be seen as representing an arithmetical majority, it could be argued that its presence was ubiquitous and influential, particularly when Standard English was less omnipresent.

Having said that, a number of the 'creole' features in StHE are present, albeit in a smaller scale distribution, throughout the English-speaking world (and often in south-east England). From Trudgill's viewpoint, it could be argued that these 'pushed' the 'creole' features close to the majority usage. In any event, it seems likely that, in an isolated community with a highly mixed population linguistically, like St Helena, features which would seem marked to speakers of more mainstream varieties might actually have been considered fairly unmarked. With all this in mind, it is useful to make a comparison with a much more recently established South Atlantic English variety.

6.3.2 Tristan da Cunha English

Tristan da Cunha, a volcanic island chain in the South Atlantic (only one of whose islands is permanently inhabited) is probably the most isolated community on Earth. With a population of 264 (at the 2010 census), it is a British dependency, administered as part of the widely flung British Overseas Territory of Saint Helena, Ascension and Tristan da Cunha. Tristan da Cunha English has some similarities to St Helenian English, but is much more mainstream (in relation to other Southern Hemisphere Englishes) than its northern neighbour. This is surprising given how isolated the settlement is and how little contact, until very recently, the archipelago has had.

There are, however, some features which are either unusual or entirely unknown in these contexts. Verb/subject concord, for instance, is rarely that of the standard; instead, it might be argued that a number of features, both southern and northern British English, are at work in the system. Some features, such as completive *done*, a construction which is, apart from St Helenian English, unusual in the Southern Hemisphere, are relatively common.

Arguably the most striking morphosyntactic feature is the construction *usta went* (and other past tense/past participle) constructions. In habitual situations, the mainstream *used to go* is common: *Sometimes we **used to go** round together, all round the beaches we **used to go**.* With other contexts, however, an unusual feature shows itself: *I useta went Nightingale with my father when I was a boy, we never had no good schooling . . . all we usta done was sums an' a bit of reading.* The use of past tense in infinitival constructions, even when only one verb can trigger it, is most unusual in the English-speaking world. It is probably not chance, we might posit, which has caused this phenomenon to occur in two island communities which have a long, albeit spasmodic, relationship with each other.

Again, something of the settlement history of Tristan da Cunha needs to be known to interpret this type of data. The population of the island has never been high (at times it has been perilously low) and involuntary immigration (shipwreck or stranding) has had a considerable impact upon the make-up of the society while 'official' immigration has not always been a central feature in the island's demographic pattern in the way it was in St Helena. On the other hand, Tristan da Cunha has less than half the settlement time-depth St Helena has.

While, as with St Helena, settlement of people from southern England was probably the largest single input into Tristan da Cunha English, Scottish and Northern English settlers were also present in the early colony. New Zealand and South African English (and Afrikaans) speakers have also been present at times during the colony's history, the South African influence being more prevalent, perhaps, given its 'proximity' to the island. Interestingly, speakers of Dutch, Danish and Italian have also had extended stays on the island. Indeed one Italian speaker, Gaetano Lavarello (resident 1892–1952), became spokesman for the islanders and a veritable patriarch; interestingly, his English was praised by outsiders. Under normal circumstances, we would not expect the English of non-native speakers to affect that of native speakers. In a situation where speakers of any variety could be numbered in the (low) decades, and non-native speakers may be well respected within the community and there is little direct influence from Standard British English, in particular in spoken form, such barriers may have been much lessened, or even broken down entirely.

One further feature of early Tristan da Cunha demographic history must be recognised. In the first years of settlement men outnumbered women considerably; this led to quite serious social problems. Women on St Helena were given the opportunity to come to Tristan da Cunha as wives to the single men. A number of women availed themselves of this opportunity, arriving in 1827. Most if not all of today's Tristanians are descended from these founding mothers. We do not know what social backgrounds these women had, although their willingness to jump into the unknown in this way is, perhaps, evidence that they were

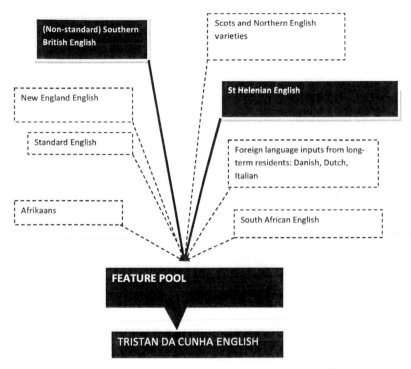

Figure 6.2 The feature pool of Tristan da Cunha English

from backgrounds where the opportunity for economic and social betterment was perhaps not assured on their native island. This would suggest, then, that many of them came from a recent slave background. In any event, as we have seen, all St Helenian English varieties have elements which could be described as creole-like. This final population input may well explain the presence (albeit in a limited way) of past-tense marking on infinitives in Tristan da Cunha English.

Following Schreier's system for describing the inputs into St Helenian English I have produced this schematisation for Tristan da Cunha English (Figure 6.2).

From what has been said, it becomes apparent that the population which had the largest input in the early stages of a variety's development has the whip hand in producing the final 'product'. Again, however, and perhaps particularly because of the small number of settlers involved, the linguistic effects of a large minority, speakers of St Helenian English, particularly when distributed regularly demographically and geographically, while limited in comparison, can break through on regular occasions. Thus Trudgill's model works to a large degree with this type of formation. Nevertheless, particularly perhaps because of the intimate nature of the creation of the new dialect, founder effect is vital. As we will see with Shetland Scots, indeed, founder effect(s) are central to the importation and creation of features.

6.3.3 Shetland Scots

Shetland lies in the north Atlantic, some 150km north of the Scottish mainland and around 300km from both the Faeroe Islands and Norway. It is an archipelago, with the Mainland physically dominant. A number of the islands are a considerable distance from the centre – most notably Fair Isle and Foula. There are around 22,000 permanent inhabitants, some 8,000 of whom live in Lerwick, the only sizable town. Until the advent of North Sea Oil in the 1970s, most people were involved in a combination of fishing and subsistence farming. Although on the very edge of the European continental shelf, human habitation goes back well over 2,000 years, and potentially much longer (the following is based primarily on the discussion in Millar 2007a: Chapter 5).

The dialects of Shetland are particularly difficult to analyse typologically. In many ways this is the most northern of the Northern dialects, forming part of a dialect continuum which passes through Orkney, Caithness and the Black Isle into the north-east of Scotland. Although these dialects differ sometimes considerably in relation to morphosyntax, phonology and lexis, they also regularly unite in opposition to more southerly varieties of Scots, such as in the use of *this* and *that* with plural nouns, or *riach* for 'greyish-white, drab, brindled'.[3] Understandably, the geographical and cultural proximity of Shetland and Orkney (and, to a degree, Caithness on the Scottish mainland) has meant that many features not found in other Northern dialects are common to two or three of the grouping. Thus both Orkney and Shetland dialects preserve /y/ in the equivalent of English *moon* and *school*, when practically all other Scots dialects have an unrounded equivalent (thus, in the north-east, /min/ and /skwil/ and in west central areas /mɪn/ and /skɪl/); a second person singular familiar pronoun is found (*du* in Shetland and *thoo* in Orkney). A great deal of vocabulary is also held in common. But there are elements of Shetland dialect which represent a close relationship to the north-east of Scotland, such as the raising of Central Scots /e/ to /i/ in *een* 'one' (in comparison to Orcadian *ane*) and the use of vocabulary items such as *cair* 'mix together'. which are not used anywhere else apart from these regions. Moreover, although the archetypal North East (and on this occasion Caithness) change of /ʍ/ to /f/ in words like *where* and *whale* (*faar* and *faal* in the north-east), one <wh> word – *how* – is *foo* in Shetland, suggesting a borrowing due to intimate contact. Other features appear to represent rather more geographically distant connections, however.

There are, for instance, a large number of similarities between Shetland Scots and the dialects of the counties of east central Scotland – in particular Angus, Fife and the Lothians. These correspondences are largely lexical (although see the discussion of Knooihuizen 2009 in the following) and include words like *en-wye* 'progress (v)'. The survival of /y/ in some rural Angus dialects in forms cognate to *moon* and *school* needs also to be mentioned. But the connections go further. There are a smaller number of similarities in lexical use between Shetland dialects and the West Central, South Western and Ulster dialects of Scots. These include the use of *wan* 'one' (alongside *een*), which may have an Irish English origin.

It seems likely that what we have here is an example of new dialect formation. We need to be certain that we are not finding evidence because we are looking for it, however. Can other explanations be put forward?

In the first instance, we might have to consider whether anything unusual *is* happening in the history and present state of Shetland dialect. It is quite possible that what we have here is primarily a relict zone where features from earlier periods in the history of Scots have been retained, perhaps because Shetland lies at the very end of the dialect continuum and was also, until relatively recently, a world unto itself (although, as we will see, too much could be made of this).

Thus it could be argued that the survival of a second person familiar singular pronoun in Orkney and Shetland is due to the form's retreat over the last few centuries. This would be very difficult to argue against, since in living memory *thoo* and its variants were used in some Northern dialects and it is reported for the nineteenth-century dialect of my home town, Paisley, in the West Central dialect area. Although other arguments could be made for this type of usage, there can be little doubt that retreat has caused the Insular dialects' prominence in their survival. Indeed, the fact that *thoo* appears to be confined now in Orkney to older speakers, in particular from the northern islands of the archipelago appears to support this view.

But there are problems with complete acceptance of this analysis, primarily because it does not explain why concordances with the north-east are quite common in Shetland dialect. The presence of east central and other features in the dialect need also to be borne in mind. While it is entirely possible that *some* of these similarities are either chance or, more likely, relict survivals, the number and variety of examples would appear to argue against this hypothesis, as would the fact that some of the areas where similarities are found are major centres, such as Aberdeen and in particular Edinburgh and its environs, where linguistic innovation must have been more normal.

We should assume, therefore, that, ignoring the Scandinavian influence upon Shetland dialect, the present nature of that dialect can be analysed in relation with migration from Scotland and that, as Trudgill appears to have achieved with New Zealand English, we can consider how migrants' origins affected the present state of the dialect.

6.3.3.1 Shetland as a Scots tabula rasa

In many of the new varieties discussed in recent years, such as Tristan da Cunha (as analysed above) or the Falkland Islands (Sudbury 2001), a literal *tabula rasa* existed before colonial settlement, since hardly anyone had lived on those islands before. With others, such as Australian and New Zealand English or the French of Canada (Mougeon and Beniak 1994), sizeable aboriginal populations did live in the new colonies. Their linguistic influence on the 'colonial' variety is not great, however, being confined largely to a token set of culture-specific lexical borrowings. Obviously by either of these definitions, Shetland did *not* represent a *tabula rasa*. But it is informative to analyse the nature of Shetland Scots as if this were the case.

Even before the official transfer of power in the Earldom of Orkney (including Shetland) from Denmark-Norway to Scotland in 1468–9 (due to the inability of the former to pay a dowry), Scottish influence was considerable in both Orkney and Shetland. As Donaldson (1983) points out, the last native ruling house of the Earldom was originally from the Lowlands of Scotland and, more than a generation before the handover of the islands, legal decisions made by the *thing*, the local court and assembly, were occasionally recorded by the native *lawspeaker* in Scots (although Norn – or more often a Danicised Norwegian – was officially recorded for a considerable period after the transfer of power). There is considerable evidence throughout of immigration by people from northern Scotland in general and Caithness in particular.

With the transfer to Scottish rule and the replacement of the native ruling house by a cadet branch of the Scottish royal family, these connections were encouraged. Many immigrants either came from the populous south-east of Scotland or had been educated there; their Scots is likely to have reflected this connection. Indeed, the spread of the Scots of the Edinburgh area as something approaching a standard national variety would have encouraged its use, at least in writing, by people from many parts of Scotland. The Protestant Reformation, active in Scotland from the 1540s on, also brought metropolitan Scots speakers to the islands (although it should be noted that more isolated parts of Shetland in particular, such as Fair Isle, did not have regular contact with the State Church until the nineteenth century).

More importantly, the economic attractions of the islands led to the immigration of merchant venturers. In the case of Shetland, this movement was largely associated with the development of the local fishing and fish-processing industries, already tapped into by Dutch companies on a large scale. Until the first decades of the eighteenth century, in fact, it could be argued that Shetland enjoyed a boom, much of which was associated with the development of the natural harbour at what is now Lerwick. With the establishment of central government control over the use of salt in particular, however, this boom quickly faded; remnants of the immigration remained. Although incomers came from all over Lowland Scotland, many came from the eastern counties of Fife and Angus; in particular from the coastal burghs of Kirkcaldy and Dundee. The same origins were also common among their servants and assistants who followed them onto the islands; they may well have had more to do with the majority of Shetlanders.

We can readily connect some of what we know about Shetland dialect and its connections to other Scots dialects to this series of historical developments. Knooihuizen (2009) places modern Shetland phonology firmly in a line of descent from an early modern Angus system. While this is very likely for the majority elements of the Shetland systems, it does not explain the exceptions, apparently derived from other Scots sources, however. As we have seen, there appears to be a considerable amount of north-eastern Scottish influence upon Shetland dialects. These are primarily lexical; nevertheless, some word sets, such as those associated with mainstream Scots /e/ to /i/ before /n/, as in *been*, equivalent to Central Scots (and also Orcadian) *bane* 'bone', correspond in Shetland and the north-east, as do occasional single words, such as *foo* 'how'. Indeed what is interesting with these apparently north-east features in Shetland dialect is that they exist in a system which largely avoids such features: the verb negativiser in Shetland dialect is, for instance, always *no* rather than *nae*, found only in the north-east.

This suggests a situation not dissimilar to those postulated by Trudgill (2004), where marked forms are generally (but not always) avoided, even if a sizeable minority of the source population have these features.

Immigration from the north-east has been, as far as we can tell, present from early on in the Scottish period of Shetland's history, both from the mercantile centre of Aberdeen and also in connection with whaling and, in particular, fishing. The boom period for this final connection was from the early nineteenth century to the first decades of the twentieth, when herring was generally plentiful, seasonally predictable in its movements and normally well priced. Fishing fleets from around the British Isles took place in the herring fishery; the sheer number of fishing centres in the north-east of Scotland (in particular Peterhead, Fraserburgh and Aberdeen itself) would have given speakers of its dialects considerable prominence in the (relatively) near fishing grounds in Shetland. In addition, it should be noted that the seasonal prominence of north-easterners in Shetland included both men and women, the latter largely employed as fish gutters. Intermarriage was common between the two centres. While this often meant Shetlanders moving to the north-east, the opposite tendency was also present. Because of the profitable nature of the trade at the time, a considerable number of north-easterners moved to Shetland permanently. Indeed there is still a neighbourhood in Lerwick – *Scottie toun* – which commemorates just such a migration in the late nineteenth and early twentieth centuries.

Evidence of this type appears to tell us that two sets of influences – one from settlers coming from east central Scotland and another along a dialect continuum leading from Caithness through Orkney to Shetland – has been joined in the last few centuries by another from the north-east of Scotland. As we have seen, differences between these sources have been worked out according to processes suggested by Trudgill and other scholars concerned with koineisation.

So to a large extent we can say that Shetland Scots, while having its own nature and not being merely a product of 'mixing', does bear traces of its history as a place where speakers of different Scots dialects came and intermingled over a considerable period. Interesting as this is, however, this analysis only presents a partial and rather surface explanation for the origins of Shetland dialect. Historical evidence might suggest which extraterritorial elements came first. It does not explain all the unique features of Shetland Scots.

This point is important. Scots speakers did not enter a *tabula rasa* environment in Shetland. Unlike St Helena or Tristan da Cunha, a considerable number of people were already resident on Shetland; unlike

New Zealand or the United States, moreover, most Shetlanders are at least partly descended from these 'natives'. The language that they spoke – Norn, a western North Germanic language – was also a fairly close relative of Scots, with a fair amount of lexical correspondence (although it should be noted that, unlike the contact between Viking Norse and Old English in the ninth and tenth centuries discussed in the previous chapter, there is no reason to suspect that anything like mutual comprehension was possible between the two languages). We need, therefore, to investigate the nature of Norn's decline and disappearance on Shetland and what effects it might have had on the developing dialects of Shetland Scots.

6.3.3.2 Norn: an alternative founder dialect?

The extralinguistic reasons for the process of decline of the Scandinavian dialects of Northern Scotland and the Northern Isles are fairly well-known (see Barnes 1998 and 2010). As we have already seen, Scots came to have a dominant place in the Earldom of Orkney as a whole and, eventually, in Shetland. In written, and in the end spoken, domains, of course, Standard English from early on also had a powerful presence in the islands. Inevitably these new language varieties had an effect on when Norn was use and, eventually, on whether it was used at all or not. It does appear, for instance, that many originally Norn-speaking members of the land-holding class shifted fairly quickly to the new language of power as well, meaning that Norn became primarily associated with the subsistence level fishing and farming populations of the islands.

How quickly, and the process by which, Norn 'died' is rather more of a vexed question. There is no evidence (apart from some potentially questionable place name material) for when language shift occurred in Caithness (although the general consensus – for what it's worth – is some time in the fifteenth century). The language appears to have survived for longer in Orkney, probably still having some first language speakers at the end of the seventeenth century in the landward parishes of the Mainland (see Millar 2012b for more discussion). There is considerable debate over Shetland. The southern Mainland appears to have switched relatively early to Scots; there is every reason to suspect, however, that there were considerable numbers of native speakers of Norn still found on Foula and the northernmost of the isles at the start of the eighteenth century. How long after this the language survived is a question to which I will return on a number of occasions in the course of this section.

We have rather more evidence than we might expect of what late Shetland Norn was like. In 1774, the Rev. George Low recorded a version of the Lord's Prayer, some phrases and a thirty-five stanza ballad – the 'Hildina ballad' – in Norn, the last from William Henry, an elderly resident of Foula. But there are problems with this evidence: Low knew no Scandinavian language, so his transcription has been interpreted in a variety of ways by different scholars. Interestingly, Henry appears not to have understood fully what he was saying: he could only give a paraphrase of the ballad, not a translation.

The other major fragments of late Norn were recorded by the Faeroese dialectologist Jakob Jakobsen during his fieldwork on Shetland in the 1890s (there are a small number of examples of late Norn recorded by others in the nineteenth century which are too 'corrupt' for interpretation). As a gifted linguist, and also a native speaker of a variety which must have been a close relative of Shetland Norn, his witness of what he had heard is obviously considerably more trustworthy than that of Low. Jakobsen hints that Norn might have been spoken by a few people in the outlying isles in the middle of the nineteenth century. It is not entirely clear what he meant by *Norn*, however – perhaps a heavily Scandinavianised Scots; perhaps a fully functional North Germanic variety – or even whether he was suggesting that Norn was still used as a first language when his informants remembered its being spoken.

Barnes (1998: 21–31; see also 2010) suggests that three separate interpretations of how Scots replaced Norn are possible. The first, which he associates with Jakobsen (1932), Flom (1928–9) and Marwick (1929), was that the Scots element in the Shetland dialect gradually 'swamped' the Scandinavian element; from this point of view, it is difficult to perceive the change in language: over time, the originally Scandinavian structure of the dialect was altered by borrowing of structures from Scots (along with considerable amounts of lexis) to the extent that it became a dialect of Scots with considerable phonological and lexical Norse residual features. Barnes dismisses this view:

> . . . if for no other reason than that the imperceptible melting of one language into another they envisage seems to be without parallel. There is in addition the weakness that none of the three scholars argues a clear case for fusion; all the reader is offered is a series of inexplicit assumptions. Crucial terms such as 'Norn', 'Scots', 'dialect', 'language', etc. are used in a disconcertingly vague manner, to the extent that one is led to doubt whether the writers themselves always knew precisely what they had in mind (Barnes 1998: 23)

While many of Barnes' points are well made, particularly since at least two of the scholars – Jakobsen and Marwick – were primarily lexicographers, it is worth noting that such a 'melting' *is* known elsewhere in the world; particularly in the famous case of Michif, discussed in Chapter 5, although it is certainly true that this particular language merger cannot be described as 'imperceptible', at least in terms of its speakers' attitudes. Barnes also appears to ignore the fact that the language contact which existed in Shetland was between languages which were quite close relatives.

The second viewpoint Barnes discusses is that of Rendboe (1984 and 1987). Rendboe interprets the evidence to suggest a brutal takeover by Scots speakers which was met with considerable resistance by the native Shetlanders. Using the 'hints' made by Jakobsen about survival of Norn in some areas of Shetland well into the nineteenth century, mentioned above, he makes a case for the 'purity' of the Norn recorded by Jakobsen in 1890s, as being used by people who had heard – perhaps even used – Norn in their early years. As Barnes (1998: 23–4) puts it, '[whilst] it must be said Rendboe does his best to demonstrate the purity of Norn at different stages of its existence . . . the evidence he adduces can often be shown to point in precisely the opposite direction'.

I make no claims to being an expert on the dialectology of the west Norse diaspora, as undoubtedly Rendboe is. But I would take Barnes' argument further. A number of the short 'conversational fragments' which Jakobsen recorded can be explained – with, it has to be stressed, considerable goodwill – as being systemically grammatical. For example:

> Jarta, bodena komena ro'ntəna Komba, 'My heart, the boat has come round "de Kaim" ["the Comb", a distinctive rock formation]'

which Rendboe gives as equivalent to Nynorsk,

> Hjarta, båten er komen rundt om Komba,

although even in this example there seems to be at least one extra suffix present in the Norn, without the benefit of an elision argument being possible.

But there are many such verses which do not make anything but the barest of semantic rather than rhythmic sense: for example, the following riddle, recorded by Jakobsen in northern Yell, which the speaker could not translate, but knew had the answer 'flakes of snow being melted in the sun' (Jakobsen 1932: cvii):

> flɔkəra flūra *fedderless*,
> ut kɔm modərə häŋa*less*,
> häŋæ beŋæ gōra*less*

(with last line apparently lost: the forms in italics are Scots rather than Norn).

It is also illustrative that a number of the verses (or versions thereof) have been reinterpreted according to Scots lexical and semantic models, for instance:

> White fool fedderless,
> ut kɔm modərə häŋtaless,
> sotsa gōa benderless
> and plucked awa White fool fedderless,

which, with a knowledge of both languages, is just about comprehensible (a translation would be roughly along the lines of 'White bird [flock of birds] featherless, out came a handless mother which also went without legs, and plucked away white bird featherless'). How can a language both be 'pure' and not (fully, if at all) understood by its speakers? The rather 'distorted' state of most Norn recorded during the crucial eighteenth and nineteenth centuries seems to imply not the survival of a living, 'natural', language, but rather a barely remembered and understood cultural item.

The third interpretation which Barnes cites – and the one he seems to support most – is that of Smith (Smith, B. 1990 and 1996), who perceived the Shetlanders as, in the course of the seventeenth and early eighteenth centuries, losing their earlier multilingual and multicultural identity, largely due to the end of the boom in fishing and whaling discussed above, with the concomitant rise of Scots in speech and English in writing. What followed, Barnes argues, was a quite normal example of language shift, with the perception among speakers of Norn that Scots varying in relation to domain and register with English was 'the language of the future', a view which eventually led to what Fishman terms the breach of intergenerational transfer of the mother tongue. Rejecting Rendboe's 'late date' hypothesis for the death of Norn, Barnes (1998: 26) favours the end of the eighteenth century for when '... the last native speakers (those whose first language had been Norn) went to the grave'.

While this sifting of the evidence does seem the most reasonable, there are a number of problems with complete acceptance of this viewpoint. If the Scots to English continuum during this crucial period was so attractive to native speakers of Norn, why is it that, some eighty or ninety years after Norn stopped being effectively anyone's mother tongue, Jakobsen could have recorded so much 'Norn', which was often very willingly and proudly offered? Of course, as we have seen, what language ideologies a group of people or a community claim to espouse, and what associations speakers actually have for particular varieties, may often be diametrically opposed. This is easier to contain within one language, however, rather than in the transfer from one language to another.

This is a conundrum: how can a language continue to be given voice when it has no native speakers?

One way to move forward is by returning to Sasse's (1992) theoretical model discussed in the last chapter. There are a number of points in this model where we might pause and reflect in relation to the death of Norn. Certainly, there are elements, such as 'increase of collective bilingualism because of restriction of domains', which appear to be in concord with Smith and Barnes' views on the language's decline. Another is 'negative attitude towards A'. To what extent can such negative attitudes be found in Shetland at the time? Of course we are, as ever, at the mercy of what has come down to us. Nevertheless, some evidence of such views can be found, at least from Rendboe's viewpoint, in the views expressed by middle class commentators in the eighteenth century that the use of Norn in their circles was quite 'worn out', no longer in fashion. But is this the whole story? At this point it is worth concentrating on one of the most famous fragments of late Norn (in Jakobsen's transliteration):

> De vaar e (vera) gooa tee,
> 'when' sona min 'guid to' Kaadanes:
> haayn kaayn ca' *russa* 'mare,'
> haayn kaayn ca' *bigg* 'bere'
> haayn kaayn ca' *eld* 'fire'
> haayn kaayn ca' *klovandi* 'taings'
> 'That was a good time, when my son went to Caithness: he can call *russa* 'mare', he can call *bigg* 'bere' [a form of barley], he can call *eld* 'fire', he can call *klovandi* 'taings' [tongs]' [my translation].

At face value, this looks like it is hymning the praises of Scots as the language of the future. It might, however, be a good example of what is termed *skyimpin* in Shetland Scots (Schei 1988: 68): a lampooning of externally fashionable values frowned upon by the in-group. Moreover, modern Shetlanders – at least until the last generation – have been particularly careful to avoid *knappin* (Melchers 1985), speaking like a *sooth-moother*. Many fieldworkers – from Jakobsen on – have remarked on the awareness among Shetlanders of at least some of the Scandinavian elements in their present dialect. Of course we have to accept that a post-Romantic and, at least in recent years, relatively affluent Shetland is inevitably very different from the demoralised archipelago of two hundred years ago. Nevertheless, there must have been some 'national' feeling associated with the language to encourage Shetlanders from all over the islands to remember sometimes quite lengthy pieces of Norn which they could not understand – and which, by the end of the nineteenth century, the people who taught them probably did not understand either. We could therefore claim that two competing language ideologies – one overt, the other covert, with the former dominant – existed in Shetland during the period.

A partial explanation for this continuation can also be found towards the end of Sasse's model: after the 'end of regular communication in A' there is 'use of residue knowledge for specialized purposes = ritual, group identification, joke secret [sic] language'. Might this not be what we have in the recording of Norn by both Low and Jakobsen? This seems to be connected by Sasse with 'residue, substratum knowledge, continuation of a T_A dialect' (where T_A is a variety of the target language affected by the abandoned language) which, again, is more likely to be what lies behind a great deal of the 'word-list' recorded by Low on Foula in the late eighteenth century and discussed by Rendboe, rather than the entire survival of a language.

But why should this residue knowledge have survived so long in Shetland? As we have already touched upon, it is important to note that Scots and Norn, being Germanic varieties, have much in common with each other, amplified by the former's being descended from a close secondary Norse contact dialect in the early Middle Ages, although, of course, there would have been little or no chance of immediate mutual comprehension. We can see mixing of this type in the examples we have already considered. This, in its more potent Scots-Norn contact phenomenon role, could be seen as having a performative side to it – the 'ritual' aspect discussed by Sasse. A seriously intended attempt at the expression of Shetland identity may be found in the use of half-understood, but well-remembered, phrases. It cannot be ruled out, in fact, that, even in the eighteenth century, some Shetlanders had learned to 'package' their culture, to turn it into a heritage item.

A further possible spur can be found in the well-reported taboo-avoidance language of Shetland fishermen. Given the dangerous nature of their trade, taboo-avoidance strategies are common to fishing communities around the world, as are, to a considerable extent, those taboo subjects for which avoidance terms must be used. What is striking, however, is the level of Norn vocabulary used by Scots-speaking Shetland fishermen well into living memory to avoid taboo topics. A mouse was, for instance, *bohonnin*, 'good dog' (Fenton 1968–9: 119 and 1978), which includes a fossilised example of the typically North Germanic enclitic definite particle (Knooihuizen 2007).

This taboo-avoidance argument might seem special pleading. How could the argot of one occupation affect the language use of an entire community? It must be borne in mind that, in an environment like Shetland, there must have been very few people – particularly among the descendants of recent Norn speakers, given the social stratification of the islands – who were not intimately connected with the fishery. Therefore, knowledge of words not part of the common Scots/Norn lexis was perpetuated, and fed into the long-term retention of elements of the 'lost' language.

In some ways this discussion asks more questions than it answers, however. One of the most central is: what happens to ethnic identity when a language dies? If the abandoned language shares much in common with the replacement target language, is it possible for a 'half-life' to ensue, where speakers who do not have a language as an active part of their repertoire are still able to produce something which sounds – at least to an external ear – like a fair approximation to the ancestral language? The Norn phrases recorded in the eighteenth and particularly nineteenth centuries probably represent an attempt to express a Shetland or 'local' identity. Despite this, there was obviously a point where the meaning of what was being said had been so thoroughly garbled that intergenerational transfer was no longer possible. In places where traditional ways of life persisted, however, this complete cessation may have occurred two – possibly even three – generations after the language ceased having native speakers.

To what extent, then, can we say that the modern Scots dialects of Shetland have been affected by the long-term presence of Norn in the same relatively circumscribed area? As we have seen, Scots had a long-term presence in the islands, from the fifteenth century on at least. During this period these Scots speakers and their descendants assumed considerable power, political and economic, even if, as we assume, many Scots speakers and their descendants were employed in rather more menial ways. The latter, while sharing in some of the reflected force of their better heeled compatriots, were more likely to come into contact with the indigenous, Norn-speaking, peasantry. This suggests, perhaps, that their linguistic influence would over this period have been most effective in reaching the largest number of people. Beyond a considerable number of loanwords, often central to the everyday experience of Shetlanders well into the twentieth century, some phonological and morphosyntactic features of Shetland Scots have been argued to be of Norn origin. These include:

1. the use of /t/ and /d/ for Central Scots /θ/ and /ð/, in particular in initial and medial position
2. *possibly* the survival of Norwegian vowel length in some words (van Leyden 2004)
3. the use of *be* in perfective constructions along the lines of *I am worked here for twinty year* (Pavlenko 1997; although this construction is occasionally found elsewhere in the English-speaking world: Yerastov 2010)
4. the continuing use of *du* as an intimate second person singular pronoun, just as is the case in the modern North Germanic languages (although, as we have already noted, this form also used to be present in earlier varieties of many dialects of Scots; moreover, the object form is not North Germanic – something along the lines of *deg, dek* or *dej*, perhaps; instead, it is the equivalent of English *thee*, with the expected Shetland sound change in the first consonant)
5. the survival of grammatical gender through the use of male and female pronouns to refer to inanimate objects and states (although it would have to be noted that this use is not consistent – in the way a healthy grammatical gender system has to be – and could also be interpreted as an extension of the occasional English language practice of referring to modes of transport – ships in particular – using female pronouns).

As can be seen, therefore, there are often reasonable language internal explanations for why a particular form or structure is realised in the dialect. Indeed the only example of potential Norn influence which is probably entirely due to the influence of Norn is probably example one. That does not mean, however, that at least some of the other examples suggested did not come into being through the contact, with the presence of similar features in the two source languages encouraging the survival or development of features which might otherwise have slipped entirely from the dialect. In a sense this is at the heart of koineisation.

One other point might be made, however. The survival of some of these koine-produced forms might be seen as expressing local identity. With example one, for instance, there would have been a generation of Norn speakers who could not pronounce interdental fricatives. The survival of the plosive pronunciation now, when all Shetlanders are able to speak Scottish Standard English, must be associated therefore with local identity. Indeed, since it is a feature which all Shetlanders share, it can be assumed that Shetlanders whose first tongue was Scots must have chosen to acquire the local feature as a marker of group solidarity (see Thomason and Kaufman 1988:41 for a discussion of these features).

This point leads us on to the final concern of this section: how did what is now Shetland Scots come into being?

6.3.3.3 Historical representations of Shetland dialect

Scots has been spoken on Shetland since at least the sixteenth century (and probably significantly before). Unfortunately, early representations of the dialect are not forthcoming. When local records were written in Scots (rather than a Dano-Norwegian chancery variety with some Norn phonological influence), it was the emerging metropolitan near standard variety, in a largely legal context, which was used, as the documents in Ballantyne and Smith (1994 and 1999) demonstrate. We have to turn, therefore, to reports on language use by visitors to the island. In the seventeenth and eighteenth century reports collected by Flinn (1989) and others, little is said about language, except that many people still speak 'Danish' and that the local Scots variety is less 'provincial' than that found on the Scottish mainland, suggesting a variety somewhat more like Standard English than many Scots varieties were. There are also occasions, such as that reported by the Rev. George Low (whom we have met before) on his visit to Foula in 1774, where the local dialect represented has left little if any remnants in any modern Shetland dialect:

> Here the Pronunciation differs a good deal from the rest of Schetland, both in the tone and manner, and pronouncing particular words. To a man they misplace the aspirate, affixing it where it should not be, and leaving it out where it should, *e.g.*, one of the most sagacious of the natives was teaching his son to read the Bible, and to know the numbers of the Psalms; he told the boy the Vorty'th and Zaxt Z'am, XLVI, was a Hex, a Hell, a Hu, and a Hi. (Low 1879: 104–5)

The initial voicing of fricatives and the apparently variable use of /h/ described are (with the exception of the Black Isle dialect for the latter feature) foreign to Scots varieties. Given how many Dutch and Low German speakers there were in Shetland in the early modern period and the documentary evidence that at least locals in the area around what is now Lerwick spoke Dutch, influence from these languages might be possible; it is also possible that sailors from parts of England where these phenomena were common visited Shetland on their way to the Arctic. There is a danger, however, of these explanations being after the fact; indeed, of their being special pleading (although this does not mean that these phenomena might not contribute to the development of such a variety). Bearing in mind the lack of much evidence in the period, it might very tentatively be suggested that descriptions of this type appear analogous to the extreme variability described by Trudgill in the first generation of native-born Pakeha New Zealanders. If that is the case, then it might tell us a considerable amount about what was going on linguistically at the time, in particular in a place like Foula where, as we have seen, Low met people who could recite a considerable amount of Norn, even if they could not fully understand it.

Other evidence from the later eighteenth century continues the argument that Shetland speakers of Scots were generally less Scots in their speech than mainland Scots speakers were. One of the examples from the first *Statistical Account of Scotland*, a late eighteenth-century Scotland-wide report, normally by the local Church of Scotland ministers, on the business and life of parishes, often including language use (Millar 2000b and 2003), part of the report from Delting on the Mainland of Shetland, can stand for all:

> The language is the same as in the Continent of Scotland. The inhabitants, however, have less of a provincial brogue than many parts of North Britain. (Sinclair 1978: 424)

Similar evidence of relatively 'thin' dialect can be gained from Walter Scott's *The Pirate*, set mainly in the southern parts of the Mainland of Shetland and based upon fieldwork he had carried out in the islands in 1814 (Scott 1822 [2001]: 393–5). Again, the lack of density of the dialect is emphasised. Scott had a particularly good ear for language use (Tulloch 1980), so it is noteworthy that, in distinction to the Scots-speaking immigrants into Shetland depicted in the novel, the Shetlanders speak a somewhat 'colourless' dialect.

Very different to these descriptions is one reported by Christopher Thomson, travelling north on a Hull whaler in 1820. Describing a 'whiskey shop' in Lerwick, he says:

> Around the glimmer, in the ingle, were seated a troop of crones, attired in course grey Woolsey petticoats; over their heads was thrown a dark plaid, just shewing their brown profiles; some of them were knitting; each had a short black pipe, blowing away their ''bacca' and chattering in broad Gaelic. (Flinn 1989: 77)

It is possible that Gaelic was actually spoken by a small minority of Lerwick residents at the time: there was some contact with the west coast of Scotland through the herring fishery, for instance. Much more likely, however, is that Thomson did not recognise the local Scots dialect as a close relative of his native (possibly northern) English dialect. He may have been singularly inept linguistically; even if that were the case, however, it still raises issues with this evidence in relation to the numerous statements about the generally comprehensible nature of Shetland dialects in the immediately preceding period. What is at work here?

In the following year, Captain James Vetch of the Royal Engineers visited Foula, in relation to the mapping of the island for the Ordnance Survey. He observes that

> ... probably the omission of native names to minute parts will not be regretted, as many of them can only be pronounced by a native, of which the *Snuke* is an instance, as it is somewhat difficult to say whether the concluding consonant should be *k*, *g*, or *d*, though I think the *k* comes considerably the nearest. (Flinn 1989: 130)

These comments appear to suggest something like lenition, a feature not strongly associated with either the Scots or Norn input (unless there was considerable south-west Norwegian or Danish influence, the latter being particularly unlikely on such a remote island). Like the other example, also collected on Foula, from some 40 years earlier, where initial voicing of fricatives is described, these are highly distinctive developments which have had little or no effect on the present-day Shetland dialects – including that of Foula. They can therefore be analysed, as has already been suggested, as examples of the large-scale variation found in the earliest forms of a new variety.

Little more than ten years later, however, in 1832, Edward Charlton, an eighteen-year-old medical student from Newcastle, makes the following comment:

> I little thought that this day would be one ever-remembered with terror in Shetland, and that da grit gale, as it has always since been termed, was then dealing such destruction among the poor Shetland fishermen. (Flinn 1989: 184)

Here Shetland dialect as we now understand it is represented without comment, merely as an example of 'local colour'. As the nineteenth century drew on, moreover, it becomes apparent to an observer that this stability with a set of varieties essentially close to what we have now has become the norm (as a consultation of Tudoe 1883 demonstrates). By this point we are in the period observed by Jakobsen and, somewhat later, the period whose language was enshrined in the poetry of Vagaland (T.A.Robertson, 1903–73).

6.3.3.4 Discussion

Although we have brought together a considerable amount of information about earlier forms of Shetland Scots, it is self-evident that our understanding of what happened is decidedly patchy and inevitably open to interpretation. Nevertheless, it *is* possible to put together a narrative which seems to suit both the evidence we have and our theoretical understanding of new dialect formation and language change due to language shift.

As we have seen in the preceding sections, Scots-speaking settlers moved into Shetland from a variety of different parts of Scotland, although there was probably a predominance of east central speakers. In this period – reaching up to at least the middle of the eighteenth century – a new variety came into being, influenced by all inputs but particularly by the majority usage. It appears to have been less 'dialectal' than mainland Scottish dialects, perhaps because of the relatively loose ties its speakers shared in their new environment. We should also bear in mind the influence which the Standard English of Church and State must have had when other ties were less strong. This is reminiscent of the state of early American English discussed in Chapter 4. This variety is not wholly the ancestor of present day Shetland Scots, however.

Of course throughout this period Norn continued to be spoken. Reports suggest that there was considerable bilingualism – quite probably in both directions, although it is likely that social realities made Norn speakers more likely to learn Scots than vice versa. It would be very surprising if no features from A entered T during this period; this would have become much more prevalent during the period when speakers of Norn finally and irrevocably shifted to Scots. During this period, considerable variation was possible in the Scots dialects, as seen in the phonological descriptions from Foula. The 'Gaelic' description from the early nineteenth century also suggests that a heavily T$_A$ Norn-influence basilect was also present during this period. As we have already recognised, there is no evidence for this type of dialect today. Why is this the case?

What I would suggest is that the phonological variability on Foula was the result of first-generation variability after language shift. All of the features found in today's Foula dialect were already present in the Scots of locals; the level of variability is considerably greater, however. The basilect variety is, in origin, a contact variety produced by native speakers of Norn. When the final shift to Scots took place, it only survived for a couple of generations in its densest form, but was sufficiently used that, in combination with the original Scots dialects of the islands, more Norn features were incorporated into the mesolectal dialect, the ancestor of all present-day Shetland dialects. There would also originally have been an acrolectal Scots; as elsewhere in the Scots-speaking

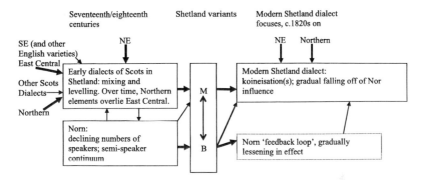

Figure 6.3 sources for, and the development of, Shetland Scots

world, although with different social associations, perhaps, this was replaced by Standard English in the course of the eighteenth century. Throughout this process we can recognise many of Trudgill's benchmarks for the creation of a colonial variety – although it is impossible to decide which inputs are the most influential.

A final input of some importance needs to be mentioned: North East Scots. Although it is likely that people from the north-east of Scotland settled in Shetland from an early period, changes in the economics of the North Sea and North Atlantic world in the nineteenth century, in particular in relation to the herring fishery, led to a greater influence upon Shetland demographically and linguistically from that direction. Although the marked nature of North East Scots in Shetland makes its contribution to modern Shetland Scots rather less obvious than it might be, this influence is considerable and ongoing.

With Mufwene's concept of the *founder principle* in mind, it become quickly apparent that not one but two (potentially three) founder populations had particular influence on the Scots of Shetland. From the Scots side, it can be seen that East Central dialects were at least initially dominant, although North East Scots dialects took on a dominant role in more recent times. This could be said to demonstrate that, particularly in relatively remote areas with low populations, founder effect is not a once-and-for-all event but rather a matter of ongoing influence and measurement. Norn also acts as a founder influence, even if the language was abandoned. As we have already seen, however, elements of identity association in Shetland were connected to Norn despite the shift and a 'feedback loop' was established for elements of survival for at least a century after the language's becoming moribund.

6.4 Conclusion

In this chapter we have considered how new varieties have come into being, how they are similar to each other and also different from each other and what forces may be at work guiding their *drifts* in the post-colonial period. We saw, moreover, that while no one theoretical model matches the experience of these developments completely, a number of them are helpful in interpreting what might actually have been going on when a change took place. It would, perhaps, be interesting to trace a new example of this type of phenomenon. This has, of course, been attempted over the last few decades (Kerswill and Williams 2000 springs to mind); the problem is the high level of literacy and the ease of travel and remote communication which we now have, even in comparison with much of the twentieth century.

Further reading

As with the last chapter, Thomason and Kaufman (1988) remains a central theoretical prop to our understanding of what is going on linguistically in colonial situations. Trudgill (in particular 2004), Mufwene (in particular 2001) and Schneider (2007) are all, in their own ways, brilliant. In particular with the first two scholars' work on this matter, a degree of unpacking is necessary in some of their conclusions.

Some issues to consider

1. Research the history of one English-speaking country or region which has been settled in the last 200 years. Now consider its local English varieties. Can the nature of the variety be related to the history of its speakers? Would you like to rephrase this last question in some way?

2. New Zealanders are often very pleased when people recognise that they are not Australian. People do this largely through listening for highly marked local pronunciations on vowels such as /ɪ/ in words like *chips*. Since pronunciations of this type now act as identity markers for both New Zealanders and outsiders, how can this be squared with Trudgill's theory that new varieties develop largely unconsciously?

3. How far back in time could we push dialect contact and creation

theories? Would it be possible to talk about a Latin colonial variety in Gaul in the last decades of the pre-Christian era or of a colonial West Germanic in Britain in the fifth and sixth centuries? What are the main issues in attempting this?

Notes

1. There is a further complication to this. Both the New Zealand recordings already mentioned and recordings of the speech of Australians born in the late nineteenth century suggest that at least some informants were (variably) rhotic. Trudgill (2010: 146–9) suggests that the lack of full rhoticity in these varieties should be read not as a lack of rhoticity being brought fully-formed from England but rather a propensity for it, a sign of linguistic *drift*. This view is supported by the evidence for rhoticity from well into the twentieth century in largely rural areas in the south-east of England which are now universally non-rhotic.
2. It should be noted that this is *my* interpretation. My impression is that Trudgill would at least be uncomfortable with an explanation which involves personal and societal attitudes and also assumes input from schoolteachers and others on the matter. With the second point these views are understandable. Schoolteachers have probably attempted to correct 'unacceptable' features in their students' language since the profession was first established. The amount of success such campaigns have had is, to be charitable, very limited indeed. But 'frontier' settlements, where there is a great deal of societal movement and anomie, generally have (and, before mass communication had, to an even greater extent), at their heart, lower middle class professionals as authority figures to be emulated – the schoolteacher, the lawyer, the religious minister – whose influence would not have been so great in a situation of long-term settlement, as I have suggested for the development of American English (Millar 2005: 162–4 and Chapter 4 above).
3. Most examples throughout this section are derived from Millar (2008), where this argument is made in greater detail; the corpus upon which it is based is derived from the *Scottish National Dictionary* (Grant and Murison 1929–76), the *Linguistic Atlas of Scotland* (Mather and Speitel 1985), local dictionaries such as Graham 1993; phonological information comes from Johnson 1997 and Millar 2007a; grammatical material from Macafee 2011 and following and Millar 2007a.

7 Some final thoughts

In this book I have attempted to bring together elements of both micro- and macrosociolinguistic theory and analytical methodology with aspects of the historical development of the various dialects of the English language. This is not, as we saw in Chapters 1 and 2, the first time that such an interweaving has been attempted. This book is at least close to being the first to concentrate in depth on particular aspects of this history rather than attempting to paint a broad canvas.

In most ways this cross-fertilisation has worked. Of course the initial doubts about transferring the expectations of sociolinguistic disciplines into other time periods with different cultural norms, as commented upon in Chapter 1 and 2, remain present and are a constant threat to meaningful analysis. This is particularly the case because, even for the relatively recent past, we do not have as much information on the structure of society and how this affected the lives of individuals as we would wish. Coupled with this is the reality that, with a number of exceptions associated with the recording of thieves' argot and other underworld 'patter' (which goes back into the early modern period: Coleman 2004), the language use of those with access to power is likely to be recorded far more often than the language of the poor and powerless. Moreover, literacy affects how language is recorded. Before it becomes widespread, only the language use of the minority is recorded, from which we extrapolate the usage of the whole community. In addition, because of standardisation, which featured so strongly in this book, we have fewer ways of telling how people actually spoke as literacy became the norm in the nineteenth century, so powerful are centripetal forces, at least until dialectology became methodologically potent and the invention of portable recording devices meant that essentially neutral evidence could be analysed and retained.

In the case of the history of English it is certainly true that linguistic evidence going back as far as the eighth century is available. We can never be entirely sure, however, to what extent what we have is representative. We are very much at the mercy of what has survived. The language of the *Peterborough Chronicle* continuations is a case in point. The linguistic evidence is unique and useful. But to what extent can we be sure that the people involved were not linguistically eccentric, given that choosing to continue the *Chronicle* was in itself a somewhat eccentric act? On this occasion we can be fairly certain that the evidence supplied by the continuators merely encapsulates a series of changes which are all readily demonstrated by other texts from across England at a variety of times. But with the discussion of the survival of Brittonic dialects in lowland Britain and their effects upon English in the Old English period, discussed in Chapter 5, the possibility of having wildly different interpretations of the same material is considerable. This naturally lends itself to conclusions which may be based as much on personal views as on what evidence there is. This is a problem which all historical linguists live with on a day-by-day basis. English is a well-documented language historically: working out patterns of change in a language which has rarely if ever been recorded is a much more dangerous (but also admirable) specialisation. And yet people shape their analyses of language change under these circumstances with ability and perseverance.

What this suggests is that, with caution and reinterpretation, it is possible to produce a sociolinguistically informed analysis of specific events or sets of events in the history of the English language. Without wishfully perceiving patterns which are not quite there in the evidence, it is possible to use contemporary sociolinguistic insights in a systematic way in an attempt to explain change in the past. The fact that this is possible tells us something about the nature of sociolinguistics itself: variation implies change; contemporary society cannot be explained without reference to the past. In that sense, an historical interest is in the 'genes' of the central research traditions of the field.

Nevertheless, we need to consider whether a book-length history of the English language as a whole could be produced along these lines. As was discussed in the Foreword, a number of impressive attempts have been made to carry this out. What has held them back, however, is that the historical linearity so necessary to an introductory university course cuts through more profoundly sociolinguistic patterns which transcend eras. It would be most interesting to see whether this book might encourage non-linear courses not just, as is intended here, for advanced students but also lower down the university curriculum.

Another feature is central to what is covered here. There is a great deal that still needs to be done in terms of documenting and explaining change in the English language. My belief is that both micro- and macrosociolinguistic methodologies and analyses provide a profound means of pushing explanation forward. I encourage anyone interested to consider this field as a potential focus for postgraduate research. There is also much to be done in developing historical linguistics in general and the various sub-fields of historical sociolinguistics in particular beyond English. Unlike English, other languages may not yet have received the detailed analysis they deserve.

Further reading

The central historical (micro-)sociolinguistic books, in particular Nevalainen and Raumolin-Brunberg (2003), have been regularly referenced in this book. There is no macrosociolinguistic equivalent, although Millar (2012a) *may* give some sense of the field. A summative volume is certainly overdue.

In this book I have assumed a basic understanding of the patterns of linguistic change. If you would like to research this more thoroughly, a number of excellent historical linguistics textbooks are available. Particularly recommended because of their strong sociolinguistic basis are Campbell (2004) and Millar (2007b).

References

Aitken, A. J. (1979), 'Scottish Speech: a Historical View with Special Reference to the Standard English of Scotland', in Aitken and McArthur (1979), pp. 85–118.

Aitken, A. J. (1992), 'Scottish English', in McArthur (1992), pp. 903–5.

Aitken, A. J. and T. McArthur (eds) (1979), *Languages of Scotland*, Edinburgh: W. and R. Chambers.

Algeo, John (ed.) (2001), *The Cambridge History of the English Language*, Vol. VI. *English in North America*, Cambridge: Cambridge University Press.

Angle, Stephen C. (2002), *Human rights and Chinese thought: a cross-cultural inquiry*, Cambridge: Cambridge University Press.

Bakker, Peter (1997), *A language of our own: the genesis of the Canadian Métis*, Oxford: Oxford University Press.

Ballantyne, John H. and Brian Smith (eds) (1994), *Shetland Documents 1580–1611*, Lerwick: Shetland Islands Council and The Shetland Times.

Ballantyne, John H. and Brian Smith (eds) (1999), *Shetland Documents 1195–1579*, Lerwick: Shetland Islands Council and The Shetland Times.

Barnes, Michael P. (1998), *The Norn Language of Shetland and Orkney*, Lerwick: The Shetland Times.

Barnes, Michael P. (2010), 'The Study of Norn', in Millar (2010b), pp. 26–47.

Baugh, Albert C. and Thomas Cable (1993), *A History of the English Language*, 4th edn, London: Routledge.

Beal, Joan C. (1999), *English pronunciation in the eighteenth century: Thomas Spence's Grand Repository of the English Language*, Oxford: Clarendon Press.

Beal, Joan C. (2004), *English in Modern Times 1700–1945*, London: Arnold.

Bebbington, D. W. (1989), *Evangelicalism in Modern Britain: A History from the 1730s to the 1980s*, London: Unwin Hyman.

Bennett, David H. (1988), *The Party of Fear: From Nativist Movements to the New Right in American History*, Chapel Hill, NC: The University of North Carolina Press.

Bennett, Henry Stanley (1932), *The Pastons and their England: Studies in an Age of Transition*, Cambridge: Cambridge University Press.

Benskin, Michael (1997), Review of Wright (1996), *Medium Ævum 66*, pp. 133–5.

Bex, Tony and Richard J. Watts (eds) (1999), *Standard English: The Widening Debate*, London: Routledge.

Bonfiglio, Thomas Paul (2002), *Race and the Rise of Standard American*, Berlin: Mouton de Gruyter.

Bourdieu, Pierre (1986), 'The Forms of Capital', in Richardson (1986), pp. 241–58.

Bragg, Melvyn (2004), *The Adventure of English*, 2nd edn, London: Sceptre.

Brenzinger, Matthias (ed.) (1992), *Language Death. Factual and Theoretical Explorations with Special Reference to East Africa*, Berlin: Mouton de Gruyter.

Britain, David (1997), 'Dialect contact and phonological reallocation: "Canadian Raising" in the English Fens', *Language in Society* 26, pp. 15–46.

Britnell, R. H. (1993), *The Commercialisation of English Society, 1000–1500*, Cambridge: Cambridge University Press.

Campbell, Lyle (2004), *Historical Linguistics*, Edinburgh: Edinburgh University Press.

Cameron, Deborah (1995), *Verbal Hygiene*, London: Routledge.

Chambers, J. K. (2009), *Sociolinguistic Theory*, 2nd edn, Chichester: Wiley-Blackwell.

Chambers, J. K. and Peter Trudgill (1998), *Dialectology*, Cambridge: Cambridge University Press.

Chambers, R. W. (1957), *On the Continuity of English Prose from Alfred to More and his School: An Extract from the Introduction to Nicholas Harpsfields Life of Sir Thomas More*, Oxford: Oxford University Press.

Cheshire, Jenny (1982), *Variation in an English Dialect: A Sociolinguistic Study*, Cambridge: Cambridge University Press.

Chibnall, Marjorie (2000), *The Normans*, Oxford: Blackwell.

Claridge, Claudia and Merja Kytö (2010), 'Non-standard language in earlier English', in Hickey (2010), pp. 15–42.

Coleman, Julie (2004), *A History of Cant and Slang Dictionaries*, Vol. 1, 1567–1784, Oxford: Oxford University Press.

Crowley, Tony (1996), *Language in History: Theories and Texts*, London: Routledge.

Crowley, Tony (1999), 'Curiouser and curiouser: falling standards in the Standard English debate', in Bex and Watts (1999), pp. 271–82.

Crowley, Tony (2003), *Standard English and the Politics of Language*, Basingstoke: Palgrave Macmillan.

Crystal, David (2006), *The Fight for English: How Language Pundits Ate, Shot, and Left*, Oxford: Oxford University Press.

Davis, Norman (1952), 'A Paston Hand', *Review of English Studies* 3, pp. 209–21.

Denison, David (1993), *English Historical Syntax*, London: Longman.

Denison, Norman (1977), 'Language Death or Language Suicide', *International Journal of the Sociology of Language* 12, pp. 13–22.

Devitt, A. J. (1989), *Standardizing Written English: Diffusion in the Case of Scotland*, Cambridge: Cambridge University Press.

Dobson, E. J. (1968), *English Pronunciation 1500–1700*, 2 vols, 2nd edn, Oxford: Clarendon Press.

Dominigue, Nicole Z. (1977), 'Middle English: Another Creole?', *Journal of Creole Studies* 1, pp. 89–100.

Donaldson, Gordon (1983), 'The Scots settlement in Shetland', in Withrington (1983), pp. 8–19.

Dorian, Nancy (1981), *Language Death: the Life Cycle of a Scottish Gaelic Dialect*, Philadelphia: University of Pennsylvania.

Dossena, Marina (2005), *Scotticisms in grammar and vocabulary: 'Like runes upon a standin' stane?'*, Edinburgh: John Donald.

Dossena, Marina and Charles Jones (eds) (2003), *Insights into Late Modern English*, Bern: Peter Lang.

Dziubalska-Kołaczyk, Katarzyna and Joanna Przedlacka (eds) (2008), *English Pronunciation Models: A Changing Scene*, Bern: Peter Lang.

Eckert, Penelope (2000), *Linguistic Variation as Social Practice*, Oxford: Blackwell.

Eckert, Penelope (2005), 'Variation, convention, and social meaning'. Paper presented at the Annual Meeting of the Linguistic Society of America, Oakland, California, 7 January 2005. Downloaded from http://www.just inecassell.com/discourse09/readings/EckertLSA2005.pdf (accessed 26 July 2011).

Ekwall, E. (1956), *Studies on the Population of Medieval London*, Stockholm: Almqvist & Wiksell.

Ejerhed, E. and I. Henrysson (eds) (1980), *Tvåspråkighet: Föredrag från tredje nordiska tvåspråkighetssymposiet 4–5 juni 1980, Umeå universitet*, Umeå: Umeå University.

Farrell, R. T. (1982), *The Vikings*, London and Chichester: Phillimore.

Fennell, Barbara A. (2001), *A History of English: A Sociolinguistic Approach*, Oxford: Blackwell.

Fenton, Alexander (1968–9), 'The Tabu Language of the Fishermen of Orkney and Shetland', *Ethnologia Europaea* 2–3, pp. 118–22.

Fenton, Alexander (1978), *The Northern Isles: Orkney and Shetland*, Edinburgh: Donald.

Ferguson, Charles (1959), 'Diglossia', *Word* 15, pp. 325–40.

Fernandez, Francisco, Miguel Fuster and Juan José Calvo (eds) (1994), *Historical Linguistics 1992*, Amsterdam: John Benjamins.

Filppula, Markku, Juhani Klemola and Heli Paulasto (2008), *English and Celtic in Contact*, London: Routledge.

Finegan, Edward (1998), 'English Grammar and Usage', in Romaine (1998), pp. 536–88.

Finkelberg, Margalit (2005), *Greeks and Pre-Greeks: Aegean Prehistory and Greek Heroic Tradition*, Cambridge: Cambridge University Press.

Fisher, John H. (1996), *The Emergence of Standard English*, Lexington, KY: University Press of Kentucky.

Fisher, John H. (2001), 'British and American, Continuity and Divergence', in Algeo (2001), pp. 59–85.

Fisiak, Jacek (ed.) (2002), *Studies in English Historical Linguistics and Philology. A Festschrift for Akio Oizumi*, Bern: Lang.

Fishman, Joshua A. (1967), 'Bilingualism with and without diglossia; diglossia with and without bilingualism', *Journal of Social Issues* 23, pp. 29–38.

Fishman, Joshua A. (1991), *Reversing Language Shift*, Clevedon: Multilingual Matters.

Flinn, Derek (ed.) (1989), *Travellers in a Bygone Shetland: An Anthology*, Edinburgh: Scottish Academic Press.

Flom, George T. (1928–9), 'The transition from Norse to Lowland Scotch in Shetland, 1600–1850. A study of the decay of one language and its influence upon the language that supplanted it', *Saga Book of the Viking Society* 10, pp. 145–64.

Franklin, Benjamin (1961), *The Papers of Benjamin Franklin*, Vol. 4, ed. Leonard W. Labaree, New Haven: Yale University Press.

Franzen, Christine (1991), *The Tremulous Hand of Worcester: A Study of Old English in the Thirteenth Century*, Oxford: Clarendon Press.

Gal, Susan (1979), *Language Shift: Social Determinants of Linguistic Change in Bilingual Austria*, New York: Academic Press.

Gienapp, William E. (2002), *Abraham Lincoln and Civil War America: A Biography*, Oxford: Oxford University Press.

Giles, Howard, Justine Coupland and Nikolas Coupland (1991), *Contexts of Accommodation: Developments in Applied Sociolinguistics*, Cambridge and Paris: Cambridge University Press and Editions de la Maison des Sciences de l'Homme.

Gneuss, Helmut (1972), 'The origin of Standard Old English and Æthelwold's school at Winchester', *Anglo-Saxon England* 1, pp. 63–83.

Gneuss, Helmut (1996), *Language and History in Early England*, Aldershot: Variorum.

Godden, Malcolm, Douglas Gray and Terry Hoad (eds) (1994), *From Anglo-Saxon to Early Middle English. Studies Presented to E. G. Stanley*, Oxford: Clarendon Press.

Gordon, Elizabeth, Lyle Campbell, Jennifer Hay, Margaret Maclagan, Andrea Sudbury and Peter Trudgill (2004), *New Zealand English: Its Origins and Evolution*, Cambridge: Cambridge University Press.

Görlach, Manfred (ed.) (1985), *Focus on: Scotland*, Amsterdam: Benjamins.

Görlach, Manfred (1999), *English in Nineteenth-Century England: An Introduction*, Cambridge: Cambridge University Press.

Görlach, Manfred (2001), *Eighteenth-Century English*, Heidelberg: Universitätsverlag C. Winter.

Graddol, David (ed.) (2007), *Changing English*, Abingdon: Routledge, in association with the Open University.

Graddol, David, Dick Leith and Joan Swann (eds) (1996), *English: history, diversity and change*, London: Routledge.

Graham, John J. (1993), *The Shetland Dictionary*, 3rd edn, Lerwick: The Shetland Times.

Grant, William and David D. Murison (eds) (1929–76), *The Scottish National Dictionary*, Edinburgh: Scottish National Dictionary Association.

Gumperz, John J. and Robert Wilson (1971), 'Convergence and creolization: a case from the Indo-Aryan/Dravidian border', in Hymes (1971), pp. 151–67.

Haugen, Einar (1962), 'Schizoglossia and the linguistic norm', in Woodworth and DiPietro (1962), pp. 63–9.

Hellinga, L. (1977), 'The Malory Manuscript and Caxton', *British Library Journal* 3, pp. 91–101.

Hernández-Campoy, J. M. and J. C. Conde-Silvestre (1999), 'The social diffusion of linguistic innovation in fifteenth century England: chancery spellings in private correspondence', *Cuadernos de Filología Inglesa* 8, pp. 251–74.

Hickey, Raymond (2004a), 'Dialects of English and their transportation', in Hickey (2004), pp. 33–58.

Hickey, Raymond (ed.) (2004b), *Legacies of colonial English: Studies in Transported Dialects*, Cambridge: Cambridge University Press.

Hickey, Raymond (ed.) (2010), *Varieties of English in Writing: The Written Word as Linguistic Evidence*, Amsterdam: John Benjamins.

Higham, Nicholas (ed.) (2007), *Britons in Anglo-Saxon England*, Woodbridge: Boydell and Brewer.

Hindle, Steve (2000), *The State and Social Change in Early Modern England, 1550–1640*, Basingstoke: Macmillan.

Hofstetter, Walter (1987), *Winchester und der spätaltenglische Sprachgebrauch*, Munich: Fink.

Hofstetter, Walter (1988), 'Winchester and the standardization of Old English vocabulary', *Anglo-Saxon England* 17, pp. 139–61.

Hogg, Richard and David Denison (eds) (2008), *A History of the English Language*, Cambridge: Cambridge University Press.

Honey, John (1991), *Does Accent Matter? The Pygmalion factor*, 2nd edn, London: Faber and Faber.

Hope, Jonathan (2000), 'Rats, bats, sparrows and dogs: biology, linguistics and the nature of Standard English', in Wright (2000), pp. 49–56.

Hopkins, Eric (2000), *Industrialisation and Society: A Social History, 1830–1951*, London: Routledge.

Hornsby, Michael (2010), 'From the periphery to the centre: recent debates on the place of Breton (and other regional languages) in the French Republic', in Millar (2010a), pp. 171–97.

Horobin, Simon (2007), *Chaucer's Language*, Basingstoke: Palgrave Macmillan.

Howlett, David R. (1996), *The English Origins of Old French Literature*, Blackrock, Co. Dublin: Four Courts Press.

Humphrys, John (2004), *Lost For Words: The Mangling And Manipulating Of The English Language*, London: Hodder and Stoughton.

Hymes, Dell (ed.) (1971), *Pidginization and Creolisation of Languages: Proceedings of a conference held at the University of the West Indies, Mona, Jamaica, April 1968*, Cambridge: Cambridge University Press.

Jack, G. B. (1979), 'Archaizing in the Nero Version of the *Ancrene Wisse*', *Neuphilologische Mitteilungen* 80, pp. 325–6.

Jackson, Kenneth (1953), *Language and History in Early Britain: A Chronological*

Survey of the Brittonic Languages First to Twelfth Century AD, Edinburgh: Edinburgh University Press.

Jakobsen, Jakob, (1932), *An Etymological Dictionary of the Norn Language in Shetland*, 2 vols, London: David Nutt; Copenhagen: Vilhelm Prior.

Johansson, S. and B. Tysdahl (eds) (1981), *Papers from the First Nordic Conference for English Studies, Oslo, 17–19 September 1980, Oslo*, Oslo: University of Oslo, Institute of English Studies.

Johnson, Paul (1997), 'Regional variation', in Jones (1997), pp. 433–513.

Jones, Charles (1967a), 'The Functional Motivation of Linguistic Change', *English Studies* 48, pp. 97–111.

Jones, Charles (1967b), 'The Grammatical Category of Gender in early Middle English', *English Studies* 48, pp. 289–305.

Jones, Charles (1988), *Grammatical Gender in English 950–1250*, London: Croom Helm.

Jones, Charles (ed.) (1997), *The Edinburgh History of the Scots Language*, Edinburgh: Edinburgh University Press.

Joseph, John Earl (1987), *Eloquence and Power*, London: Frances Pinter.

Joshel, Sandra R. (2010), *Slavery in the Roman World*, Cambridge: Cambridge University Press.

Kastovsky, Dieter and Gero Bauer (eds) (1988), *Luick Revisited*, Tübingen: Narr.

Kastovsky, Dieter and Arthur Mettinger (eds) (2000), *The History of English in a Social Context: A Contribution to Historical Sociolinguistics*, Berlin: Mouton de Gruyter.

Katz, Dovid (2004), *Words on Fire: The Unfinished Story of Yiddish*, New York: Basic Books.

Kay, Christian J., Carole Hough and Irené Wotherspoon (eds) (2004), *New Perspectives on English Historical Linguistics*, Volume II, *Lexis and Transmission*, Amsterdam: John Benjamins.

Keene, Derek (2000), 'Metropolitan values: migration, mobility and cultural norms, London 1100–1700', in Wright (2000), pp. 93–114.

Keller, Rudi (1994), *On Language Change: The Invisible Hand in Language*, trans. Brigitte Nerlich, London: Routledge.

Kerswill, Paul (1994), *Dialect Convergence: Rural Speech in Urban Norway*, Oxford: Clarendon Press.

Kerswill, Paul and Ann Williams (2000), 'Creating a New Town koiné: Children and language change in Milton Keynes', *Language in Society* 29, pp. 65–115.

Kloss, Heinz (1967), '"Abstand Languages" and "Ausbau Languages"', *Anthropological Linguistics* 9, pp. 29–41.

Kloss, Heinz (1978), *Die Entwicklung neuer germanischer Kultursprachen seit 1800*, 2nd edn, Dusseldorf: Pädagogischer Verlag Schwann.

Knooihuizen, Remco (2007), 'Fishing for words: The taboo language of Shetland fishermen and the dating of Norn language death', *Transactions of the Philological Society* 106, pp. 100–13.

Knooihuizen, Remco (2009), 'Shetland Scots as a new dialect: phonetic and phonological considerations', *English Language and Linguistics* 13, pp. 483–501.

Knowles, Gerald (1997), *A cultural history of the English language*, London: Arnold.

Labov, William (1966), *The Social Stratification of English in New York City*, Washington, DC: Center for Applied Linguistics.

Labov, William (1972a), *Language in the Inner City. Studies in the Black English Vernacular*, Philadelphia: University of Pennsylvania Press.

Labov, William (1972b), *Sociolinguistic Patterns*, Philadelphia: University of Pennsylvania Press.

Labov, William (1994), *Principles of Linguistic Change: Social Factors*, Oxford: Blackwell.

Laing, Margaret (ed.) (1989), *Middle English Dialectology: Essays on Some Principles and Problems by Angus McIntosh, M. L. Samuels and Margaret Laing*, Aberdeen: Aberdeen University Press.

Langer, Nils (2001), *Linguistic Purism in Action: How Auxiliary Tun was Stigmatized in Early New High German*, Berlin: Mouton de Gruyter.

Language in Society (2008), 37: 2, pp. 241–80.

Larson, Pier M. (2009), *Ocean of Letters: Language and Creolization in an Indian Ocean Diaspora*, Cambridge: Cambridge University Press.

Lass, Roger (1999a), 'Introduction', in Lass (1999b), pp. 1–12.

Lass, Roger (ed.) (1999b), *The Cambridge History of the English Language*, Vol. III: *1476–1776*, Cambridge: Cambridge University Press.

Leith, Dick (1997), *A social history of English*, 2nd edn, London: Routledge.

Lewis, Geoffrey L. (1999), *The Turkish Language Reform: A Catastrophic Success*, Oxford: Oxford University Press.

Llamas, Carmen and Dominic Watt (eds) (2010), *Language and Identities*, Edinburgh: Edinburgh University Press.

Lodge, R. Anthony (1993), *French: from Dialect to Standard*, London: Routledge.

Low, George (1879), *A Tour through the Islands of Orkney and Schetland, containing hints relative to their Ancient, Modern and Natural History collected in 1774*, Kirkwall: William Peace & Son.

Loyn, H. R. (1991), *Anglo-Saxon England and the Norman Conquest*, 2nd edn, Harlow: Longman.

Lucas, Peter J. (1994), 'Towards a Standard Written English? Continuity and change in the orthographic usage of John Capgrave, O.S.A', in Fernandez, Fuster and Calvo (1994), pp. 91–103.

Lumiansky, R. M. (1987), 'Sir Thomas Malory's Le Morte Darthur, 1947–1987: Author, Title, Text', *Speculum* 62, pp. 878–97.

Macafee, Caroline I. (2002), 'A History of Scots to 1700', in: *A Dictionary of the Older Scottish Tongue* 12, xxi–clvi, Oxford: Oxford University Press.

Macafee, Caroline I. (2011) *Characteristics of Non-standard Grammar in Scotland*, http://www.abdn.ac.uk/~enl038/Scotsgrammar.pdf (accessed 9 January 2012).

McArthur, T. (ed.) (1992), *The Oxford Companion to the English Language*, Oxford: Oxford University Press.

McClure, J. Derrick (1979), 'Scots: Its Ranges of Uses', in Aitken and McArthur (1979), pp. 26–48.

McIntosh, Angus and Michael Samuels (1968), 'Prolegomena to a study of medieval Anglo-Irish', *Medium Aevum* 37, pp. 1–11.

McIntosh, Angus, M. L. Samuels and Michael Benskin (1986), *A linguistic atlas of late mediaeval English*, Aberdeen: Aberdeen University Press.

McWhorter, J. H. (2009), 'What else happened to English? A brief for the Celtic hypothesis', *English Language and Linguistics* 13, pp. 63–91.

Malkiel, Yakov (1981), 'Drift, Slope and Slant: Background of, and Variations upon, a Sapirian Theme', *Language* 57, pp. 535–70.

Marwick, Hugh (1929), *The Orkney Norn*, Oxford: Oxford University Press.

Mather, J. Y. and H. H. Speitel (eds) (1985), *The Linguistic Atlas of Scotland, Scots Section Volume 1*, London: Croom Helm.

McCrum, Robert, Robert MacNeil and William Cran (2011), *The Story of English*, 3rd edn, London: Faber and Faber.

Melchers, Gunnel (1985), '"Knappin'", "Proper English", "Modified Scottish": some language attitudes in the Shetland Isles', in Görlach (1985), pp. 86–105.

Meurman-Solin, Anneli (1993), *Variation and Change in Early Scottish Prose: Studies Based on the Helsinki Corpus of Older Scots*, Helsinki: Suomalainen Tiedeakatemia.

Meurman-Solin, Anneli (1997), 'Differentiation and Standardisation in Early Scots', in Jones (1997), pp. 3–23.

Millar, Robert McColl (2000a), *System Collapse, System Rebirth: The Demonstrative Systems of English 900–1350 and the Birth of the Definite Article*, Bern: Peter Lang.

Millar, Robert McColl (2000b), 'Covert and Overt Language Attitudes to the Scots Tongue expressed in the *Statistical accounts of Scotland*', in Kastovsky and Mettinger (2000), pp. 169–98.

Millar, Robert McColl (2002), 'After Jones: some thoughts on the final collapse of the grammatical gender system in English', in Fisiak (2002), pp. 293–306.

Millar, Robert McColl (2003), '"Blind attachment to inveterate custom": language use, language attitude and the rhetoric of improvement in the first *Statistical Account*', in Dossena and Jones (2003), pp. 311–30.

Millar, Robert McColl (2004), 'Kailyard, conservatism and Scots in the *Statistical Account of Scotland*', in Kay, Hough and Wotherspoon (2004), pp. 163–76.

Millar, Robert McColl (2005), *Language, Nation and Power*, Basingstoke: Palgrave Macmillan.

Millar, Robert McColl (2007a), *Northern and Insular Scots*, Edinburgh: Edinburgh University Press.

Millar, Robert McColl (2007b), *Trask's Historical Linguistics*, London: Hodder Arnold.

Millar, Robert McColl (2008), 'The origins and development of Shetland dialect in light of dialect contact theories', *English World-Wide*, 29 (2008), pp. 237–67.

Millar, Robert McColl (ed.) (2010a), *Marginal Dialects: Scotland, Ireland and*

Beyond, Aberdeen: Forum for Research on the Languages of Scotland and Ireland.

Millar, Robert McColl (ed.) (2010b), *Northern Lights, Northern Words: Selected Papers from the FRLSU Conference, Kirkwall 2009*, Aberdeen: Forum for Research on the Languages of Scotland and Ireland.

Millar, Robert McColl (2010c), *Authority and Identity: A Sociolinguistic History of Europe before the Modern Age*, Basingstoke: Palgrave Macmillan.

Millar, Robert McColl (2010d), 'An historical national identity? The case of Scots', in Llamas and Watt (2010), pp. 247–56.

Millar, Robert McColl (2012a), 'Social History and the Sociology of Language', in Hernández-Campoy and Conde-Silvestre (eds), *The Handbook of Historical Sociolinguistics*, Oxford: Wiley-Blackwell, pp. 41–60.

Millar, Robert McColl (2012b), 'The death of Orkney Norn and the genesis of Orkney Scots', forthcoming in *Scottish Language* 29 (2012), pp. 16–26.

Millar, Robert McColl (forthcoming a), '"To bring my language near to the language of men?" Dialect and dialect use in the eighteenth and early nineteenth centuries: some observations', in John Kirk and Iseabail MacLeod (eds), *A Festschrift for J. Derrick McClure*.

Millar, Robert McColl (forthcoming b), 'Scots', in Alexander Bergs and Laurel Brinton (eds), *HSK – Historical Linguistics of English*, Berlin: Mouton de Gruyter.

Millar, Robert McColl and Alex Nicholls (1997), 'Ælfric's *De Initio Creaturae* and London, British Library, Cotton Vespasian A. xxii: omission, addition, retention and innovation', in Szarmach and Rosenthal (1997), pp. 431–63.

Miller, Thomas P. (1997), *The Formation of College English*, Pittsburgh: University of Pittsburgh Press.

Milroy, James (1992), *Linguistic Variation and Change*, Oxford: Blackwell.

Milroy, James and Lesley Milroy (1999), *Authority in Language: Investigating Standard English*, London: Routledge.

Milroy, Lesley (1987), *Language and Social Networks*, 2nd edn, Oxford: Blackwell.

Milroy, Lesley and Matthew Gordon (2003), *Sociolinguistic Method and Interpretation*, Oxford: Blackwell.

Mitchell, Bruce (1994), 'The Englishness of Old English', in Godden, Gray and Hoad (1994), pp. 163–81.

Mokyr, Joel (2009), *The enlightened economy: an economic history of Britain, 1700–1850*, New Haven: Yale University Press.

Montgomery, Michael (2001), 'British and Irish Antecedents', in Algeo (2001), pp. 86–153.

Mougeon, Raymond and Édouard Beniak (eds) (1994), *Les origines du français québécois*, Sainte-Foy: Les Presses de l'Université Laval.

Mufwene, Salikolo S. (2001), *The Ecology of Language Evolution*, Cambridge: Cambridge University Press.

Mugglestone, Linda (ed.) (2006), *The Oxford History of English*, Oxford: Oxford University Press.

Nevalainen, Terttu and Helena Raumolin-Brunberg (2003), *Historical Sociolinguistics: Language Change in Tudor and Stuart England*, London: Longman.

New Statistical Account (1841), *The New Statistical Account of Scotland, by the ministers of the respective parishes*, Edinburgh: no publisher given.

Nurmi, Arja (1999), *A Social History of Periphrastic DO*, Helsinki: Société Néophilologique.

Overton, Mark (1996), *Agricultural Revolution in England: The Transformation of the Agrarian Economy, 1500–1850*, Cambridge: Cambridge University Press.

Pauwels, Anne (2011), 'Planning for a global lingua franca: challenges for feminist language planning in English(es) around the world', *Current Issues in Language Planning* 12, pp. 9–19.

Pavlenko, Alexander (1997), 'The origin of the *be* perfect with transitives in the Shetland dialect', *Scottish Language* 16, pp. 88–96.

Pollard, A. J. (2000), *Late Medieval England, 1399–1509*, New York: Longman.

Poplack, Shana (ed.) (2000), *The English History of African American English*, Oxford: Blackwell.

Poplack, Shana and Sali Tagliamonte (2001), *African American English in the Diaspora*, Oxford: Blackwell.

Poppe, Erich (2009), 'Standard Average European and the Celticity of English intensifiers and reflexives: some considerations and implications', *English Language and Linguistics* 13, pp. 251–66.

Przedlacka, J. (2002), *Estuary English? A Sociophonetic Study of Teenage Speech in the Home Counties*, Bern: Lang.

Rendboe, Laurits (1984), 'How "worn out" or "corrupted" was Shetland Norn in its final stage?', *NOWELE* 3, pp. 53–88.

Rendboe, Laurits (1987), *Det gamle shetlandske sprog: George Low's ordliste fra 1774*, Odense: Odense universitetsforlag.

Richards, J. D. (2010), *Viking age England*, Stroud: History Press.

Richardson, John G. (ed.) (1986), *Handbook of theory and research for the sociology of education*, New York and London: Greenwood Press.

Rickford, John R. (1999), *African American Vernacular English: Features, Evolution, Educational Implications*, Oxford: Blackwell.

Riddy, Felicity (ed.) (1991), *Regionalism in Late Medieval Manuscripts and Texts: Essays Celebrating the Publication of* A Linguistic Atlas of Late Mediaeval English, Cambridge: D. S. Brewer.

Roberts, Jane (1970), 'Traces of Unhistorical Gender Congruence in a late Old English Manuscript', *English Studies* 51, pp. 30–7.

Romaine, Suzanne (ed.) (1998), *The Cambridge History of the English Language*, Vol. IV. *1776–1997*, Cambridge: Cambridge University Press.

Rosen, David (2006), *Power, Plain English and the Rise of Modern Poetry*, New Haven: Yale University Press.

Sales, Roger (2002), *John Clare: A Literary Life*, Basingstoke: Palgrave Macmillan.

Samuels, M. L. (1972), *Linguistic Evolution: With Special Reference to English*, Cambridge: Cambridge University Press.

Samuels, M. L. (1989a), 'Some applications of Middle English Dialectology', in Laing (1989), pp. 64–80.

Samuels, M. L. (1989b), 'Chaucerian Final -*e*', in Smith (1989), pp. 7–12.

Samuels, M. L. (1989c), 'Spelling and Dialect in the Late and Post-Middle English Periods', in Smith (1989), pp. 86–95.

Sandved, A. O. (1981), 'The Rise of Standard English', in Johansson and Tysdahl (1981), pp. 398–404.

Sapir, Edward (1921), *Language*, New York: Harcourt, Brace and World.

Sasse, Hans-Jürgen (1992), 'Theory of language death', in Brenzinger (1992), pp. 7–30.

Saussure, Ferdinand de (1916), *Cours de Linguistique Générale*, ed. Charles Bally and Albert Séchehaye, Paris: Payot.

Sawyer, P. H. (1982), 'The Causes of the Viking Age', in Farrell (1982), pp. 1–7.

Schei, Liv Kjørsvik (1988), *The Shetland Story*, London: Batsford.

Scholtmeijer, Harrie (1999), 'Taalontwikkeling in een nieuwe polder', *Cultuurhistorisch Jahrboek voor Flevoland* 9, pp. 71–83.

Schneider, Edgar W. (2007), *Postcolonial English: Varieties Around the World*, Cambridge: Cambridge University Press.

Schreier, Daniel (2003), *Isolation and Language Change: Contemporary and Sociohistorical Evidence from Tristan da Cunha English*, Basingstoke: Palgrave Macmillan.

Schreier, Daniel (2005), *Consonant Change in English Worldwide*, Basingstoke: Palgrave Macmillan.

Schreier, Daniel (2008), *St Helenian English: Origins, Evolution and Variation*, Amsterdam: John Benjamins.

Schrijver, Peter (2009), 'Celtic influence on Old English and phonetic evidence', *English Language and Linguistics* 13, pp. 193–211.

Scott, Sir Walter (1822 [2001]), *The Pirate*, ed. Mark Weinstein and Alison Lumsden, Edinburgh: Edinburgh University Press.

Sherborne, James (1994), *War, Politics, and Culture in Fourteenth-century England*, London: Hambledon Press.

Siegel, Jeff (1985), 'Koinés and koinéisation', *Language in Society* 14, pp. 357–78.

Simpson, Grant G. (ed.) (1990), *Scotland and Scandinavia 800–1800*, Edinburgh: John Donald.

Sinclair, Sir John (ed.) (1978), *The Statistical Account of Scotland* 19: Orkney and Shetland, Wakefield: EP Publishing.

Smith, Brian (1990), 'Shetland, Scandinavia, Scotland 1300–1700: the changing nature of contact', in Simpson (1990), pp. 25–37.

Smith, Brian (1996), 'The development of the spoken and written Shetland dialect: a historian's view', in Waugh (1996), pp. 30–43.

Smith, Jennifer and Mercedes Durham (2011), 'A Tipping Point in Dialect Obsolescence?' *Journal of Sociolinguistics* 15, pp. 197–225.

Smith, Jeremy J. (ed.) (1989), *The English of Chaucer and His Contemporaries: Essays by M. L. Samuels and J. J. Smith*, Aberdeen: Aberdeen University Press.

Smith, Jeremy J. (1996), *An Historical Study of English: A Dynamic Approach*, London: Routledge.

Smits, Caroline Jeannine Martine (1996), *Disintegration of Inflection: The Case of Iowa Dutch*, The Hague: Holland Institute of Generative Linguistics.

Spolsky, Bernard (2004), *Language Policy*, Cambridge: Cambridge University Press.

Stanley, E. G. (1969), 'Laȝamon's Antiquarian Sentiments', *Medium Ævum* 38, pp. 23–37.

Stanley, E. G. (1988), 'Karl Luick's "Man schrieb wie man sprach" and English Historical Philology', in Kastovsky and Bauer (1988), pp. 311–34.

Starnes, De Witt T. and Gertrude E. Noyes (1991), *The English Dictionary from Cawdrey to Johnson 1604–1755*, 2nd edn, with an introduction and a select bibliography by Gabriele Stein, Amsterdam: John Benjamins.

Steadman, J. M., Jr (1926), 'The language consciousness of college students: a study of conscious changes in pronunciation', *American Speech* 2, pp. 115–32.

Strikwerda, Carl (1997), *A House Divided: Catholics, Socialists, and Flemish Nationalists in Nineteenth-century Belgium*, Lanham, MD: Rowman & Littlefield Publishers.

Sudbury, Andrea (2001), 'Falkland Islands English: a southern hemisphere variety?' *English World-Wide* 22, pp. 55–80.

Sundkvist, Peter (2007), 'The pronunciation of Scottish Standard English in Lerwick, Shetland', *English World-Wide* 28, pp. 1–21.

Swift, Jonathan (1957), *A Proposal for Correcting the ENGLISH TONGUE, Polite Conversation, etc.* [1712], ed. H. Davis with L. Landa, Oxford: Blackwell.

Szarmach, Paul E. and Joel T. Rosenthal (eds) (1997), *The Preservation and Transmission of Anglo-Saxon Culture*, Kalamazoo: Medieval Institute Publications.

Taavitsainen, Irma (2004), 'Scriptorial "house-styles" and discourse communities', in Taavitsainen and Pahta (2004), pp. 209–40.

Taavitsainen, Irma and Päivi Pahta (eds) (2004), *Medical and Scientific Writing in Late Medieval English*, Cambridge: Cambridge University Press.

Thomas, George (1991), *Linguistic purism*, London: Longman.

Thomason, Sarah G. (2001), *An Introduction to Language Contact*, Edinburgh: Edinburgh University Press.

Thomason, Sarah Grey and Terrence Kaufman (1988), *Language Contact, Creolization, and Genetic Linguistics*, Berkeley: University of California Press.

Tolkien, J. R. R. (1929), '*Ancrene Wisse* and *Hali Meiðhad*'. *Essays and Studies* 14, pp. 104–26.

Tristram, Hildegard (2007), 'Why don't the English speak Welsh?', in Higham (2007), pp. 192–214.

Trudgill, Peter (1974), *The Social Differentiation of English in Norwich*, Cambridge: Cambridge University Press.

Trudgill, Peter (1975), 'Sex, covert prestige, and linguistic change in urban British English of Norwich', *Language in Society* 1, pp. 179–96

Trudgill, Peter (1983), *On Dialect: Social and Geographical Perspectives*, Oxford: Blackwell.

Trudgill, Peter (1986), *Dialects in Contact*, Oxford: Blackwell.

Trudgill, Peter (2004), *New-Dialect Formation: the Inevitability of Colonial Englishes*, Edinburgh: Edinburgh University Press.

Trudgill, Peter (2010), *Investigations in Sociohistorical Linguistics: Stories of Colonisation and Contact*, Cambridge: Cambridge University Press.

Truss, Lynn (2003), *Eats, Shoots & Leaves: The Zero Tolerance Approach to Punctuation*, London: Profile.

Tudoe, John R. (1883), *The Orkneys and Shetland: Their Past and Present State*, London: Edward Stanford.

Tulloch, Graham (1980), *The Language of Walter Scott: A Study of his Scottish and Period Language*, London: André Deutsch.

Tulloch, Graham (1989), *A History of the Scots Bible*, Aberdeen: Aberdeen University Press.

Tyler, Elizabeth and M. Jane Toswell (eds) (1996), *Studies in English Language and Literature: Doubt Wisely. Papers in Honour of E. G. Stanley*, London: Routledge.

Twining, Mary A. and Keith E. Baird (eds) (1991), *Sea Island Roots*, Trenton, NJ: Africa World Press.

Upton, Clive, Lawrence M. Davis and Charles L. Houck (2008), 'Modelling RP: a Variationist Case', in Dziubalska-Kołaczyk and Przedlacka (2008), pp. 409–20.

Van Dam, Raymond (1985), *Leadership and Continuity in Late Antique Gaul*, Berkeley and Los Angeles: University of California Press.

van Leyden, Klaske (2004), *Prosodic Characteristics of Orkney and Shetland Dialects: An Experimental Approach*, Utrecht: Lot.

van Windekens, A. (1952), *Le Pélasgique*, Louvain: Publications Universitaires.

Wales, Katie (2006), *Northern English. A Social and Cultural History*, Cambridge: Cambridge University Press.

Walton, John (1987), *Lancashire: A Social History*, Manchester: Manchester University Press.

Watts, Richard and Peter Trudgill (eds) (2002), *Alternative histories of English*, London: Routledge.

Waugh, Doreen J. (ed.) (1996), *Scotland's Northern Links: Language and History*. Edinburgh: Scottish Society for Northern Studies.

Webster, Noah (1789), *Dissertations on the English Language*, Boston: Printed for the author, by I. Thomas.

Wells, J. C. (1982), *Accents of English*, 3 vols, Cambridge: Cambridge University Press.

Williamson, Keith (1982), 'Lowland Scots in Education: An Historical Survey – Part I', *Scottish Language* 1, pp. 54–77.

Williamson, Keith (1983), 'Lowland Scots in Education: An Historical Survey – Part II', *Scottish Language* 2, pp. 52–87.

Withrington, Donald J. (ed.) (1983), *Shetland and the Outside World 1469–1969*, Oxford: Oxford University Press.

Wood, Gordon S. (2003), *The American Revolution. A History*, London: Phoenix.

Woodworth, E. D. and R. J. DiPietro (eds) (1962), *Monograph Series on Languages and Linguistics*, Washington, DC: Georgetown University Institute of Languages and Linguistics.

Woolf, Alex (2007), 'Apartheid and Economics in Anglo-Saxon England', in Higham (2007), pp. 115–29.

Wright, Laura (1994), 'On the Writing of the History of Standard English', in Fernandez, Fuster and Calvo (1994), pp. 104–15.

Wright, Laura (1996), 'About the evolution of Standard English', in Tyler and Toswell (1996), pp. 99–115.

Wright, Laura (ed.) (2000), *The Development of Standard English 1300–1800*, Cambridge: Cambridge University Press.

Yerastov, Yuri (2010), '*Done, finished,* and *started* as reflexes of the Scottish transitive *be* perfect in North America: their synchrony, diachrony, and current marginalisation', in Millar (2010a), pp. 19–52.

Index